MALE FRIENDSHIP IN SH
AND HIS CONTEMPC

CW00547066

Renaissance Humanism developed a fantasy of friendship in which men could be absolutely equal to one another, but Shakespeare and other dramatists quickly saw through this rhetoric and developed their own ideas about friendship more firmly based on a respect for human difference. They created a series of brilliant and varied fictions for human connection, as often antagonistic as sympathetic, using these as a means for individuals to assert themselves in the face of social domination. Whilst the fantasy of equal and permanent friendship shaped their thinking, dramatists used friendship most effectively as a way of shaping individuality and its limitations. Dealing with a wide range of Shakespeare's plays and poems, and with many works of his contemporaries, this study gives readers a deeper insight into a crucial aspect of Shakespeare's culture and his use of it in art.

TOM MACFAUL is a lecturer at Merton College, University of Oxford. He has written reviews for *The Times Literary Supplement* and *Notes and Queries*. This is his first book.

MALE FRIENDSHIP IN SHAKESPEARE AND HIS CONTEMPORARIES

TOM MACFAUL

CAMBRIDGE
UNIVERSITY PRESS

CAMBRIDGE UNIVERSITY PRESS
Cambridge, New York, Melbourne, Madrid, Cape Town, Singapore,
São Paulo, Delhi, Dubai, Tokyo

Cambridge University Press
The Edinburgh Building, Cambridge CB2 8RU, UK

Published in the United States of America by Cambridge University Press, New York

www.cambridge.org
Information on this title: www.cambridge.org/9780521123174

First published 2007
Reprinted 2008
This digitally printed version 2009

A catalogue record for this publication is available from the British Library

ISBN 978-0-521-86904-1 Hardback
ISBN 978-0-521-12317-4 Paperback

To Alex

Contents

Acknowledgements	*page ix*
Note on the text and list of abbreviations	*xi*

1 True friends?	1
2 Momentary mutuality in *Shakespeare's Sonnets*	30
3 Friends and brothers	48
4 Love and friendship	65
5 Servants	91
6 Political friendship	116
7 Fellowship	141
8 False friendship and betrayal	169
9 Conclusion: 'Time must friend or end'	196

Notes	198
Bibliography	213
Index	221

Acknowledgements

This book has taken a long time to write, and many people have offered ideas and sugestions; I apologize to any who are omitted.

My debts of gratitude go back a long way: the first is to the series of exceptional teachers who have guided my literary interests: at Queen Elizabeth Grammar School, Wakefield, Dave Howson introduced me to Shakespeare and an enthusiasm for drama, and Derek Coates fostered my abiding interest in the Classical languages; at Pembroke College, Cambridge, Colin Wilcockson (amongst other things) alerted me to the significance of the thou/you distinction in early modern drama, Mark Wormald fuelled my wider literary enthusiasms, and Howard Erskine-Hill provided (and continues to provide) a marvellous example of critical rigour and sensitivity. My first thoughts on friendship in the Renaissance began during my doctoral work on Edmund Spenser, under the supervision of Richard A. McCabe, who has continued to give me much-valued advice and support. My D. Phil. examiners, A. D. Nuttall and Colin Burrow, suggested that I pursue the topic of friendship, and I am grateful to them for setting me on such a stimulating path.

I am grateful to the Provost and Fellows of Oriel College, Oxford, for giving me a sabbatical term in 2004, during which I did a substantial amount of the work on the book.

I have enjoyed conversations about various issues related to the book with many friends and colleagues in Oxford, particularly Cliff Forshaw, Glenn Black, David Wormersley, David Maskell, Richard Cross, James Methven, Diarmaid MacCulloch and Amanda Holton.

My editor at Cambridge University Press, Sarah Stanton, has been wonderfully patient and supportive as the book has gone through its various drafts. The Press's anonymous readers provided extremely helpful suggestions as to how the book might be improved. Many thanks also to Rebecca Jones for seeing the book through the press, and to Kay

McKechnie for her scrupulous copy-editing, which has saved me from many infelicities.

I am grateful to my students at various colleges in Oxford for many stimulating discussions of Renaissance and other literature; I continue to believe that tutorial teaching can provide one of the best ways to hone and reconsider one's research work. It is also tremendous fun.

My parents have given me immense love and support, without which this book could hardly have been written. Finally, a book on friendship would not be complete without a gesture of appreciation to all of my friends, some of whom I have, ironically, seen too seldom during the gestation of this work.

Note on the text and list of abbreviations

Quotations from Shakespeare's plays are from *The Riverside Shakespeare*, 2nd edition, ed. G. Blakemore Evans et al. (Boston: Houghton Mifflin, 1997); I have also consulted Arden, Cambridge and Oxford editions of various plays, and have on occasion silently preferred their spelling in insignificant matters; I have also anglicized American spellings of words such as *honour*. I have tried to refer to the best readily available modern-spelling texts of early modern authors.

The following journal abbreviations have been used:

EC	*Essays in Criticism*
ELH	*ELH: A Journal of English Literary History*
ELR	*English Literary Renaissance*
HLQ	*Huntington Library Quarterly*
NQ	*Notes and Queries*
PQ	*Philological Quarterly*
RES	*Review of English Studies*
RQ	*Renaissance Quarterly*
SEL	*Studies in English Literature*
Sh. St.	*Shakespeare Studies*
Sh. Surv.	*Shakespeare Survey*
SP	*Studies in Philology*
SQ	*Shakespeare Quarterly*

CHAPTER I

True friends?

'Most friendship is feigning', sings Amiens in *As You Like It* (II. vii. 181);
this reflects a sense common in Shakespeare's time that friendship was on
the wane, becoming increasingly untrustworthy. At the risk of over-
interpretation, though, we might find other meanings here: the aphorism
contains a deeper truth – that friendship is a *fictional* relationship, artificial rather than natural, despite Humanist attempts to make it into the
most natural of human relationships; further, that most ideas about
friendship, derived from the dominant Humanist tradition, were a kind
of fakery. Yet the song only suggests that *most* friendship is feigning, and
therefore that some true friendship remains somewhere. Despite the
surface cynicism, then, there is a persistent belief that true friendship *does*
exist. Most of Shakespeare's plays and much of the writing of the period
are shaped by the Humanist ideal of true friendship, even when they are
aware that it is a will o' the wisp, but its main effect is to create a self-
assertive individuality coloured and limited by the failure of this ideal.

The Humanist ideology of friendship tries to make friendship the most
important thing in the world; the fact that it cannot ever really be the
centre of the world – after all, it can hardly even be defined – enables the
emergence of a new way of looking at individuality in the literature of this
period. People seek to discover themselves in their friends, and the central
mirage of friendship affects the shape of all other relationships. Moments
of connection with others are seen as pivotal, more important than any
other events in life; family is compromised (though not ultimately driven
away); romantic love is seen as inadequate; servile and political relationships are distorted by an ideal of friendship; larger social groups
bend towards the ideal of one-to-one friendship; even if these other
social priorities drive out ideal friendship, they are reshaped by it.
The new attitude to individuality that emerges from this is alienated,
self-consciously fictionalized, torn between solitude and company, but, in
the end, ironically self-assertive. There may be a movement towards

isolation in tragedy, and towards social integration in comedy, but the effect on the individual is at root the same: coming out on the other side of friendship the individual feels alienated from himself, but also alone, even when most in company. Having identified with another, even when this identification is exploded as a fiction, the self will never quite feel one's own. Hoping to find a stable and ennobled self in the friend or in friendship, there is always disappointment, but a more precise, if diminished and alienated self does emerge – a poor thing, but one's own. By insisting, ideally, that a friend should be 'another self' Humanism affirmed that there was such a thing as the self, whilst at the same time alienating this sense of self, which can only be found in or through others. In the end, one is thrown back on one's own resources – 'simply the thing I am / Shall make me live', as Parolles concludes in *All's Well that Ends Well* (iv. iii. 333–4). He has come to himself, because he has abandoned the fictions or feigning of friendship. The crucial fictions of friendship in Humanist texts were of equality and permanence, fictions which obviously impact on the individual's sense of selfhood: the fiction of equality enables a belief in the validity of social aspiration; that of permanence bolsters the individual's sense of his own integrity. The drama of the period recognizes the emotional force of these fictions but tends rather to demonstrate the importance of difference in friendship and the impermanence of any individual friendship. In doing so, it forces the individual to recognize the precise nature of his own selfhood, dependent on his differentiated and impermanent symbiotic connections to others. The alternative to the Humanist idea of perfect friendship is this idea of symbiosis – never fully articulated, and certainly not in modern biological terms. This model has its own problems, however: whilst it provides the individual a certain social and dramatic role and stresses the importance of his connection to others, it necessarily emphasizes the limitations of the individual and challenges his sense of integrity, and only creates tenuous or contingent links to others.

These ideas will be explored in detail in the main chapters of this book, which address the relationship of ideal friendship to other social structures. This chapter will consider some crucial foundational concepts: the emergence of ideal friendship from older familial models and the persistence of such feudal models alongside it; the structure of the Humanist ideal and its roots in classical thought; the use of friendship for dramatic self-assertion; the relation of the ideal to supposedly imperfect friendships of pleasure and utility; and the supposed corruptions of friendship by homoerotic desire. We will also consider the kinds of individuality that emerge from friendship and the use of a limited but symbiotic model of friendship to achieve this.

A word about gender issues: the Renaissance praise of friendship tended to emphasize its importance for a *man*'s life. A woman had other priorities, in her duties to her father or husband and in her role as a mother, thus making female friendship an entirely separate issue, affected by different codes of values.[1] Consequently, my focus in this book will be on male friendship only. In an age when men and women were strongly differentiated by education and men feared the 'feminizing' influences of women,[2] friendship with other men was crucial to a man's sense of identity. Eve Kosofsky Sedgwick presents homosocial bonds as the means by which men sustain their power over women in any particular society; but this fails to capture the nature of the subjective experience of friendship. Sedgwick makes important points about the effects of male relations on women, but when she argues that 'for a man to undergo even a humiliating change in the course of a relationship with a man still feels like preserving or participating in a sum of male power, while for a man to undergo any change in the course of a relationship with a woman feels like a degeneration of substance',[3] she fails to capture the experience of most men: they are more anxious about being humiliated in front of other men. No one, in our society or Shakespeare's, feels much personal stake in 'a sum of male power'. If anything, humiliation at the hands of another man is more powerfully felt because more power is at stake. Whilst Sedgwick is certainly right that 'the status of women, and the whole question of arrangements between genders, is deeply and inescapably inscribed in the structure even of relationships that seem to exclude women',[4] such relationships are obviously not *only* about women; men do have direct needs for emotional support from other men, more so in the early modern world, owing to the relative powerlessness of women to help them in an unequal society.

The relationship of friendship to romantic love of women will be explored in chapter 4, below. For now, we should note that friendship, because of the Humanist emphasis on it, is at least as important for identity-formation as romantic love – or, indeed, the family. W. Thomas MacCary (from a psychoanalytic standpoint) argues that 'Shakespeare's comedies . . . are not only about marriage. They are also about the beginnings of desire in the search for the self in mirror-images of the self and the gradual acceptance of difference and independence in the other.'[5] This acceptance can be traumatic in friendship as well as in sexual love, because it makes a man realize the limitations of his identity even as he is offered the possibility of greater wholeness. MacCary also argues that 'Shakespeare deals with desire in such a way that he is dealing with identity, and no Shakespearean male character is ever satisfied with the identity mere possession of a female can bring him'; men yearn for friendship as a buttress for identity that goes beyond the economic, the social or the sexual. As Coppélia Kahn observes, Shakespeare's 'male characters are engaged in a continuous struggle, first to form a masculine identity, then to be secure and productive in it'.[6] She emphasizes the importance of the father to this identity-formation, but if friendship groups are at least as important as the nurturing family in forming the individual's social identity and inner life, it is clear that being productive in one's identity involves the social group at least as much as the family. If, as Kahn says, 'Shakespeare rarely portrays masculine selfhood without suggesting a filial context for it',[7] he even more rarely leaves out a friendly social context.

Even as the order of traditional society was breaking down in the Renaissance, friendship was clung to as one last bastion of wholeness and unity; but for that very reason it was also the subject of particular anxiety, because if friendship failed there was no unity left. For Burton, friends are more important than family, as (he says) 'The love of kinsmen is grown cold.'[8] The failure of friendship has correspondingly disastrous consequences:

Where this true love is wanting, there can be no firm peace, friendship from teeth outward, counterfeit, or, for some by-respects, so long dissembled till they have satisfied their own ends, which upon every small occasion breaks out into enmity, open war, defiance, heart-burnings, whispering, calumnies, contentions, and all manner of bitter melancholy discontents.[9]

So much, then, is riding on friendship, for the health of both the individual and the nation. It is both the cause of anxiety and its hoped-for cure. For melancholic individuals, such as Hamlet, or Antonio the merchant of Venice, friendship has a critical importance.

Partly this is because these men are alienated from family. Hamlet's mother has become untrustworthy, his uncle has become 'more than kin' (i. ii. 65), and his father has been murdered; Bassanio is Antonio's 'cousin', but that is the only family he has, and cousinship is in any case a decidedly imprecise relationship, its optionality bordering with that of friendship – Antonio has chosen to think of himself more as friend than family member. Considering the Gothic novel, Sedgwick argues that 'it is the ideological imposition of the imaginary patriarchal Family on real, miscellaneous, shifting states of solitude, gregariousness, and various forms of material dependence, that rationalizes, reforms, and perpetuates, in the face of every kind of change, the unswerving exploitations of sex and of class'.[10] Although it is not clear that such vigorous ideological promotion of the family as bastion of class and gender domination was present in Shakespeare's England, the Protestant Church of England was clearly beginning to impose ideas of the nuclear family as the foundational unit of society.[11] With the destruction of other modes of allegiance, the family became an increasingly monolithic commitment for the individual – and friendship, the one remaining alternative mode of allegiance, therefore came to be presented in stark opposition to family.

Shakespeare's plays, then, were performed at what seems a particularly important time in the history of friendship, as older feudal modes of allegiance gave way to modern friendship of affection. Broadly stated, in the medieval world people knew where they stood with regard to one another: their friends were their neighbours and their familial attachments, through being 'god-sibs' (co-godparents) or through marital attachments. This meaning of the word *friend*, in fact, persists until the nineteenth century, and can be found prominently in the works of Jane Austen, and even of Trollope. It was, however, no longer the necessary or primary meaning. Alan Bray's splendid re-examination of the history of friendship shows that

As England passes into the sixteenth century, an apparently quite different kind of friendship becomes visible and is far more familiar: a noninstrumental friendship, based in affinity, that does not (and should not) obtrude on a wider world of public affairs. With its quite different assumptions, modernity seems to arrive, with a world we can recognize.[12]

It is notable for example that Wendoll, in Heywood's *A Woman Killed with Kindness* (1607), explicitly states that Frankford's friendship for him is based on 'no alliance' (vi. 33), and this is meant to prove the friendship particularly sacred.[13] The play's subplot articulates the sense that kin alliance is no longer reliable when Old Mountford says of his newly impoverished nephew 'He lost my kindred when he fell to need' (ix. 17). There is a suggestion then that 'friends' from old-style alliances are not to be trusted, and that betrayal of modern friendship of affection is a much greater sin. On the other hand, Bray's study also shows that older practices of friendship persisted well beyond the sixteenth century, involving rituals of friendship that were ethically if not legally binding:

> The kinship of two godbrothers or two sworn brothers could be as indisputable as that formed by marriage; but kinship of this kind shared a crucial distinction to that of betrothal or marriage in its ability to forge links across social divisions where marriage would have been unthinkable.[14]

Several modes of friendship were in existence and could often be confused with one another (after all, one could have a friendship of affection with a cousin as Antonio does). The traditional familial mode, however, is more straightforward and unambiguous, and is therefore easier to represent as a priority in drama, and can be used more readily for plot purposes. In Middleton's *A Trick to Catch the Old One* (*c*. 1605), Witgood's marriage to Hoard's niece is validated by the fact that Hoard and he (supposed rivals for the affections of a non-existent widow) have declared themselves to be friends, forming a 'league' (IV. iv. 264) before witnesses; this is taken to be dramatically and almost legally binding.[15] Once a friendship has been founded, it cannot be easily renounced. Friendship could also be inherited, like kinship. In Massinger's *A New Way to Pay Old Debts*, Welborne tells Alworth, 'Thy father was my friend, and that affection / I bore to him, in right descends to thee' (I. i. 117–18).[16] It is clear, then, that an older obligatory mode of friendship persisted, at least in dramatic plots (though Shakespeare, notably, does not make much use of it).

Set against this, the ideal of friendship informed what men at least claimed to want from relationships with other men. Renaissance Humanism had a clear if fragile ideology of friendship as the centre of man's life, which can be summed up fairly simply: a friend is a second self with whom one shares everything, friends are virtuous and similar to one another, and the friend is chosen after long and careful assessment of his virtues; the purpose of such friendship is the promotion of virtuous thought and action; it may contribute to the public sphere, but it is ultimately independent of it. This is clearly an idealization, and was often recognized as such, but even so it had a persistent ideological force.

The central aspect of the Humanist ideology of friendship was a belief in friendships of *virtue*, which promoted manliness (practically as well as etymologically): for Cicero, the crucial influence on ideas of friendship, these were the only true friendships. What he calls (in *Laelius* / *de Amicitia*) friendships of pleasure or of utility are in his view not just inferior to virtuous friendship but actually false versions of it. This contrasts with Aristotle, to whom Cicero owes many of his ideas, but whose conceptions he simplifies. In the *Nicomachean Ethics*, Aristotle presents friendships of pleasure or utility as different, inferior, but none-theless allowable forms of friendship, so much so that A. W. Price has argued that in the case of friendship 'Aristotle was never closer to the concept of family resemblance': that is, he sees friendship as a range of cognate possibilities rather than as one precise and perfectible form.[17] The potential confusion between these forms was fruitful for drama. Cicero, on the other hand, created a unitary, authoritative version of what friendship is, and he was often taken as an authority by early Renaissance Humanists. Such an ideal, then, has a certain cultural centrality in this period, but the homogeneity it promotes means that it soon disappears from more complex drama. It is the Ciceronian model that Laurens J. Mills calls 'the friendship theme',[18] but, as we shall see, there are many other ways of treating friendship. Laurie Shannon argues that the fiction of equal friendship provides a space of freedom for the individual to 'shape him-self',[19] but when friendship is too rigorously conceived in a Ciceronian manner it can become just as obligatory and stifling as any other set of rules. In plays like *The Two Gentlemen of Verona* it becomes an absurd and arbitrary 'law' that must be overturned. Like the friendly aristocrats of Navarre, friendship cannot isolate itself in virtuous contemplation, and the drama often (as in the case of *Love's Labour's Lost*) satirizes the absurd effects of a belief in the autonomy of friendship. *Shakespeare's Sonnets* explore the pleasures of isolated friendship, but are also consumed with the difficulties of establishing and sustaining such a relationship, which can perhaps only exist in a sonnet, and is liable to collapse across a sonnet sequence, let alone when set in the larger context of a drama.

Although Cicero's idea of friendship was much more directly influ-ential on English Humanists than that of his Greek predecessors, Plato and Aristotle were increasingly available to an English audience, and their presentation of friendship has some similarity to that in Shakespearean drama, however indirect their influence may have been. At the conclusion of *Lysis* Socrates says:

O Menexenus and Lysis, how ridiculous that you two boys and I, an old boy, who would fain be one of you, should imagine ourselves to be friends – this is what the bystanders will go away and say – and as yet we have not been able to discover what is a friend![20]

The emphasis here on the age difference is as important as that on the impossibility of defining friendship: there is an ironic suggestion that it is ultimately difference that makes friendship. The *Symposium* demonstrates the power of educative pederasty (in any case a subcategory of *philia*), seeing friendship as a mode of cultural transmission that subverts the biological and the primary means by which humanity develops beyond mere biological need; again, this is a use of friendship that is predicated on difference. Francis Bacon develops the idea in 'Of Parents and Children':

> The perpetuity by generation is common to beasts; but memory, merit, and noble works, are proper to men. And surely a man shall see the noblest works and foundations have proceeded from childless men, which have sought to express the images of their minds, where those of their bodies have failed. So the care of posterity is most in them that have no posterity.[21]

Our affections guide us to transmit our ideas. The dialogue of the *Symposium* demonstrates this more dramatically and precisely than that of the *Lysis*. In a simple sense, the mere expression of different ideas about *eros* in the *Symposium* shows the value of *philia* (friendship) in promoting philosophy, as each speech feeds off the others' ideas. The arrival of Alcibiades at the dialogue's end shows the results of educative pederasty and presents a comic picture of its limitations. Alcibiades is drunk when he and his gang enter and this in itself, along with Alcibiades' decidedly ambiguous later reputation, hardly shows Socrates' educative methods in the best light. Alcibiades' sexual desire for Socrates might also somewhat undermine the latter's claims to chaste educative friendship. Nonetheless, a more subtle point is being promoted: Socrates tells us that he started off by loving the boy's beauty, but now the boy loves him, despite his ugliness. Such friendship therefore demonstrates the superior beauty of ideas. Even though it still carries with it the freight of physical desire and personal affection, this friendship is nonetheless valuable. Flawed though it necessarily is, and requiring careful sexual restraint on Socrates' part, human affection remains a crucial part of self-improvement. The friendship is not equal, but its balance changes over time, to the enrichment of both. It is hard not to think that Shakespeare had Socrates and Alcibiades in mind when he created what amounts to a parodic picture of them in Hal and Falstaff. The concept of friendship as a balancing act that has noble aims but may fail, existing firmly in time-based conditions, is more dramatically fruitful and a better representation of social reality than soul-connection. It is the very differences between Socrates and Alcibiades, or between Hal and Falstaff, that give these friendships their emotional power – differences that the Ciceronian concept of friendship would erase. Aristotle, although he was Cicero's main source, also valued difference in friendship, seeing it as involving a complex balancing act, taking place over time; it therefore involves rather more of a *process* than Ciceronian friendship. For Aristotle, friendship was a matter of moral competition, in which one sometimes increased one's friend's *eudaimonia* (moral well-being) at the expense of one's own, but this was envisaged very much as a two-way process;[22] in Cicero there is less stress on the dynamic nature of this process.

Nevertheless, Cicero's ideas dominated Humanist thought and verse (and even drama) for most of the sixteenth century. In the Middle Ages, friendship was a theme rarely treated for its own sake, being taken for granted as part of the feudal system,[23] but in the early sixteenth century there was a sudden flowering of interest in the subject. This began when Cicero's *De Amicitia* was first printed in 1481, and its ideas were popularized partly by the inclusion of many friendship aphorisms in Erasmus's *Adagia* (1525), and partly by the works of Sir Thomas Elyot, whose *Boke Named the Governour* (1531) can be seen as the key text in the English Renaissance discovery of friendship. He is particularly emphatic about the centrality of friendship to man's life – it sustains society, buildings, agriculture, and is the sun of man's life.[24] His rhetorical enthusiasm is powerful in its attempts to yoke people and their emotions together: 'Verely it is a blessed and stable connection of sondrie willes, makinge of two parsones one in hauinge and suffringe' (pp. 129–30). This fantasy of unity can only be sustained by a fantasy that it escapes from mutability, and therefore from the social mobility he seems keen to promote. The emphasis here on stability cannot but be challenged in a dramatic context. Elyot's own narrative of friendship (between Titus and Gisippus), which we shall address in a later chapter, seems designed to prove this stability, but it is a circular and undramatic narrative. It avoids the sense of a wider society embraced by Shakespearean drama.

Later writers used Elyot's rhetoric in order to present friendship as a resource for legitimate social aspiration, appropriating the rhetoric of perfect friendship between equals for more instrumental purposes. Thomas Churchyard says that friendship

is a certaine felicitie of the minde, a sweete ensence that burnes before GOD, a preseruer of mans renowne and life, a willing bondage that brings freedom for euer, a steadfast staffe that all good people doe stay on, the mother and nurse of mutuall loue, the conqueror of hate, the pacifier of quarels, the glorie of kings, and the suretie of subjects.[25]

This is the peak of the idealizing tradition, ripe for debunking, so little does it have to say about the subtleties of human life, except in that paradox of 'willing bondage', which emphasizes that the bonds of friendship are chosen (as opposed to familial ones), and thus enable one to escape from the unfree conditions of one's social position. There is an almost desperate confidence in the power of friendship here. This relates to the fact that the text, dedicated to Sir Walter Ralegh, is geared towards patronage: it is designed to 'requit a good turne receiued' (A2r). Churchyard defends himself from the potential charge of flattering Ralegh by arguing that to turn towards the powerful is *natural*. Patronage is as natural as friendship, and is indeed one of its forms.

Thomas Breme's *Mirror of Friendship* (1584 – translated from Italian, it signals its traditional nature) is also concerned with patronage. It is addressed to Thomas Kyrton, chief Serjeant of London, a man whom Breme had clearly not met, but one whom he wishes 'good will' (Aiiv), 'hauing heard you so notably commended and well spoken of' (Aiir). It argues that a friend is someone who gives one what one lacks, and that one gives one's heart to one's friend. Emotional loyalty, then, is given in return for material favours. One of the primary burdens of Breme's work is that friendship is a bulwark against misfortune (indeed his text is accompanied by 'a briefe treatise, or caueat, not to trust in worldly prosperitie'). Nicholas Grimald takes a similar line in his 'Of friend-shippe', in which friendship is represented as the only absolutely steady thing in life:

> When fickle fortune fayles, this knot endureth still,
> Thy kin out of their kind may swerue, when friends ow the good [will?]
> What sweeter solace shall befall then one to finde
> Upon whose brest thou maist repose the secrets of thy minde
> He waileth at thy woe; his teares with thine be shed;
> Behold thy frend and of thy selfe the patter[n] see
> One soule a wonder shall it seeme in bodies twaine to bee
> In absence, present rich in want in sicknes sounde
> Ye after death aliue maist thou by thy sure friend be founde.[26]

He also observes, following Cicero and Aristotle, that 'nothing is more kindely for our kinde'. This emphasis on the naturalness of friendship (in the old meaning of the word *kind*) is an attempt to make it supersede familial attachments. At the same time Grimald acknowledges the rarity of friendship, a view which seems strangely in tension with the supposed naturalness of friendship and which will provide the seeds of a more sceptical outlook. For Aristotle it was perfect friendship that was rare: for these followers of Cicero, who think the perfect form the only true form, friendship *tout court* is rare. Perhaps this is designed to persuade potential patrons that the rarity of their good deeds will give value to them. Even if the idealization is sincere, it is deployed for persuasive purposes. As Bray observes, 'the ideals of friendship themselves appear as . . . instruments, precisely because of their capacity tactfully to efface and negotiate the dangers of friendship'.[27] Texts on friendship, then, become little more than extended dedications designed to shore up the patronage system.[28]

The Humanist rhetoric of friendship, as such scholars as Alan Stewart and Lisa Jardine have argued, is really a rhetoric of social aspiration, providing a means by which writers could gain patronage whilst simultaneously arguing for a fiction of equality with their patrons.[29] In Shakespeare's time, these ideas, which had been extremely popular for much of the sixteenth century, were coming to be treated with downright scepticism;[30] they came to be explicitly condemned as a mode of self-advancement. Francis Bacon, for example, wrote that 'There is little friendship in the world, and least of all between equals, which was wont to be magnified. That that is, is between superior and inferior, whose fortunes may comprehend the one the other';[31] and Thomas Nashe wrote that 'there is no friendship to be had with him that is resolute to doe or suffer anything rather than to endure the destinie whereto he was borne; for he will not spare his owne Father or Brother, to make himself a gentleman'.[32] In the case of drama, whilst friendship is often used for social self-advancement, it is also used for the assertion of an individual's importance within the play. Advancement within the play world is often parallel to prominence in the play, but is not necessarily so; sometimes the opposite is the case. As Enobarbus says in *Antony and Cleopatra*, it is through friendship that an ordinary man, 'earns a place i' th' story' (III. xiii. 46), but, ironically, he earns his place through betraying Antony rather than by staying loyal to him. It is through friendship with Antony, of course, that he has come to our attention at all, and a high valuation of friendship is required for betrayal to have dramatic force. At such moments we can see a crucial aspect of Shakespeare's dramatic genius – his ability to give life to even the most minor characters, which is commonly effected by his use of friendship, preventing excessive prominence being given to central figures, and giving emotional resonance to the complex affiliations of the characters on stage, and meaning to the groups we see presented there.

The Humanist tradition presents friendship as absolutely central to human life, at a time when traditional, 'natural' affiliations were losing some of their force. The vaunted freedom of friendship, however, makes it imprecise; in its liberating force, it may mean everything to the self, but in its imprecision, it may ultimately mean nothing. This ideal of friendship is almost by definition voluntary, and therefore constitutes an assertion of the individual will, whereas the older sense of friendship as rooted in family and feudal obligation is an expression of social determinism. We can, therefore, see the negotiation of friendship in Shakespeare's time between ideas of fixed social hierarchy and the new voluntarism as providing the seeds of a more egalitarian vision of society, as Laurie Shannon has done.[33] But this, in turn, is complicated by the fact that one major comfort of friendship is the reinforcement of one's social place, by the affirmation of one's place in the dramatic story; the self is ultimately situated in relation to others, and the place of lower-status minor characters tends to be dependent on higher-status major characters. Dreams of equality give way to a recognition of difference, but the process enables individuals to assert themselves. Francis Bacon concludes his essay 'Of Friendship' by saying that a man 'may quit the stage' if he has no friends.[34] The friend here is presented as something necessary for the individual to play his *part* in life: it is not enough simply to be oneself; one's self must be performed in interaction with a friend or friends. The metaphor of the stage is crucial: friends are essential to the proper playing of one's part before others, something that is obviously accentuated in the theatre.

Friendship in Shakespeare's plays, even when it is most self-sacrificing in ethical terms, is primarily a way of asserting an individual's dramatic importance and giving us a sense of his character. Allan Bloom points out that a man's character is, if not determined, at least represented through his friends;[35] and challenges to friendship can therefore become challenges to selfhood. This worry is articulated by Castiglione's Federico:

me thinks there is an other thing that giveth and diminisheth reputation: namely the choise of friends, with whom a man must have inwarde conversation. For undoubtedly reason willeth, that such as are coupled in strayte amitie, and unspeakable companie, should be also alike in will, in minde, in judgement, and inclination.[36]

This argument is extended by Lodowick Bryskett to the idea that one is not only assumed to be the same as one's friends, but also (at least in youth) one's friends really do shape one's character:

The auncient wise men assigned to youth the plannet of Mercury, for no other cause (as I suppose) but for that Mercury being (as Astronomers say) either good or bad according as he is accompanied with another plannet good or euil: euen so youth becommeth good or bad, as the companies to which it draweth or giveth it selfe.[37]

This concern is also partly to do with the fact that friendship was genuinely important to the individual's status. One of the key features of friendship in the higher political spheres of Jacobean England was the giving of *countenance* by higher-status individuals to their clients.[38] A similar effect can be found in drama, where the countenance of the dramatically central figures compels the audience's attention to the more peripheral. Kent in *King Lear* and Antonio in *The Merchant of Venice* may wish the best for Lear and Bassanio respectively, but they also demand that their friendship be recognized, both by the object of their affectionate altruism and by a wider society presented as an on-stage audience. On stage this works very simply but effectively – our sense of a character's introversion or extraversion being clearly marked by whether we see him alone or in company, and by his attitude to company. Shakespeare's characters want to have a proper place in the story, and friendship is the best way apparently minor or subordinate characters can obtain this. Their life is that of actors trying to overplay the small roles they have been given.

Whilst the Humanists wanted friendship to be a central element in human life, the Humanist understanding of perfect sympathy in equal friendship rarely takes centre stage in the best drama; rather, it is used as a device for placing characters within the overlapping but sometimes conflicting spheres of dramatic and social importance. Dramatic characters – particularly Shakespeare's – are presented as trying to assert their dramatic importance and as making claims on the attention of other characters and that of the audience. This self-assertion is one major reason why Shakespeare's characters seem to be getting out of the playwright's control. One of Shakespeare's most effective dramatic techniques is to present characters who appear to be competing, like actors, for centre stage.[39] This gives the impression that they have real selves, but these selves can only gain credit, and a sense of roundedness, by being credited by other apparent selves on stage. Friends are required to recognize the self, and to round it out, by recognizing its limitations.

This is easily achieved in the forms of friendship that Aristotle regarded as imperfect but allowable, even though Cicero and the Humanists refused to call them friendship: that is, friendships of utility and/or pleasure. As we have seen, Thomas Nashe and Francis Bacon recognize that social aspiration has destroyed the conditions of peaceful equality necessary for ideal friendship. Bacon's practical idea of mutuality is partly a lament, but it also constitutes a fruitful recognition of difference and of social context. Whilst it removes the self-sufficiency of friendship, it gives it a clear value and meaning within the social world. Bacon brings friendship down into social realities as an instrument of compromise. He has a rational and pragmatic sense of the idea of the friend as second self, arguing that

If a man have a true friend, he may rest almost secure that the care of [his works] will continue after him. So that a man hath, as it were, two lives in his desires. A man hath a body, and that body is confined to a place; but where friendship is, all offices of life are as it were granted to him and his deputy. For he may exercise them by his friend. How many things are there which a man cannot, with any face or comeliness, do himself? A man can scarce allege his own merits with modesty, much less extol them; a man cannot sometimes brook to supplicate or beg; and a number of the like. But all these things are graceful in a friend's mouth, which are blushing in a man's own.[40]

Bacon constantly looks for the usefulness of friendship, but this must be rooted in affection, even if he tends to take affection for granted. Drama, having a greater concern with emotions, would negotiate between the extremes of pragmatism and idealism, seeing friendship as an essential social lubricant (as opposed to the glue it had once been), but recognizing the practical limitations as well as the emotional power of the idealizing tradition.

The significance of friendship in early modern England, then, goes well beyond the praises of it that Ciceronian humanism had promoted, though these praises had an important influence on the way people thought and talked about it. A central aspect of friendship was the economic one: a friend might provide one with loans or other material assistance. Most people in England had relationships as close with their neighbours as with their wider family, and while there is much evidence of neighbours lending each other money, we can only assume the goodwill that may have gone along with that.[41] Lorna Hutson identifies a shift in attitudes to such assistance in the late Elizabethan period, in that people came to be less trusting of one another, probably due to less secure neighbourhood structures in an urbanizing society. The rhetoric of friendship was also under a peculiar strain as a result of the economic crisis of the time, and of shifting attitudes towards usury. Whilst this made people less certain about their friendships, it opened up a range of friendship possibilities:

> in the course of the sixteenth century, the notion of 'friendship' between men was transformed from that of a code of 'faithfulness' assured by acts of hospitality and the circulation of gifts through the family and its allies, to that of an instrumental and affective relationship which might be generated, even between strangers, through emotionally persuasive communication, or the exchange of persuasive texts.[42]

Hutson argues convincingly that whilst persuasive texts could create the illusion of great intimacy, the increasing reliance on rhetoric in friendship opened up a space for considerable distrust, for who can be sure that rhetoric is sincere?[43] A further problem for the new rhetorical economy is uncertainty about the balance of reciprocation, which is less readily assessed in terms of affectionate language than it is in terms of material transactions. Robert C. Evans notes the difficulties of balance in supposedly equal friendship. His view is that it is a matter of not doing too many favours, but under the pressure of the ideal of friendship, the balance becomes still more difficult, as even small differentiations that make little difference to the economy of reciprocation can cause anxiety about the upsetting of the equal friendship.[44] Few relationships could be entirely equal in social, affective or instrumental terms. In Sir Philip Sidney's *Arcadia* (pub. 1591), for example, we encounter two princes, Musidorus and Pyrocles, who are as evenly matched as one could wish – both are noble, and they are cousins. Yet there are small differentials even here – Musidorus is the elder, but Pyrocles has a slightly higher status. These differentials may be said to cancel each other out, but it shows that a balancing trick is almost always necessary in friendship. Each further differentiation of the cousins – such as their respective disguises as a shepherd and an Amazon – threatens to unbalance their relationship. Drama provides particularly acute registers of the balance of favours and emotion in friendship.

Writers of this period regard assistance in need (what Robert Burton called 'mutual offices') as one clear sign of friendship – a friend in need is a friend indeed, goes the adage (dating back to Ennius in the second century BC) – but it can seem like a manifestation of a rather general (perhaps Christian) goodwill unless it is accompanied by a sense of common pleasure. Burton tells us:

'tis that similitude of manners which ties most men in an inseparable link, as if they be addicted to the same studies or disports, they delight in one another's company, 'birds of a feather will gather together': if they be of diverse inclinations, or opposite in manners, they can seldom agree.[45]

Walter Dorke presents a similar sentiment in insisting that pleasure shared is greater than solitary pleasure:

if a man should climbe vp to the skies, & take a ful view of the highnesse of the heauens, and contemplate the beautifulnesse of the skies: and behold all the wonderfull workes of GOD vpon the face of the earth: the admiration thereof would be but vnpleasant without some friend to whome hee might make relation of the same.[46]

Dorke, a good Ciceronian, only considers intellectual and spiritual pleasure. Aristotle pointed out that even the good need pleasure, and C. S. Lewis makes common interest the basic ground of friendship.[47] This of course reflects a modern society in which friendship is dependent on shared interests – literary, artistic, sporting – but such a society may have been emerging thanks to improving education. Drama rarely shows such common interests (perhaps because they are necessarily dull to outsiders) and represents pleasures in more basic forms, such as drinking, singing or even going to a play together, all of which, it can be assumed, are understandable to an audience. In Marston's *The Malcontent* Mendoza knowingly promotes a friendship of pleasure as a false shortcut to the impossible friendship of virtue, saying 'Let's be once drunk together, and so unite a most virtuously strengthened friendship' (II. iv. 109–10).[48] The other friendly pleasure commonly represented is the playing of practical jokes. These can be more serious, and show the continuity between pleasure and practicality for friends, but they can also show friendship's limits. Sir Toby Belch enjoys tricking Malvolio in the company of his friend Sir Andrew Aguecheek, but he also tricks Andrew and repudiates his foolish friend in the end – he marries Maria, his truer collaborator in trickery. Lorenzo's friends in *The Merchant of Venice* are on one level playing an enjoyable trick with their friend when they help him to elope with Jessica; friendship is a means to an end, but it is also enjoyed in itself; pleasure and utility go hand in hand. Lewis figures friendship as involving individuals who are 'side by side' rather than face to face,[49] and this is how we see them on stage – whilst we register their alliances, their positioning often draws our attention away from the friendship itself to the direction or purpose of the friendship. Despite Humanist attempts to make friendship an end in itself, then, there is always a tendency for it to point outwards.

The one element which might prevent this from being the case is homosexual desire. Unlike friendships of utility or pleasure, sexual desire in friendship, we might think, orients men towards one another. There might therefore be a surprising similarity between the Humanist ideal and the 'sodomitical' desires that Humanists were eager to repress; both differ from the imperfect forms of friendship in not being directed outwards. But how important a component of early modern friendship was sexual desire? This is a subject that has been given much attention in recent years, and a consensus seems to have emerged: firstly, that homosexuality as such (i.e. as an identity or exclusive sexual orientation) did not exist in the Renaissance,[50] and secondly, that homosexual acts were officially stigmatized as sodomy but were ignored in practice except when they were brought in to round out and confirm other charges against socially and politically undesirable individuals.[51] Eroticism can clearly be seen as a major component of the early modern expression of friendship: it was normal, but could easily be stigmatized as abnormal. Any friendship that was too private, and that threatened the social hierarchy, could be regarded as sodomitical; this obviously created a certain anxiety about friendship, and militated against the success of private friendship. Worries about sodomy forced friendship into the public sphere.

We might wonder, though, how far eroticism affected the nature of friendships. Mario DiGangi observes that 'homoerotic practices [e.g. kissing, hugging] were "normal" aspects of even the most socially conventional relationship',[52] and goes on to argue that 'early modern gender ideology integrated orderly homoeroticism into friendship more seamlessly than modern ideological formations, which more crisply distinguish homoeroticism from friendship, sexual desire from social desire'.[53] This means that there is always considerable uncertainty about the erotic content of an early modern friendship, which was always open to hostile interpretation from outside. It is also open to friendly interpretation by modern critics, who can call friendship practices homoerotic, even whilst arguing that such a category did not exist in the period. In such cases we are making inferences without much evidence: we cannot know if *Twelfth Night*'s Antonio has sexual desires for Sebastian, though to some readers it has seemed obvious.[54] Staging clearly makes a difference here, and actors can easily make Antonio or his namesake in *The Merchant of Venice* gaze longingly upon Sebastian and Bassanio respectively. This can be taken as a sign of excessive feeling in friendship, but this in turn raises the question – which comes first, the excess of feeling, or the homoerotic desire? The feelings of desire are normally associated with desire for possession of some sort, and real possession of another man was not possible for an early modern man. What is important to note is Antonio's emotional desire for Bassanio: he knows that Bassanio and he will not set up home together, and even helps him to find a wife, but he wants to remain more emotionally important to Bassanio than Portia is.

It is worth noting that erotic desire between males is almost always accompanied by the figuring of the desired party as a *boy* – the idea of male sexual desire for *men* seems almost unthinkable in this period. In such cases as *Shakespeare's Sonnets* erotic desire seems always to be an expression of age difference in friendship.[55] The desire is a way of balancing difference in the face of an ideology of equal friendship. Just as expressions of heterosexual desire work across gender difference (and it is the difference that creates the desire), expressions of homoerotic desire in the Renaissance work across age difference, and are not, as Freud contended, narcissistic. They also operate across social difference – the *Sonnets* are a case in point again. As Mark Breitenberg notes, 'the young man's appeal derives from the combination of his sameness and difference in relation to the poet', and he goes on to argue that this militates against homoeroticism,[56] but it is precisely this admixture of sameness and difference that provokes the poet's fascinated desire, though it need not be a desire for sexual contact as such. Desire is the consequence and expression of the inevitable differentials involved in friendship: social and political anxieties are here transformed into emotions with considerable dramatic force. The erotic side of friendship, then, is a way of expressing and representing anxieties that have little to do with what we would call sexuality. It is more to do with the public (and private) assertion of the existence of friendship. James I's caresses of his favourites were similar to his writing letters to them – they signified to the favourite and to others that royal favour persisted.[57] If homoeroticism in the Renaissance is a normal component of friendship, then we must learn to treat it casually, avoiding the modern hysteria about sexuality.

Nonetheless, there is in friendship a force of desire that cannot be fulfilled, and that consequently cannot be resolved in dramatic plots – a desire that is more compelling and intangible than the sexual. Eve

Kosofsky Sedgwick articulates the range of such desire with particular force when she argues it 'is not . . . a particular affective state or emotion, but . . . the affective or social force, the glue, even when its manifestation is hostility or hatred or something less emotively charged, that shapes an important relationship'.[58] Whilst this may seem worryingly imprecise, it captures the free-floating element that cannot be acknowledged in friendship, owing to the ideology of ideal friendship. It is not just eroticism, then, that dare not speak its name, but any element of desire in friendship that does not conform to the Humanist ideal. Friendship is bound up with social status even as it is separated from it; it is a mode of social aspiration as well as being a source of pleasure in itself. Sexuality may be a component both of simple pleasure and of social affirmation. The ideal of perfect friendship is a rhetorical way of separating friendship from these supposedly sullying factors, but such rhetoric is itself a part of social life, and cannot do away with the fact of social hierarchy and difference. In poems and prose tracts an illusion of pure and isolated friendship can be given, but drama's representation of social hierarchy puts such rhetoric back in its place. The ideal of perfect friendship suggests a beautiful particularity of relationship between individuals that becomes increasingly necessary in a socially and physically mobile society.[59] It allows other people to anchor one's identity. Yet the dreams of stasis in friendship are always just dreams. Humanist texts may present fictions of one soul in bodies twain, but the drama presents the shifting and untrustworthy nature of friendship even as it recognizes the desire for stasis.

Unlike some of his contemporaries, John Donne is not an outright sceptic of the tradition of perfect friendship; he tries in his verse letters to carve out a private space of virtue in friendship. Friendship, for Donne, focusses virtues:

> Seek we then ourselves in ourselves; for as
> Men force the sun with much more force to pass
> By gathering his beams with a crystal glass;

> So we, if we into ourselves will turn,
> Blowing our sparks of virtue, may outburn
> The straw, which doth about our hearts sojourn.
> ('To Mr Richard Woodward', lines 19–24)[60]

Emphasis on friendship here causes an inward turn – not, as we might expect, a turn from the self to the outside world. As we shall see in the next chapter, however, even Donne makes considerable rhetorical play with the ideal of perfect friendship. He gets flexibility out of the idea because of the static form of the verse letter. Shakespeare, in his *Sonnets*, finds similar and even greater possibilities in meditation on the ideal of friendship, but such meditation is out of place in drama. Ideal friendship is undramatic; it might work in chamber drama, but the Shakespearean public theatre, with its presentation of large social groups and of the whole social hierarchy, actively rejects such attempts to focus on private rarefied social relationships as the only valuable ones. Perfect friendship is hard to put into a plot; friendship has an illusion of permanence because it has no apparent teleology, and therefore has no obvious plot paradigm, but when it is put into a plot, an end to the friendship has to be assumed. From this end a sense of individualized selfhood can emerge. I do not wish to emphasize the emergence of modernity, much less the 'invention of the human' in Shakespeare, but I do think that we see a highly characteristic type of selfhood at the end of Shakespeare's plays; this involves a kind of ironically melancholic recognition that one is fundamentally alone – one has one's place in the story, but one's self will never be *fully* realized. This comes across in Iago's silence, Hamlet's recognition that 'the rest is silence', Henry V's insistence that he does not 'know' Falstaff; all these reflect on the limitation of human connectedness, but at the same time depend on some prior form of friendship with others.

Laurie Shannon convincingly demonstrates that the myth of likeness in friendship enables a fiction of parity which, if it does not anticipate modern democracy, creates a space in which the individual can feel sovereign – paradoxically self-sufficient in friendship.[61] In some respects this argument resembles Joel Fineman's contention that traditional poetry of praise (before Shakespeare) 'presupposes or anticipates the correspondence, ultimately the identification of [the poet's] ego and his ego ideal: he is therefore a full self, incipiently or virtually present to himself by virtue of the admiration instantiated by his visionary speech'.[62] Fineman goes on, however, to argue that the full self of traditional poetry is fractured in *Shakespeare's Sonnets* (and also in the tragedies). These arguments can be reconciled if we understand the peculiar rhythm of Shakespearean friendship: as Shannon notes, a relatively rigid and naturalized social hierarchy is the starting point;[63] within this structure, but driven by an ideology of equal friendship, points of equality are recognized, giving a temporary sense of parity which ennobles both parties in a friendship, producing an autonomous but paradoxically interdependent sense of selfhood; in the course of time and narrative this gives way, more or less mournfully, to a recognition of difference between the friends;

although this limits the sovereignty of the self, these limitations give each character his peculiar individual shape.

To generalize a little, one can say that Shakespeare develops the crucial truth that it is in interaction with others that we gain a personality; but he also sees the deeper problem of what we are to do with that personality when others have got through with it. Friendship, as an arena for self-assertion, is the means by which men in the best literature of this period, particularly in the works of Shakespeare, make themselves meaningful; but ultimately they have to accept that they are alone, that the framework of meaning is impermanent. This leads either to a cooling into self-reliance or to a sense of self-abandonment. In this compromised selfhood, sometimes mixed up with the characters' sense of doom, there is a sense that being oneself is a matter of indifference, that even as the plays allow individuals to assert themselves, they become aware of the limitations of the selves they are asserting. In some cases this involves a continued identification with others – as Kent in *King Lear* and Horatio in *Hamlet* express the desire to follow their royal friends to the grave – but in others it involves a defiant self-preservation. In both cases there is a mixture of self-assertion and self-abandonment based on a recognition of the self's limitations.

In the tragedies, this can take the form of an acceptance of death, as in Antony's reflection 'No matter' after his comparison of his fortunes to Octavius's (*Antony and Cleopatra*, III. xi. 40), or in Coriolanus's sense that Aufidius has 'made my heart / Too great for what contains it' (v. vi. 102). In both these cases, the intimate enemy (who has been in some sort a friend) has pushed the hero to the point of destruction but also to the point of recognition of how that destruction is inherent in his own character. 'Simply the thing I am / Shall make me live', says Parolles (*All's Well that Ends Well*, IV. iii. 333–4); but in tragedy, simply the thing I am shall make me die. In an earlier tragedy, Brutus takes a more robust but still doom-laden line:

> Countrymen,
> My heart doth joy that yet in all my life
> I found no man but he was true to me.
> I shall have glory by this losing day
> More than Octavius and Mark Antony
> By this vile conquest shall attain unto.
> So fare you well at once, for Brutus' tongue
> Hath almost ended his life's history.
> Night hangs upon mine eyes, my bones would rest,
> That have but labour'd to attain this hour.
> (*Julius Caesar*, v. v. 33–42)

Brutus's acceptance of himself is founded on his belief (however ill-founded) that other men have been true to him, but he must die alone – in his use of the third person, he is showing a self-assertive awareness that it is his story, not Caesar's, not Octavius's, not Mark Antony's.

Such self-assertion is not just tragic. In the histories, individuals come to see themselves in their historic significance. In the simplest version of this, Suffolk ends *1 Henry VI* talking of himself in the third person and comparing himself to the Trojan Paris. More powerfully, Richard II famously soliloquizes thus in gaol:

> I have been studying how I may compare
> This prison where I live unto the world;
> And for because the world is populous,
> And here is not a creature but myself,
> I cannot do it; yet I'll hammer it out.
> My brain I'll prove the female to my soul,
> My soul the father, and these two beget
> A generation of still-breeding thoughts;
> And these same thoughts people this little world,
> In humours like the people of this world:
> For no thought is contented. (*Richard II*, v. v. 1–11)

Richard, who has no children, defies death by making himself the progenitor of the world. Prince Hal, by contrast, in his differing responses to the death of Hotspur and the apparent death of Falstaff, seems to displace mortality onto others, making himself a kind of immortal, and thus tacitly identifying himself with the deathless kingship. To the dead Hotspur he says:

> When that this body did contain a spirit,
> A kingdom for it was too small a bound,
> But now two paces of the vilest earth
> Is room enough. This earth that bears thee dead
> Bears not alive so stout a gentleman.
> If thou wert sensible of courtesy,
> I should not make so dear a show of zeal;
> But let my favours hide thy mangled face,
> And even in thy behalf I'll thank myself
> For doing these fair rites of tenderness.
> (*1 Henry IV*, v. iv. 88–98)

What we see in both Richard and Hal is a claim to an exclusive authority on stage, though of very different kinds. These are characters who welcome isolation, but that isolation forces them to make little dramas with imaginary friends – Richard his little kingdom of multiple selves, Hal his imaginary truce with Hotspur. The difference is that Hal's confidence is as strong as Richard Duke of Gloucester's 'I am myself alone' (*3 Henry VI*, v. vi. 83). Yet Hal is not alone on stage; the apparently dead Falstaff is also there. As Hal gives him a highly ambivalent eulogy, he seems to bring his fat friend back to life. The power of human relations is reasserted (for more on this, see chapter 6, below).

These are characters who have evaded the processes of melancholy self-acceptance, owing to their preoccupation with power; as such, they seem comparatively inhuman, but even so they cannot imagine themselves without imagining other people. The more human Cardinal Wolsey, as he sees power slipping from him, is much more sympathetic; he knows that 'The King has gone beyond me' (*Henry VIII*, III. i. 408), but is able to hand on his connections to Cromwell:

> Seek the King!
> That sun, I pray, may never set! I have told him
> What, and how true, thou art; he will advance thee.
> Some little memory of me will stir him
> (I know his noble nature) not to let
> Thy hopeful service perish too. (lines 414–19)

This desire to transmit power to others (however much of a poisoned chalice it may be) is founded on his acute sense of what it is to be a sole self, a sense that is wonderfully depicted in his earlier soliloquy:

> I have ventur'd,
> Like wanton boys that swim on bladders,
> This many summers in a sea of glory,
> But far beyond my depth. My high-blown pride
> At length broke under me, and now has left me,
> Weary and old with service, to the mercy
> Of a rude stream that must for ever hide me. (lines 358–64)

That these lines may be by Fletcher rather than Shakespeare only goes to show that Shakespeare was able to hand over some of his own artistry of selfhood to a younger dramatist, as Wolsey hands over to Cromwell. It is in *loss*, half-forced, half-willed, based on an acceptance that one's connections to others are impermanent, that Shakespeare's people most assert themselves.

We can even see elements of this in the comedies, as characters recognize the limitations of their selfhood through their relationships to others. Benedick's words to his friend Don Pedro – 'Prince, thou art sad, get thee a wife, get thee a wife' (*Much Ado about Nothing*, V. iv. 122) – accept his prince's power, but with a sly dig at power's limitations; he asserts their shared humanity even as he acknowledges the prince's status. We can see in Benedick a shrug of the shoulders at the fact that one is not the master of one's own destiny, because despite this fact of fate, one remains oneself. Jaques takes on himself a greater power in pretending to arrange *As You Like It*'s conclusion by his own will; his ersatz theatrical power is founded on his melancholy withdrawal from the world, but he still accepts authority in an ironic way – attaching himself only to the disempowered whilst acknowledging the active authority:

> If I heard you rightly,
> The Duke [Frederick] hath put on a religious life,
> And thrown into neglect the pompous court?
> JAQUES DE BOIS. He hath.
> JAQUES. To him will I. Out of these convertites
> There is much matter to be heard and learn'd.
> [*To Duke Senior*] You to your former honour I bequeath,
> Your patience and your virtue well deserves it;
> [*To Orlando*] You to your love, that your true faith doth merit;
> [*To Oliver*] You to your land, and love, and great allies;
> [*To Silvius*] You to a long and well-deserved bed;
> [*To Touchstone*] And you to wrangling, for thy loving voyage
> Is but two months victuall'd. – So to your pleasures,
> I am for other than for dancing measures.
> DUKE SENIOR. Stay, Jaques, stay.
> JAQUES. To see no pastime I. What you would have
> I'll stay to know at your abandon'd cave. (v. iv. 180–96)

Even as he asserts his own solitariness, he relates himself to all the main characters on stage. Such comic characters retain their ability to assert themselves theatrically because of their recognition of their own limitations, a recognition that comes through the interaction of the conventions of friendship and of social hierarchy. Such characters have more resilience than idealizers of friendship like Antonio, who can only conclude 'I am dumb' (*The Merchant of Venice*, v. i. 279 – though he does go on to tell of his recovered argosies); their endings are more like the irony of Hamlet's 'the rest is silence' (*Hamlet*, v. ii. 358), which surely reflects a moderately contented sense of the world going on without him. Antonio is defeated in a way that Hamlet is not, and this is because he has believed too much in the ideal of friendship. Shakespeare ultimately brings out a sense of individuality founded on loneliness and loss. As Mark Antony says, 'No matter': there is no *real* human connectedness, just as there is no *real* political power, even though we have to live by its conventions.

Nietzsche argues that it is through friendship that people come to accept themselves:

Through knowing ourselves, and regarding our own nature as a moving sphere of moods and opinions, and thus learning to despise ourselves a little, we restore our proper equilibrium with others. It is true we have good reason to think little of each of our acquaintances, even the greatest of them; but equally good reason to direct this feeling back onto ourself. – And so, since we can endure ourself, let us also endure other people.[64]

Individualized selfhood is won through the loss of the sense of equality found in friendship, but retains a persistent sense of meaning and value because of the experience. Hence it is, as Maurice Blanchot and Jacques Derrida argue, both following Montaigne, that the true value and meaning of friendship can only be seen in retrospect.[65] The evanescent and nostalgic ideal of true friendship, even if recognized as a fiction, recalibrates the world, however momentarily.

If retrospective eulogies are the fullest mode of representing friendship, the present tense of friendship, much more dramatically, takes place in conversation, which is the major mode of representing friendship, from Plato, through Cicero, and into Renaissance drama. Conversation is also a mode of self-assertion, both within the friendship itself, and to a wider society; as Nietzsche observed:

In the normal conversation each thinks he is leading the way, as if two ships sailing side by side and now and then gently bumping into one another each faithfully believed the neighbouring ship was following or even being pulled along by it.[66]

This feeling was present in some form in our period. Robert C. Evans shows that 'Jonson's poems take seriously the axiom that friends provide opportunities to communicate about oneself; his praise is inherently and often subtly reflexive.'[67] Joel Fineman makes a similar point about the whole tradition of the poetry of praise, arguing that 'the rhetorical magnification praise accords its object also rebounds back upon itself, drawing attention to itself and to its own grandiloquent rhetoricity'.[68] This is still more the case in drama, where every speech, regardless of its subject, draws attention to the speaker more than to the addressee or the person spoken about. Whilst Enobarbus praises Cleopatra or Kent advises Lear, it is Enobarbus or Kent we look at, not Cleopatra or Lear. For Burton, grace of speech is the most powerful property of friendship; such speech has an almost marvellous effect on individuals, being 'a charm, like mandrake wine', which puts away our cares. Words, however, are worth less than the individuals who speak them: 'good words are cheerful and powerful of themselves, but much more from friends, as so many props, mutually sustaining each other like ivy and a wall'.[69] This insists on a value in human company which surpasses the rhetoricity that Hutson sees as provoking anxiety in friendship.

The idea of mutual sustenance between friends is an alternative model to the soul-connection of equals, and one which allows room for individual difference and self-assertion whilst still enabling and sustaining connections between individuals. This is not a permanent condition of sympathy with others, but rather an occasional capacity to feel that someone else's life has a special relation to one's own. This relation may in fact be quite significantly instrumental rather than a matter of soul-connection, but it is felt as a desire for the other's well-being and an assurance that this feeling is reciprocated. Rather than instrumentalism, this may best be thought of as symbiosis, as in Burton's image of the ivy and the wall. It is a feeling that turns very sour when it turns out not to be mutual or permanent. The image of the ivy can also easily be used as an image of parasitism: it is in these terms that Prospero uses it of his treacherous brother Sebastian (*The Tempest*, i. ii. 85–7). In his Colloquy 'Amicitia', Erasmus argues that there are natural connections or sympathetic affinities between different species;[70] this may also be applied to individuals of different classes, who develop special connections in their ability to promote and clarify each other's selfhood. To some extent, this book will argue, the Humanist ideal of equality is done away with in the drama, and replaced by a sense of sympathetic or symbiotic difference in which individuality is recognized in everyone.

The kind of inter-species sympathy that Erasmus identifies is *natural* and in clear and persistent opposition to the idea of natural antipathy. In Shakespeare's time, the word *sympathy* had an essentially physical or physiological meaning, and only a weaker and analogical psychological meaning (a later version of this can be found in Goethe's notion of elective affinities). Sympathy, of course, is a two-way process, but it is rarely exactly balanced or simultaneously reciprocated. At times the desire for sympathy may be more powerful than the willingness to sympathize, but the desire does provoke the willingness, in cases like Marlowe's Edward II or Shakespeare's Hamlet. Of course, the desire to assert one's power cuts across this sense of sympathy: Richard II wants to dominate but also wants to sympathize and be sympathized with. His extraordinary self-alienation may be the consequence of this process. The sum total of these desiring forces is the desire for *recognition*, the desire to see the total impact of the self in the other (and of the other in the self). A key motive in friendship on stage is to have one's friends – and also the audience – see that one has done good, for example in Kent's desire that Lear ultimately recognize him and his services. If this is not soul-connection, nor should human motives be taken with unmixed cynicism. There are no permanent soul-connections, but from the backdrop of more instrumental friendship it is possible for moments of connection to emerge.

These moments resemble classical recognition scenes (Aristotle's *anagnorisis*) where an individual either recognizes someone as his friend, or recognizes himself through another. Such scenes have a visceral appeal to our yearning for human sympathy and connection. Recognition is one of the great aesthetic pleasures because it is the core of perception, but there is a deeper pleasure in the surprising recognition of other human beings. Aristotle made it a core component of literature in his *Poetics*, defining it as 'a change from ignorance to knowledge, tending either to affection or to enmity'.[71] Although he acknowledges that there can be recognition of objects or of people's responsibility for deeds, he is primarily concerned with recognitions of persons. He also observed that it can either be mutual or one-way. The principal recognitions in the Athenian drama that was Aristotle's subject are of separated family members; such familial *anagnorisis* is at the centre of Shakespearean romance (*The Comedy of Errors, Twelfth Night, The Winter's Tale, Cymbeline*), but in his other plays there is a more muted but emotionally significant form of recognition which is the essence of the dramatic representation of friendship. In order to see how this works, we may first consider its opposite. The recognition that someone is really an enemy – a discovery Othello makes about Iago – or a false friend – as Bertram finds of Parolles – is an obvious enough feature of drama. Changes towards affection and friendship are less obvious; the clearest instance is Hamlet's sudden declaration that Horatio is the justest man he knows. This is because friendship rarely emerges as suddenly as enmity or romantic love; there is no equivalent of Benedick's sudden realization that Beatrice loves him (and, of course, that he loves her). Rather, what one recognizes in a friend is something deeper and subtler – an element of oneself, or a complement to oneself. In this, the friend can teach one about one's true nature, including – even particularly highlighting – one's flaws. The recognitions of friendship may not be immediate – as we have seen, they are more likely to be retrospective – but they are at least as powerful as those of love.

Erasmus was as aware as Shakespeare and his generation would be of the impossibility of the Ciceronian idealization of friendship. As his Moria declares, friendship has its true origins not in wisdom but in human folly:

Look! Conniving at your friends' vices, passing over them, being blind to them, being deceived by them, and even loving these same vices as if they were virtues – does this not seem to be folly?[72]

Moria goes on to say that inequalities are the basis of friendship, and that the only human equality is in folly; this deliberate undermining of the Ciceronian tradition, along with the idea that friendship requires a basis in foolish self-love anticipates the dramatic presentation of self-assertive, imperfect friendship, driven by peculiar affinities and oddities of personal taste which have little to do with abstract virtue.[73] In Erasmus's Colloquy 'Amicitia', Ephorinus argues that to find happiness man 'should avoid the company of those whose characters he finds incompatible with his own and associate with those to whom he is drawn by natural sympathy'.[74] Whilst Ephorinus may hate a boastful liar, others find him amusing, and Ephorinus suggests that there is nothing wrong with this. It is an indulgence that we see reflected in Hal's attitude to Falstaff. Ephorinus considers that all the different enmities and affinities could not have been set up by Nature, who 'enjoyed this spectacle, just as we find entertainment in setting cocks among quail'.[75] Similarly, dramatists will set up human affinities of great variety for the audience's amusement, not just equal friendship, which gives us no pleasure in difference or incongruity.

The following chapters show how these various aspects of the Renaissance ideology of friendship operate in a variety of contexts, some of which would not immediately seem promising for the emergence of friendship. In all cases, we can see how individual self-assertion is enabled by friendship, but also limited by it. Social difference between friends is a major part of this, as most friendships are not – indeed cannot be – quite as equal as Humanist ideology would have them. Nonetheless, the fantasy of equality is important for the individual's self-assertion, just as the fantasy of permanence is important for the sense of loss in friendship that makes it a ground for the representation of individuality. We begin not with drama, but with *Shakespeare's Sonnets*, where these issues can be seen particularly acutely, as the friendship there lacks the external complications of the plays. We then consider how family (particularly brotherhood) and romantic love – relationships which might seem to have coherent homologies with friendship – interact with and are compromised by friendship. The next chapters deal with relationships that are more obviously instrumental – service and politics – or pleasurable – groups of friends – and show how they too are affected by the ideology of friendship. Finally, I consider the way in which explicitly false friendship or betrayed friendship can be as intimate and as strikingly important for the development of selfhood as true friendship. In all these cases, there is a complex dynamic balance between self-assertion and the desire to make meaningful connections with others. The suspicion that we have as many selves as we have friends (or even acquaintances) perhaps motivates the desire to promote one particular friendship which will underpin the integrity of the self, but if such a notion is pushed at too hard, we may end up with no self at all.

CHAPTER 2

Momentary mutuality in *Shakespeare's Sonnets*

The large cast of most Elizabethan and Jacobean plays means that friendships are necessarily implicated, as in life, in a larger social structure; they cannot be taken in isolation as they are in philosophical texts. The more rarefied mode of the sonnet sequence, however, allows a laboratory-like isolation of an individual friendship. Even here, however, the 'base infection' of the social world ultimately compromises friendship: sexual desire, homoerotic as well as heterosexual, complicates ideal friendship, and all emotions are ultimately informed by social hierarchy. Nonetheless, the sonnet form allows for moments of negotiated intimacy which have greater intensity than any comparable moment in the more urgently active world of the plays.

The *Sonnets'* friendship is an unequal one. Their rhetorical strategies attempt to bridge differences between the poet's persona and the young man to whom the poems are addressed.[1] The bridges are made by fictions of mutuality, which Shakespeare often knows to be fictions, and only temporary ones at that. In the larger sequence, each creation of a bridging fiction tends in turn to open another gap between the men. In the end a respect for distance and difference emerges, but this fatally compromises any idealized friendship, which (according to the Humanists) should be based on similarity, closeness and equality. Shakespeare makes the young man radically different from himself, but in doing so, as Eve Kosofsky Sedgwick argues, he makes him passive, partly as a mode of 'anticipatory self-protectiveness'.[2] Whilst some have questioned the prevailing view that the *Sonnets* have only one male addressee,[3] the sense of discontinuity may come from the fact that Shakespeare finds himself forced to reconstruct his addressee from poem to poem: the *Sonnets* succeed in conjuring moments of mutuality and intimacy which collapse in the larger sequence. Part of this involves the poet's self-assertion; part his self-abandonment. The poet's search for mutual friendship will never quite balance out; his own desire for recognition reflects his writing back on

30

himself, carving out and clarifying his own self, giving it prominence even as it is morally diminished.

Joel Fineman's tremendously influential work on the *Sonnets*, arguing that a modern sense of selfhood emerges in the course of Shakespeare's praise of his friend, may sometimes overstate its case, but emphasizes a crucial aspect of the *Sonnets*: the object of admiration here can never quite live up to the ideal standards by which he is judged; on the other hand, the poet *feels* that it is the ideals that are not good enough for the young man. This creates self-division in the poet, a loss of 'fulness', and a distrust in language's ability to carry the burden of selfhood to another.[4] I shall argue that something of this self-division can be found in Plato's thoughts on friendship, and that Aristotle offers some provisional answers to these problems. Finally, however, Shakespeare attempts to resolve them by the extraordinary tactic of intermittently identifying himself and the young man with both the Christian God and with Christ the Saviour. This last desperate tactic of identification necessarily fails: having allowed a momentary sense of perfect mutuality, it ultimately divides the young man and the poet.

Plato's and Aristotle's views of friendship are remarkably similar to Shakespeare's ideas about his friendship in the *Sonnets*. Whether he assimilated these ideas from his university-educated friends, or thought them through for himself on the basis of classically influenced texts, Shakespeare's poems develop in directions that are illuminated by the great Greek philosophers.[5] It has been argued that 'friendship is more the environment or ethos than the subject of Plato's dialogues',[6] and it is clear that in Plato's view friendship is constituted in discourse. This may help to account for the dialogic feel that many have detected in the *Sonnets*.[7] Of course, we only get one side of a dialogue in a lyric poem, and so the poet may be engaged in a solo version of the Platonic process.[8] As A. W. Price argues, in Plato's *Symposium* 'philosophizing with and for another may be the only way of philosophizing oneself'.[9] Plato's *Lysis* inconclusively but illuminatingly considers whether friendship is merely a matter of reciprocal altruism, a pleasurable affection, or a way for the individual to fill some moral lack in himself. The dialogue reflects a clear and almost desperate desire to make friendship something more worthy of good men, for the reciprocation, pleasure and moral redress arguments would not make friendship necessary for the truly good man. The failure to come to a satisfactory answer to this problem implies, with characteristic Socratic irony, that friendship is something only needed by the morally imperfect. It is thus a means for the recognition of one's moral imperfection, and the resulting need for moral compromise with others. Similarly, the *Sonnets'* sense of mutuality is not so much a matter of equal virtue as equal sinfulness, allowing Shakespeare and the young man to bind themselves together in forgiveness. That forgiveness is not founded on absolute or external standards, but rather on the standards of the friendship itself; it consequently provides a very fragile validation of the individual.

Lysis also provides a warning for one who wants to praise a friend: Socrates tells Hippothales that the songs he intends to write in honour of his beloved are really in praise of himself:

for if you win your beautiful love, your discourses and songs will be a glory to you, and may be truly regarded as hymns of praise composed in honour of you who have conquered and won such a love; but if he slips away from you, the more you have praised him, the more ridiculous you will look at having lost this fairest and best of blessings.[10]

This combination of the risk of loss and the risk of selfishness is at the heart of the *Sonnets*. Aristotle, in the *Nichomachean Ethics*, tries to get around this problem by arguing that friends contribute to each other's moral well-being, or *eudaimonia*. For Aristotle there is no conflict between self-love and social, at least for the good man, who will strive to do what is best all the time, but who can also sacrifice his own good actions without loss of virtue: 'It is also possible to sacrifice actions to his friend, since it may be finer to be responsible for his friend's doing the action than to do it himself.'[11] Moral competition between friends promotes the increase of virtue, but it is not a zero-sum game: all gain by co-operation.[12] But the fact that the promotion of good action is somehow 'finer' than action itself is a concept that anticipates Shakespeare's ironies of self-assertion in friendship even as he lauds the young man. Shakespeare seeks a 'double vantage' (88. 12) in his friendship with the young man.[13] By proving the young man 'virtuous' (line 4), even though he has spoken ill of Shakespeare, the poet intends to give 'much glory' to him (line 8). Shakespeare, being prepared to 'bear all wrong' (line 14), ultimately wins the advantage. In this poem, the idea of winning a game in which both win is fully explicit, but it is an undertone of the whole sequence. The young man is constantly used as an object of contemplation to mutual advantage. Shakespeare gradually comes to terms with the fact that he himself gets more advantage. He builds bridges to the young man, but these bridges remain his own.

At first the advantage Shakespeare gets is merely a matter of improving his own mood through the contemplation of the young man. This can be seen most clearly in the sequence of sonnets 29–31. Sonnet 29, 'When in disgrace with fortune and men's eyes', has a simple enough core meaning – 'When the rest of the world hates me, I remember your love, and then I feel good.' But the 'disgrace' could easily suggest feeling disgraced in the eyes of the beloved. The poem is a bootstrapping exercise, in which Shakespeare's mind lifts itself from despair to joy, by using the weight of its pondered despair. The first lines' generalized terms home in on the beloved young man even though he may be the key factor of the despair. As Helen Vendler argues, the poem pivots itself on the line 'With what I most enjoy contented least'.[14] This clearly implies discontent with the beloved, but once Shakespeare thinks about the beloved, his mood lifts; he rises 'From sullen earth' and 'sings hymns at heaven's gate' (line 12). All the other discontents may be metaphors for vague discontent in his relationship, yet once the young man becomes the focus of his thoughts, the clouds lift. Thoughts of the young man are an opium, curing the discontents which have probably been caused by him. But how caused? Shakespeare's discontent is expressed thus:

> [I] look upon myself, and curse my fate,
> Wishing me like to one more rich in hope,
> Featured like him, like him with friends possessed,
> Desiring this man's art, and that man's scope.

This expression of envy is generalized, but in the context of the sequence surely suggests envy of the young man ('featured like him' calls on all the expressions of the young man's beauty, and if written for William Herbert before he came into his title as Earl of Pembroke, 'rich in hope' is particularly applicable). It is almost a blazon of the young man's attributes. Therefore one might trace the emotional movement of the sonnet thus: 'When I feel bad, I want to be like you – but then I think of you, and then I feel so good that it's as if I am you – so I don't envy you any more.' The identification is only momentary, but it is enough for the sonnet. Envy is transformed, temporarily at least, into successful emulation. The young man is both the means to get to heaven, and perhaps the heaven itself. Sonnet 30, immediately following, puts still greater weight on the despair, and the gravity-defying buoyancy that ends the poem seems still more of a last-ditch effort:

> When to the sessions of sweet silent thought
> I summon up remembrance of things past,
> I sigh the lack of many a thing I sought,

And with old woes new wail my dear time's waste;
Then can I drown an eye (unused to flow)
For precious friends hid in death's dateless night,
And weep afresh love's long since cancelled woe,
And moan th' expense of many a vanished sight.
Then can I grieve at grievances foregone,
And heavily from woe to woe tell o'er
The sad account of fore-bemoaned moan,
Which I new pay, as if not paid before;
　　But if the while I think on thee, dear friend,
　　All losses are restored, and sorrows end.

Considering all his lacks, Shakespeare can compensate for all previous woe by thinking of the young man. This overdetermines the beloved, making him bear the weight of all that has gone before, and it is hard to accept the balance. The friend is made into too much of an end in himself, as if in a desperate attempt to avoid an instrumental view of friendship; Shakespeare thus rules out the idea of friendship as a step on the Platonic ladder to the divine. The poem also recognizes the balancing difference between the immediacy of present joy and the distance of past woe. In *summoning* up remembrance of things past, in recognizing that previous woes are 'fore-bemoaned' (line 11), Shakespeare achieves a tentative balance that relies on living in the moment. As Fineman argues, the sonnets to the young man seem like elegies for the present.[15] This effect is appropriate to the immediacy of the short form of the sonnet, but cannot be sustained for a whole sequence and becomes much more fragile in the longer structures of drama. Friendship, which should (according to Sir Thomas Elyot for example) be based on long trial and is supposed to be a rational and long-term relationship, has been reduced here to the momentary. Sonnet 31 develops from the themes of sonnet 30, but takes them in a somewhat different direction. All Shakespeare's old lost loves have come together in the young man, as if he were the heaven for their dead spirits. As Burrow notes, 'The dominant mood here is of a triumph over death through the friend';[16] the young man's redemptive powers, and his victory over death, give him Christlike powers. Having started in sonnet 29 with an effort to cheer himself up, Shakespeare now finds that the only way to do this is to give 'the all of me' (line 14) to the young man. Trying to find a way to 'sing hymns at heaven's gate' (29. 12) all his eggs are put in the basket of this supposed heaven, leaving Shakespeare more vulnerable to later betrayal. Moments of self-consolation amount to a larger sequence of self-abandonment. Lars Engle aptly calls this type of stance in sonnet 88 'passive-aggressive abjection'.[17] This leads, in turn, to subtle attempts to assert the value of the poet's self. Envy is clearly a part of friendship, but one that writers on friendship are keen to erase. Donne does this particularly gracefully:

> Men say, and truly, that they better be
> Which be envied than pitied, therefore I,
> Because I wish thee well, do thee envy.[18]

In making envy voluntary, and in translating it into a matter of good will, Donne has removed the problem of underlying resentment in friendship, but it is also clear that this is a rhetorical flourish designed to emphasize the talents of the supposedly inferior friend. Donne also plays with the idea of one soul in bodies twain, undercutting it with a humility trope; he addresses his friend in some apparent confusion: 'Thou which art I, ('tis nothing to be so) / Thou which art still thyself.'[19] Shakespeare's sense of the need to present a humble self similarly undercuts absolute identification with the friend, and suggests that social status differentials ultimately undermine the realization of the friendship ideal.

One of the young man's advantages over Shakespeare, his youth, is a mixed blessing: whilst it gives him hope and beauty superior to the poet's, it also allows the poet to give advice on the basis of his superior experience. This is most obviously expressed in the first seventeen sonnets, advising the young man to marry, but it also becomes the premise of the entire sequence, as the older man speaks and the younger man, whilst notionally active, is the passive object of language. Yet this process creates a bridging fiction of mutuality. Even as he highlights and exaggerates his age in order to differentiate himself from the young man, he appropriates the young man's youth in order to explore his feelings about the age difference: 'My glass shall not persuade me I am old / So long as youth and thou are of one date' (22. 1–2). This is clearly based on the Humanist idea of one soul in two bodies; the poem relies upon the conceit of exchange between the men which goes well beyond the concept of blood-brotherhood. Having made a distinction between 'inner worth and outward fair' in sonnet 16, Shakespeare now complicates this duality, suggesting that the young man's looks are really appropriate to the poet's own self: 'For all the beauty that doth cover thee / Is both the seemly raiment of my heart, / Which in thy breast doth live, as thine in me' (22. 5–7). This assertion of their inter-dependence means that any selfishness on either part is really altruism, and that any care for another is really care of the self, an idea which resembles Aristotle's:

> O therefore love be of thyself so wary
> As I not for myself but for thee will
> Bearing thy heart, which I will keep so chary
> As tender nurse her babe from faring ill. (22. 9–12)

J. B. Leishman observed that the *Sonnets* are singularly lacking in *carpe diem* motifs,[20] but they do attempt to deny mortality and to promote greater youthfulness in both men. In making the young man an infant, Shakespeare makes him passive even as he propounds what Vendler calls 'a fantasy of mutual care'.[21] Making himself a nurse rather than a mother reflects Shakespeare's insistence on the value of extra-familial relations. As Vendler has shown, the early sonnets enact a shift from genetic to poetic reproduction of the individual,[22] just as Plato's philosophy of love in the *Symposium* moves from physical to mental procreation in its approach to immortality.[23] Shakespeare becomes the crucial agent in this process, even if it is in service of the young man. The poet, a kind of servant to the young man, like most servants subtly disables his master. The fiction of service which enables the connection between the men is ultimately destructive to their relationship.

The *Sonnets*, then, deny the young man any independence that he might naturally claim. This can be seen very sharply in sonnet 13:

> O that you were yourself! But, love, you are
> No longer yours, than you yourself here live;
> Against this coming end you should prepare,
> And your sweet semblance to some other give:
> So should that beauty which you hold in lease
> Find no determination; then you were
> Yourself again after yourself's decease,
> When your sweet issue your sweet form should bear.
> Who lets so fair a house fall to decay,
> Which husbandry in honour might uphold
> Against the stormy gusts of winter's day
> And barren rage of death's eternal cold?
>   O none but unthrifts, dear my love you know:
>   You had a father; let your son say so.

The poem is a rhetorical *tour de force*. Vendler argues that 'it is the first of many "reply-sonnets", poems which respond to an implied anterior utterance from the young man. We are to imagine that the young man has said, in response to earlier reproaches, "I am myself, sufficient to myself".[24] Shakespeare replies with a sophisticated tutorial on selfhood, into which he intrudes his first mention of *love* for the young man, as if he is emboldened by the intoxication of his own verbal ingenuity. The first lines require some paraphrase to highlight their strangeness: 'You are not your self: you only belong to yourself whilst your self is alive. You must give your substance to someone else. Then your beauty will live on; and you will be your self when your self is dead, when your son has your form.' We can fairly ask what on earth Shakespeare means by self here. *You, yourself* and *your self* all appear to be different things. Once the sestet brings in the (dynastic) house, which is associated with beauty (fairness), the confusion is heightened still further. To simplify things we have to create a binary opposition: on the one hand there is 'you', the substance of personality, sometimes confusingly called yourself; on the other is the *self*, which is glossed as semblance, beauty and the house, with its implications of status and wealth. In other words, Shakespeare is suggesting that 'what you see as yourself, as sufficient, is in fact merely accidental; it is only beauty and status, which you hold in lease: this, for it to have meaning, must be passed on to a son. But you have a deeper, more essential self, the self that I love.' Underneath the continued exhortation to beget an heir, then, is a declaration of love that transcends status and patronage, and this is one of the *Sonnets*' deepest themes: 'how can I declare my love for you, when it would be too easy to love, as you yourself love, merely your beauty and status?' What we can see here is that status and beauty are seen as unearned attributes, which reflect the young man's passivity. The poet's lower status allows him to be the only active figure in the friendship.

Another problem that this poem raises is the association of beauty and status. Sumptuary laws of the sixteenth century ensured that higher-caste men dressed more beautifully than the lowly.[25] Shakespeare does not make use of this fact, for he concentrates on the young man's facial beauty, but it is clear that he sees this beauty as a familial rather than a personal resource.[26] In sonnet 94 Shakespeare returns to the idea of whether men can be 'lords and masters of their faces' and he is continually preoccupied by the questionable association of face and personality/self. House, face and wealth are familial and genetic resources, and, insofar as Shakespeare concentrates on them, he is distanced from the young man and put in a poet–patron relationship rather than one of friendship. In an almost parasitic way, Shakespeare's verse manages to appropriate the young man's superiority of caste and wealth just as he appropriated his youth. In sonnet 37 he sees himself as a non-genetic father to the young man, making himself 'engrafted' (line 8) to his family. In this way he takes 'a part of all thy glory' (line 12) and shares in the young man's *eudaimonia*. The pose of humility, of being lame, poor and despised, allows a more subtle self-assertion.

In differentiating himself from the young man in order to praise him worthily Shakespeare acknowledges the young man's 'power to hurt' (94. 1). Even if this power is not exercised, it admits the possibility that the friendship is not entirely mutual on its supposedly fundamental level – the affective. The young man may indeed be 'as stone' (line 3), though he moves others, primarily Shakespeare. In sonnet 25 Shakespeare is able to convince himself that the friendship transcends other worldly considerations, but in the next poem he acknowledges his 'vassalage'. Shakespeare is *working* for the glory of one who only has to *be* himself for glory to accrue: this is not the Aristotelean process of *eudaimonia*. In a foreshadowing of the Hegelian struggle for recognition, it is bound ultimately to demean both master and vassal,[27] the master through his stony passivity, the poet–servant through not being allowed to keep the fruits of his labour. The nature of this dependent relationship is such that Shakespeare has to 'bear love's wrong' (40. 12), which does neither of them credit. Shakespeare's self-abasement is sly even when it is most explicit. 'The pain be mine, but thine shall be the praise' (38. 14) is a clear enough courtship/patronage sentiment, unless we consider the second clause to conceal the meaning, '*You* will praise it (and that will be ample recompense for my pains).' Even this slyness conceals a deeper compliment (that the young man's praise is valuable – he is a source of honour), by which both poet and addressee are raised a notch. That Shakespeare gets honour is proof that the young man can confer it: the young man's worth is therefore guaranteed by Shakespeare. The process is circular, however, and therefore cut off from reality. When, in sonnet 89, Shakespeare says 'speak of my lameness and I straight will halt', he is putting himself in the same position of submission that Katherina is forced to adopt in *The Taming of the Shrew*. Like the relationship between Katherina and Petruchio, that between Shakespeare and the young man has become cut off from the social world, and therefore from standards of truth, and their reality is constructed entirely in language (which, despite Shakespeare's humility, puts him in a stronger position than the young man). All the relationship's energy comes from within and it must eventually burn itself out. In this sense 'base infection' (94. 11) may enter the relationship: this may be the infection of Shakespeare's baseness of status, or even perhaps of the baseness that is caused by status differentials. The difference which sustains the relationship is the cause of its destruction; social differences make a society work, but make it impermanent. In these circumstances, friendship cannot have comedic resolution, cannot be reintegrated into the values of a larger society; we may like to believe in the perfection of a two-way, self-sustaining friendship, but it only works momentarily, through an unsustainable bridging fiction. In a sonnet, it can be sealed off from the outside world, but in a sequence, and much more in a play, such isolation is impossible.

One problem is the idea of possession in friendship: possession is a temporal concept, implying some sort of security and permanence; friendship lacks this security. Sonnet 91 reflects Shakespeare's anxieties about possessiveness in friendship particularly well. It starts with the speaker patronizing those whose sense of self-worth is materially based:

> Some glory in their birth, some in their skill,
> Some in their wealth, some in their bodies' force,
> Some in their garments, though new-fangled ill,
> Some in their hawks and hounds, some in their horse. (lines 1–4)

The equation between personal qualities and mere possessions here is subtly done. Although the primary meaning is that there are different types of people who glory in different things, the overall effect is additive rather than analytic, suggesting that there are some who have all these things (a similar effect to sonnet 29). Shakespeare, though, is able to rise above these various humours – 'these particulars are not my measure'. As Kerrigan points out, the meanings of 'measure' are threefold: '(1) the things to judge me by; (2) enough for me, sufficient to satisfy me; (3) the things I use to judge happiness.'[28] As Shakespeare doesn't have these things (according to his own lights anyway), he might be glad that he neither wants nor needs them, and particularly that they don't affect his status. His self-assertion (paradoxically *to* the friend) is based on his possession of the friend, the implication being 'you have all these things and glory in them; I bask in the reflected glory, and, what is more, I have you, the substance, as well as the attributes, to glory in. These are merely lendings to you, but I have their essence, and am therefore – through you – somehow superior to you.' The 'general best' he claims in line 8 develops this sense:

> All these I better in one general best.
> Thy love is better than high birth to me. (lines 8–9)

But the poem cannot end on this note of self-aggrandizement (which resembles the idea of standing on giants' shoulders). The end of the twelfth line 'of all men's pride I boast' is quickly modified in the couplet:

> Wretched in this alone, that thou mayst take
> All this away, and me most wretched make. (lines 13–14)

The poem sees Shakespeare climb to glory over the friend's possessions, but then tumble to earth in the recognition that he cannot truly possess the friend. The problem is simply stated by Helen Vendler: 'High birth cannot be taken away, but love can be.'[29] Friendship, which is free, is simply not a mode of possession as marriage is; its glory is its flaw. That the highest emotion is more contingent even than new-fangled garments makes any absolutism or permanence in friendship a pipe-dream. The verse can only conjure temporary self-assertions.

The strain required to balance the relationship is reflected in the emergence of a sense of sin. In *Astrophil and Stella* Sir Philip Sidney is constantly occupied with his own active virtue – does his love for Stella increase or retard it? Shakespeare is similarly preoccupied, but in an inverse way: he is more explicitly concerned with the effect of the relationship on the young man, and focusses on vice rather than virtue. The young man's sin, introduced in sonnet 33 as a stain on the sun, is vague. Lisa Freinkel may be right to argue that 'What the young man has done literally makes no difference since any report of beauty is an "ill" report',[30] so that it is the very fact of being represented that makes the young man sinful, but we are nonetheless intrigued by the mystery, which becomes another bridging fiction, and allows a theological relationship between the poet and the young man, one that may perhaps be less subject to temporal anxieties. Insofar as the young man's sin seems to involve something done with Shakespeare we may fairly wonder if the unspeakable sin is sodomy, that unspeakable category.[31] On the other hand, Shakespeare's involvement may be an aspect of the fictions of sharing that we have seen at work: as Shakespeare shares the young man's wealth, youth, beauty etc., the corollary is that he shares his sins. It is also possible, though, that the young man's sin from its first introduction involves taking Shakespeare's mistress, a fact that is only fully clarified in the Dark Lady subsequence; it is the shared sin of Old Adam, heterosexual desire, which both joins and separates the men. The commonness in Shakespeare's time of narratives putting friends into conflict over a woman (explored in chapter 4, below) makes it likely that such a narrative is to be inferred from the first. The implication, then, is that their shared sin is the sin of being men sexually drawn to women. As Jonathan Goldberg has argued, we can construe the true sodomy in the world of the *Sonnets* as sex with women.[32] Whether the woman concerned is individual or representative does not matter for the purpose of this argument: within the sequence's discourse of friendship, to turn to a woman is sinful, a 'sensual fault', against the rational 'sense' of friendship (35. 9). It is the principal and symbolic way in which the perfect circle of friendship is broken. If we read sonnet 40 as coming from a poet whose friend has taken his mistress, we can see Shakespeare as taking a pose rather similar to that of Sir Thomas Elyot's Titus when Gisippus falls for Sophronia.[33] Yet there is ill-concealed rancour here: the young man is a 'gentle thief' (line 9), in an apparently paradoxical statement of upper-class larceny. When Shakespeare insists at the end of the poem that 'we must not be foes', all he does is bring up that possibility. The implicit threat of enmity, an instance of what Christopher Ricks calls the 'cold courtesy' of Shakespeare's 'counter-threats',[34] becomes another way of equalizing the unequal friendship. The young man's sin becomes an opportunity for greater mutuality. In sonnet 41, Shakespeare speaks of the young man's 'pretty wrongs' (line 1), committed in his 'liberty': whilst this primarily implies the young man's libertinism, the qualification 'When I am sometime absent from thy heart' makes his liberty dependent on Shakespeare absenting himself. His freedom comes only from licence given by the poet.

   Whatever the sin is, Shakespeare's real interest is in using it to bring himself closer to the young man by forgiving or redeeming it. As the young man was Shakespeare's saviour from woe in sonnets 30 and 31, Shakespeare can be the young man's saviour from sin. This binding process in friendship can be found more explicitly in Donne's verse letters, when he deifies his female correspondents, and particularly when he tells 'Mr T. W.' 'I am thy Creator, thou my Saviour.'[35] The idea of a friend as Christlike saviour – the ultimate special relationship – redeems friendship from the Platonic view that there is something ignoble about needing friendship.[36] This fiction, however, creates a curious circle of mutual redemption: the process of excusing binds them together in sin, but, for the moment at least, the fact that it binds them together at all is enough to content the poet, even though the sin is against himself. In sonnet 35 ('No more be grieved at that which thou hast done'), Shake-speare's excuse is that 'All men make faults, and even I, in this, / Authorizing thy trespass with compare' (lines 5–6). As Donne claims to be the creator of his friend, Shakespeare authorizes the young man – he writes him and he gives him licence. As he appears to show humility, as he makes his own fault for the sake of the young man, he gains a moral advantage. This is a Christianized inversion of the Aristotelian idea of it being finer to cause virtue in others than to act oneself: here, we feel it is finer to take another's sins on oneself.

Sonnet 58, however, implies that Shakespeare's sacrifice has not gone far enough for the young man, and that consequently a further sacrifice must be made in allowing the young man complete independence. The tone here is of a long-suffering but obedient wife: 'That god forbid, that first made me your slave, / I should in thought control your times of pleasure' (lines 1–2). The obvious implication is that Shakespeare wants to control the young man. There is something dismissive in the concession that 'to you it doth belong / Yourself to pardon of self-doing crime' (lines 11–12). To err is human, to forgive divine: the young man is both.[37] Stephen Booth notes that 'self-doing crime' may be a crime against Shakespeare (as a supposed second self) as much as a crime committed by the young man (against himself).[38] As a 'vassal' (line 4) Shakespeare has no role here but to 'wait' (line 13). He washes his hands. Effective as it is, it is a disagreeable poem, which reduces both poet and subject; but it is also the natural development of the earlier self-sacrifice. The earlier creation of mutuality can only cool now into this deeper indifference and disconnection. The poet is not Christ and cannot absolve the young man, though for a moment he fancied that he could. Instead he takes on some of the young man's properties, becoming more like stone himself. This had already been suggested in sonnet 36, where Shakespeare says:

> Let me confess that we two must be twain,
> Although our undivided loves are one;
> So shall those blots that do with me remain,
> Without thy help, by me be borne alone. (lines 1–4)

The taint to the relationship is 'separable' (line 6), suggesting that it can be separated from the friendship, but also implying that it can only be so if they separate from each other. Shakespeare is prepared to be a scapegoat: he has appropriated the young man's sin here, calling it 'my bewailed guilt' (line 10) because he has bewailed it, not because he is really guilty himself. In sonnet 39, he worries that he cannot rightly praise the young man because the young man is himself, albeit 'all the better part' (line 2). In saying that they must 'divided live' (line 5) in order that Shakespeare not be guilty of self-praise, he is able to assume that love is guaranteed and permanent, but the 'thoughts of love' (line 11) that he fondly hopes will compensate him for absence cannot last. The response, in order to recover equality and make them inseparable, is for the poet to sin himself. In sonnet 117, Shakespeare accepts the accusation (which he himself supplies) that he has gone out into the world 'with unknown minds' (line 5) and has 'hoisted sail to all the winds' (line 7), while the young man stays as a still centre. As well as both suggesting and enacting the young man's passivity, this poem also, in its reply to the accusations, insists that Shakespeare's movements 'prove' (line 13) the young man's love. It is by Shakespeare's testing of the young man that the latter's godlike constancy is asserted. Only through Shakespeare can the young man be realized. This develops in sonnet 120 in a splendidly half-ironic recovery of friendship in shared vice:

> That you were once unkind befriends me now,
> And for that sorrow, which I then did feel,
> Needs must I under my transgression bow,
> Unless my nerves were brass or hammered steel. (lines 1–4)

Shakespeare starts here with his conclusion – 'you did it and I forgave you; so you owe me forgiveness now I've done it too'. The assumption that the young man is feeling the same 'sorrow' that Shakespeare felt is ironic but hopeful. The insistence at the end 'that your trespass now becomes a fee; / Mine ransoms yours, and yours must ransom me', is commanding. In sinning, Shakespeare has become 'a tyrant' (line 7) and regained power in the relationship – an appropriation of the power to hurt, however fictive. As Shakespeare is the sinner, the young man is now the redemptive Christ-figure. Yet in sonnet 109 the poet, in returning, brings 'water' for the 'stain' of his absence (line 8). He is as self-pardoning as the young man. Friendship has become a mode of excusing one's own sins. The Aristotelian friendship of virtue is replaced by a Christian version, which is now in turn replaced by a parodic version of itself, a tainted version of the ideal. It has become transactional and is based on failures in both men. This is exactly what Socrates in *Lysis* feared that friendship might really be.

In addition to using ideas of Christlike redemption to validate friendship, Shakespeare makes the flawed young man an idol, an alternative deity. 'Moving others' (94. 3) but not moving himself, he takes on the properties of God, the Prime Mover. Shakespeare may insist in sonnet 105 that his love is not 'idolatry', but that is only because in his terms the young man is actually a God.[39] This has the advantage of removing the humiliating element of being a servant to the young man; service to a human master may be demeaning, but service to a divinity ennobles. Unable to wash away the young man's sins in human terms, Shakespeare makes a move of stunning audacity: he absolves him by making him God, and therefore, by definition, always right, incapable of wrong. There is a fundamental theological problem in praising God, in that it is hard to see how flawed human praise can be of any worth to a flawless deity. John Donne tries to get round this by arguing that honour can only come from flawed humans:

> Honour is so sublime perfection,
> And so refined; that when God was alone
> And creatureless at first, himself had none;
>
> But as of the elements, these which we tread,
> Produce all things with which we'are joyed or fed,
> And, those are barren both above our head:
>
> So from low persons doth all honour flow.
> ('To the Countess of Bedford', lines 1–7)[40]

In a similar manner Shakespeare suggests that though he is himself unworthy, his praise has value. The movement of sonnet 84 is a fascinating wrestle with the same problem of praise as Donne's, and with the same theological backdrop. The truest praise for the young man is 'that you alone are you' (line 2), giving him divine uniqueness,[41] but in writing that 'lean penury within that pen doth dwell / That to this subject lends not some small glory' (lines 5–6), Shakespeare insists that there is some merit in the god-praising human. In the case of the young man, however, 'he that writes of you, if he can tell / That you are you, so dignifies his story' (lines 7–8). The real art is pure representation of the young man's godlike perfection, but the entertaining and dismissal of the idea that the pen can add to this glory at least brings up the notion of mutuality of advantage, even with a God. Shakespeare gives the young man glory (or at least, in normal circumstances, should be able to) and the young man dignifies Shakespeare's verse. Dignity, with its class suggestions, comes from the countenance of the upper-class man; glory (or as Donne puts it, honour), more abstract, comes from low persons, those penurious souls like Shakespeare who give the dignified upper class their place in the world and history. After all, superior people would not be superior if they did not have anyone to be superior to. Yet the poem has a further sting in its tail. Shakespeare says that the young man has one flaw, thus giving some worth to his praise. This flaw is exactly the excessive love of praise: 'You to your beauteous blessings add a curse, / Being fond on praise, which makes your praises worse' (lines 13–14). As in Donne, the fact of the deity wanting praise implicitly diminishes that deity. But that lack is to be celebrated, for it allows the relationship to exist and gives it meaning. Socrates' wrestling, in *Lysis*, with the problem of how a good man can need a friend – doesn't it imply a lack? – presents the same problem when he asks,

What place then is there for friendship, if, when absent, good men have no need of one another (for even when alone they are sufficient for themselves), and when present have no use for one another? How can such persons ever be induced to value one another?[42]

In the end both Shakespeare and Plato suggest that we must accept the imperfection of the apparently perfect, because it is the only way that more imperfect souls can relate to it. The poet must pretend that the young man is perfect, even though he knows that it is his praise that makes him so.[43] This is something that he comes close to acknowledging in sonnet 108. His sonnets here are 'like prayers divine' (line 5) and he insists on the constancy of their love: 'thou mine, I thine / Even as when first I hallowed thy fair name' (lines 7–8). The hallowing here is not just reverence: it suggests something more actively transitive – that he *makes* the young man holy. When he denies in sonnet 105 that he *shows* him as 'an idol' (line 2), he is engaged in the necessary double-think of all idolaters: he has made his God, but must pretend that he has not. The process of making the fiction to give the two men a real, extra-temporal relationship is ultimately destructive of any human, social connection between them.

The poet may accept his dream, as Theseus suggests in *A Midsummer Night's Dream* (v. i. 2–22). The impossible 'possessing' of that which is 'too dear' (87. 1) makes Shakespeare 'In sleep a king' (line 14), even if waking he is no such matter. Momentary possession, however, is not true possession, even if it may be something finer. Though power is given to the young man, the tension at the heart of the *Sonnets* is that temporary feelings of mutuality are conjured by strategies that distance the two men until they become opposites. This allows a genuine respect for individual particularity, and a sense of the men's peculiar importance for one another, but it is lonely. The last full sonnet to the young man, number 125, rejects all the gains that Shakespeare has appropriated from him, insisting that the poet is 'poor but free' (line 10) and thus able to praise properly. No longer wanting 'increase' (1. 1) or 'double vantage' (88. 12), he despises those who seek for 'compound sweet' (line 7) from friendship. He is 'a true soul', not in the 'control' of the 'suborned informer' (lines 13–14), whom Duncan-Jones construes as Time.[44] As Sedgwick argues, an 'external agent' is needed so that the young man cannot be blamed for his changes.[45] All Shakespeare wants is 'mutual render, only me for thee' (line 12), a momentary, dreamlike creation of a deity in whom one believes absolutely and to whom one can give oneself up. Shakespeare tries to create intensity of feeling in friendship partly through the Ciceronian notion of one soul in two bodies, but such identification does not seem sufficient to the feeling. A grander identification can be found through the Christian doctrine of the incarnation, mixing perfect deity with imperfect man, to redeem the latter: 'mutual render' resembles Gerard Manley Hopkins's sudden identification with Christ: 'I am all at once what Christ is, / since he was what I am' ('That Nature is a Heraclitean Fire and of the comfort of the Resurrection', line 22).[46] Like Hopkins's, Shakespeare's intense identification relies on a collapse of temporality and must come all at once. This can, however, only take place in the realm of lyric isolation, and the *Sonnets* ultimately constitute a regretful critique of the dangers of such isolated friendship, which is as lonely as the 'truly parallel' love of Marvell's 'Definition of Love',[47] which can never meet. Such friendship is not enough – its lyric intensities must give way to friendship that is part of the larger social structure. Whilst such friendship provides recognitions of selfhood in the other and, above all, in the poet himself, and these recognitions may have some of the dramatic force of Aristotelian *anagnorisis*, it is side-by-side friendship rather than face-to-face engagement with the other that dominates drama. Although we shall see moments of recognition in drama, they are only momentary, swept aside by larger social forces and by personal desires that have greater priority than friendship. Nonetheless, even when not idolizing one another, characters in drama give each other honour, something that can only exist in relation to others.

The problem that ideal, equal and permanent friendship has in this respect is that the friends are presumed to be too similar for this to emerge; they tend to cancel each other out, thus diminishing rather than augmenting the self. The other relationship with other men that can only diminish the self is that with one's brothers – they dilute, diminish and share out one's selfhood in a way that demonstrates, by contrast, the additive power of friendship. If difference is ultimately what makes the friendship of the sonnets creative for selfhood, it is similarity between brothers that is a major social and dramatic problem, as we shall see in the next chapter.

CHAPTER 3

Friends and brothers

Whilst it can be argued that a crucial aspect of the transition from the medieval world to the modern is the move from a kin-based model of society to one based on friendship of mutual advantage, we must be wary of inferring too great a break. Alan Bray has shown that the idea of 'sworn brotherhood' persisted much longer than was previously acknowledged;[1] the model of family as the basis for friendship persisted. Montaigne, though arguing that friendship is superior to brotherhood, acknowledges that 'Verily the name of Brother is a glorious name, and full of loving kindnesse, and therefore did he [his friend Etienne de la Boëtie] and I terme one another sworne brother.'[2] If friendship is to some extent modelled on brotherhood, to understand the problems of brothers will help us to see both what friendship was competing against and what it was based upon. There is a more obvious tension between brothers than between friends: Sir Thomas Elyot argued that there is a crucial difference between friendship and kinship in that 'from kynrede may be taken ben-euolence, from frendship it can neuer be seuered. Wherfore beneuolence taken from kynrede yet the name of kinseman remayneth. Take it from frendship and the name of frendship is utterly perrished.'[3] The tension between brothers as represented in Shakespeare's plays is deeply related to friendship. As a one-to-one relationship between similar men of necessarily similar status, it resembles the Humanist ideal of friendship, but with the crucial difference of competition for familial resources. Whilst friends enable individual self-assertion (both social and dramatic), brothers tend to dilute one another's individual social and dramatic importance.

Friends can, in Bacon's words, have fortunes that 'comprehend the one the other'.[4] This is more difficult for brothers, given the importance of inheritance in a society still largely driven by the laws of primogeniture. Put simply, brothers get in each other's way more than friends do. There is therefore a natural competition or even enmity between brothers, even if there is also a natural similarity and affinity – the former is of course more dramatically interesting. If brotherhood is a model for friendship then the enmity as well as the affinity may carry across in the metaphor. One of the key features of the narrative and dramatic representation of brothers is the elimination of superfluous brothers. Bacon observed that

A man shall see, where there is a house full of children, one or two of the eldest respected, and the youngest made wantons; but in the midst some that are as it were forgotten, who many times nevertheless prove the best.[5]

Narrative economy means that such large numbers are rarely represented; normally when we see large fraternal groups the middle brothers are forgotten. Drama prefers contrasts and extremes, and tends to make brothers either unnaturally dissimilar or uncannily and confusingly similar. This may also inform the dramatic representation of friendship, in that a dramatist may also want friends either to be so similar that they compete for the same things, or so dissimilar that dramatic tensions arise. Rather than focussing on the internal dynamics of families with large numbers of brothers, most literature of this period relegates brothers in comparison to friendship or to exogamous love, whilst often seeing the relations between brothers as the starting point for a development into more social bonds. Whilst lost brothers may be recognized at the end of romance plots, there is not always the change to affection that Aristotle predicted in recognitions. Indeed, a brother's true nature may be recognized and found wanting in comparison to the recognition of a friend's nature: in this way the individual may come to recognize himself as more akin to his friends than his family. Such competing affiliations are an important aspect of the drama's representation of the individual's development. If friendship most fully develops his personality, this is first honed on the conflicts involved in brotherhood.

The deepest thoughts about kinship and friendship in the literature of Shakespeare's time come not in drama, but in the greatest poem of the period, Spenser's *The Faerie Queene*. Spenser's 'Legend of Friendship', in book iv of his poem, provides a particularly acute reflection on the displacement of kin bonds by social bonds; brotherhood is a matrix for friendship, but may also be the source of strife in friendship. As we shall see, the drama presents similarly ambivalent views on the relative value of different male bonds. The story of Cambell and Triamond in cantos ii–iii is a story of the primal origins of friendship, which can only be enacted in a more civilized form by other characters. Usually, in friendship narratives, friendship is the starting condition, having evolved prior to the narrative's beginning. Some difference or contradiction upsets the friendship and sets off a narrative which will end with the death of one or both of the friends or in the restoration of the friendship. Here, we are given a rather different picture: we are shown Cambell and Triamond riding together as friends, but we are then given their back-story, a story of conflict. The narrative structure moves into conflict, as it does in so many friendship narratives, but here that conflict is already securely in the past: the trial of the friendship was at its origin, and friendship has its origin in strife. The back-story itself is relatively simple, if very mysterious; it is told at some length, as a considerable deviation from the onward thrust of Spenser's main narrative. Triamond and his brothers Priamond and Diamond fight with Cambell for the love of his sister Canacee; Cambell strikes down and kills the older two brothers, but thanks to a magical protection given by their mother Agape, the three brothers' souls are interlinked, passing from the dead ones into the living, by a process called 'traduction' (iv. iii. 13. 6);[6] the combat is concluded by the arrival of the brothers' sister Cambina, who stills the men's strife with the potion Nepenthe and her healing caduceus. Cambell marries Cambina, and Triamond Canacee; the knights become the poem's exemplars of friendship, and fight marvellously at the ensuing tournament. The extraordinary lengths to which Cambell goes in fighting for his sister here suggest something incestuous in his attitude towards her. These are the first characters in the whole of *The Faerie Queene* to marry, and it seems reasonable to see this legend as involving not only the origins of friendship, but also the origins of exogamy. The extraordinary violence of the episode suggests the inherent conflict between men when there are not enough women to go round. When Cambell and Diamond fight, they are compared to tigers fighting over spoil, making both their desires for Canacee seem appetitive. This startling suggestion of the incest taboo is further extended into a suggestion of another great taboo, cannibalism: 'they both together fiercely met, / As if that each ment other to deuoure' (iv. iii. 21). Only when Cambina (never mentioned before, and of obscure origins) miraculously arrives, and when the excess trio of brothers has been trimmed back to one, can social bonds be formed between men. Friendship and marriage are linked: both involve going outside the family. Friendship, in this primal case, needs marriage as a guarantee, replacing the destructive idea of blood-brotherhood.

Brothers in *The Faerie Queene* tend to be in conflict or doomed. Notably, Bracidas and Amidas (v. iv) demonstrate why brothers have to be removed from the poem, reduced to one representative from each family: their quarrel over land, women and treasure shows the jealousies that can be provoked by too close a familial relation. Artegall settles the dispute, but only to one party's satisfaction. There is an inherent conflict between brothers that must be replaced by friendship. As Montaigne observes, describing friendship's superiority to brotherhood: 'this com-mixture, dividence, and sharing of goods, this joyning wealth to wealth, and that the riches of one shall be the povertie of another, doth exceedingly distemper and distract all brotherly alliance, and lovely conjunction'.[7] It is significant that the allegorical brothers outside the Temple of Venus in book IV canto x, Love and Hate, have to be held together by force on Concord's part: concord cannot easily be brought to bear on brothers. Concord's own twin sons, Peace and Friendship, are not presented in the poem, merely mentioned. These two sets of brothers are highly symbolic: when it comes to active characters the poem eradi-cates brotherhood so that some form of unified judgement may be made. That Artegall is Arthur's half-brother is a theme the poem fails to realize, and one which may suggest that a further resolution of the claims of friendship and brotherhood may have been planned.

The most extraordinary aspect of the Cambell and Triamond episode is the traduction of souls between the brothers. Spenser, normally such a magpie, appears to have invented this myth himself. It establishes the notion that brothers have to be fundamentally the same, and so if one survives, all survive in a way, continuing the family line and preventing proliferation. It contributes a great and significant uncertainty to the tale: Priamond and Diamond die (IV. iii. 12, 21), and their souls enter the next brother; Triamond then suffers two wounds (Stanzas 30, 33) which appear to lose him a soul apiece. This means that their mother's whole elaborate magic has been in vain (as Spenser implies at the canto's beginning); providing a sister is much more effective magic. This may not be the whole import of the story, however; we are uncertain as to which soul is in Triamond, and therefore, in a sense, all three brothers are in him. The finality of their reconciliation and marriages (the first in the poem) is undercut by uncertainty. Whom has Canacee married? Who is Cambina, the sister never before mentioned? Who is her father (it surely can't be the knight who raped the sleeping Agape, unless he raped her again . . .)? By injecting these mysteries into his narrative, Spenser gains a strong sense of miraculous grace in the origins of friendship. I can see two possible sources for the story. Firstly Montaigne's essay 'On Friendship', in which we are told:

this perfect amity I speake of, is indivisible; each man doth so wholly give himselfe unto his friend, that he hath nothing left to divide else-where: moreover he is grieved that he is [not] double, triple, or quadruple, and hath not many soules, or sundry wils, that he might conferre them all upon this subject.[8]

Triamond is able to perform this multiplication literally. The second is the text from which Montaigne had derived the tale he relates in support of his assertion, Lucian's *Toxaris*, where Toxaris tells Mnesippus that a man can only make three close (blood-brother) friends in his life.[9] Cambell is enacting the Scythian custom in triplicate, making all his friendships at once. Brotherhood, the original relation between men, tainted by the Sin of Cain, is replaced, through a combination of violence and magical grace, by the civilized bond of friendship. It is also significant that the image of the triple-bodied Geryon is used for friendship at the end of *Toxaris*: 'For the union of two or three friends is like the pictures of Geryon that artists exhibit – a man with six hands and three heads. Indeed, to my mind Geryon was three persons acting together in all things, as is right if they are really friends.'[10] There is therefore something monstrous in the original image of friendship that must be purged. The violence of the battle makes for a form of blood-brotherhood which is ratified by marriage. Both Scythian barbarism and civilized ceremonies are necessary. By Cambell and Triamond's participation in the tournament of the girdle, this hard-won friendship is handed on to the other characters of the poem. The fellowship of the other knights, which was enacted without affective relations in the earlier books, is infused with the virtue of friendship, enriching the later stages of the poem with more complex social relations. Drama cannot present such large allegorical development, but there is often a similar sense in Shakespeare and his contemporaries that brotherly relations are either irrelevant or need to be replaced with other social or sexual bonds.

Bacon tells us at the end of 'Of Parents and Children' that 'Younger brothers are commonly fortunate, but seldom or never where the elder are disinherited.'[11] Cyril Tourneur's *The Atheist's Tragedy*, presenting two pairs of brothers in two generations of the same family, takes for granted the enmity of younger brothers to elder. The play is more explicitly driven by man's need for posterity than most other Renaissance drama. As D'Amville says:

> Here are my sons . . .
> There's my posterity. My life in them
> And their succession shall for ever live,
> And in my reason dwells the providence
> To add to life as much of happiness. (I. i. 123–7)[12]

He is so concerned with this that he is prepared to sleep with his impotent son's wife in order to ensure the propagation of his line. To add to the prosperity of this line he kills his elder brother Montferrers without a pang, after sending his nephew Charlemont to the wars and having a false report of his death brought. So obsessed is he with producing a unitary and secure line that he refuses to split his money by giving his younger son an annuity. This younger son Sebastian has opposed his elder brother's marriage to Charlemont's betrothed Castabella, calling the enforced marriage a 'rape' (I. iv. 116), but it is not just his opposition to his father's plans that enrages D'Amville: a younger son is simply an irrelevance. Sebastian decides to take the side of Charlemont (after they have fought). His stance is not explicitly against his brother, being rather directed in favour of virtue (or at least so he claims), but he certainly has no fraternal loyalty. Although Sebastian has gained more trust (and some money) in fighting Charlemont, his father does not trust him as a continuer of his line:

> his loose humour will endure
> No bond of marriage. And I doubt his life;
> His spirit is so boldly dangerous. (IV. ii. 36–8)

This is odd, given that D'Amville has contrived marriage for his sickly and weak elder son. We may infer beneath these apparent motives a sense that a younger son is irrelevant. Sebastian is indeed an adulterer, and is killed by the man he has been cuckolding. He is his father's son, and that is the problem, as he has a younger son's bold spirit. In the deaths of his sons D'Amville's plans all come to nought, and the proper line of primogeniture survives when D'Amville providentially kills himself in attempting to execute Charlemont, who gets the girl and the money. Aided by a character called Borachio, D'Amville reminds us of Don John in *Much Ado* (who had an identically named assistant). Both are figures of pure, if easily defeated malice – a malice that is rooted entirely in brotherhood.

Pairs of brothers are relatively rare in the rest of Jacobean drama – perhaps because one of them always seems superfluous. In Webster's *The White Devil*, Flamineo kills his virtuous and superfluous brother Marcello for the spurious reason that the younger brother has cursed the whole family by breaking a crucifix as an infant. It seems more like tidying up. The murder is casual and replaces a planned duel: whereas the killing of a friend is worthy of ritual combat (as in *The Two Noble Kinsmen*), killing a brother is not worth the dramatic candle. Flamineo's allegiance is to himself and (when expedient) to his patron Brachiano; his sister Vittoria is a resource for his advancement, his brother a drag on his ambitions. In contrast, perhaps the most striking use of brothers in other Jacobean drama is *The Revenger's Tragedy* (or should that be *Revengers'*?), a play that harps constantly on brotherhood, as Vindice and Hippolito and the Duke's sons (one of them bastard) and stepsons address one another as *brother* with insistent regularity. In having a brother Vindice seems less isolated than the earlier avenger Hamlet, for the brother is a more closely involved ally than the friend Horatio. Hamlet's friend will vindicate him after death in telling his story and is not himself tainted by the murders of Elsinore; Hippolito will be executed with Vindice at the end of their play. Whereas Horatio provides a sounding board for Hamlet and a guarantee of sanity in a mad world, Hippolito is nearly as involved as his brother. Horatio is dissuaded from suicide to do his friend verbal service; a 'just' and rational friend is not expected to be pulled into the bloody catastrophe as a brother is. Hippolito is not enough of an audience for Vindice: for justice to be seen to be done it is not enough for him that his brother knows – it must be more public, and so he dooms himself by boasting of his deeds to the new Duke Antonio. The brotherly alliance in revenge contrasts with the mutual treachery of the Duke's various 'sons', but it is only a small and ultimately meaningless alliance in a world driven by fratricidal violence.

The problems of brothers with regard to inheritance are particularly acute in royal families. That Claudius has killed his brother to take the throne is the central premise of *Hamlet*, but that play is much more concerned with relations between a son and his dead father than it is with the 'primal eldest curse' (III. iii. 37) of fratricide. However, Hamlet's choice of Horatio as a rational friend hints that this play considers friends more reliable than treacherous brothers. Fraternal conflict is the mark of a selfishness and isolation that can only be mitigated by friendship, if at all. The titular hero of *Richard III* never explicitly compares himself to his elder brothers, but his preoccupation with his own crooked form and his hatred for 'these fair well-spoken days' (I. i. 29) imply an unfavourable comparison of himself to Edward and Clarence. Richard feels isolated in his family, claiming to have 'no friends' to back his suit to Anne Neville, suggesting that his brothers cannot be counted as the friends/supporters traditional society would assume they were. Clarence asks his murderers to remind Richard of the paternal blessing that should bind the brothers and prevent fratricide, but to no avail – the bonds are broken and meaningless to the self-reliant Richard:

> Tell him, when that our princely father York
> Blest his three sons with his victorious arm,
> And charg'd us from his soul to love each other,
> He little thought of this divided friendship.
> Bid Gloucester think of this, and he will weep. (1. iv. 235–9)

With the paternal injunction to love gone, there is no inherent bond between brothers. As we will see in a later chapter, friendship in the world of politics is an empty category, based on rhetoric rather than affection, but the rotting of affection starts with the erosion of fraternal bonds. Richard claims allegiance to 'our house' (*3 Henry VI*, v. vi. 65; and *Richard III*, 1. i. 3), but this is a mere cover for his absolute selfishness. In *3 Henry VI*, Richard's character is set up in his differentiation of himself from his brothers:

> I have no brother, I am like no brother;
> And this word 'love', which greybeards call divine,
> Be resident in men like one another,
> And not in me: I am myself alone. (v. vi. 80–3)

Richard's insistence here on his own uniqueness is couched in terms which in themselves justify his lack of fraternal feeling: because he is unique in himself, with no brotherly semblance, he needs not be kind to his brother, and it is in this that he is unique. The assertion of one's dramatic and social importance depends on the denial of anyone similar to oneself. Underlying Richard's circular logic is the assumption that fraternal love is the norm; if it weren't, Richard would not be unique. *Richard III* enacts the breaking of traditional familial bonds (called friendship), which will have to be replaced by more pragmatic modern friendship, but even the latter is betrayed when Richard has Buckingham killed. Fraternal bonds are nearly as unimportant to Richard III's opposite in the cycle of English history plays, Henry V, who takes a very distant attitude to his brother John of Lancaster, preferring to spend his time with his tavern companions. When he comes to the throne he signals his distance from his brothers even as he appears to reconcile himself with them. Elevated to the throne, Hal can talk down to the other members of the court not only on the basis his new external authority but also based on his unfamiliarity. Fear rather than affection is the basis of his rule, despite his pretence that the courtiers should not fear him.

> Brothers, you mix your sadness with some fear:
> This is the English, not the Turkish court,
> Not Amurath an Amurath succeeds,
> But Harry Harry. Yet be sad, good brothers,
> For by my faith it very well becomes you.
> ... For me, by heaven (I bid you be assur'd)
> I'll be your father and your brother too.
> Let me but bear your love, I'll bear your cares.
>   (2 *Henry IV*, v. ii. 46–50, 56–8)

There is nothing truly brotherly about these words, delivered in a tone of command, asserting his authority over even their emotions, and in dismissing the threat of Turkish-style regal fratricide he actually brings the idea up with a certain menace. Brotherhood certainly does not imply equality in this world. Hierarchical enmity or competition becomes a paradoxical norm, with only lip-service paid to the idea of fraternal love, which is to be *borne*, as if it were something of a burden. Henry's assertion of selfhood comes more through his friendships, but here he demonstrates that it involves the clear subordination of brothers.

Two of the mature comedies, *Much Ado about Nothing* and *As You Like It*, are premised on fraternal conflicts, but neither foregrounds this aspect. Don John has already been defeated and forgiven when the action of *Much Ado* begins. He is full of self-disdain, and hates the honest world as much as Richard III, but he seems to have no particularized dislike for his half-brother Don Pedro. His 'discontent' is vague, and he can make no 'use' of it (I. iii. 38). His plot is also vague: 'Grow this to what adverse issue it can, I will put it in practice' (II. ii. 51–2). He even seems to lack Richard III's ambition, merely wanting licence to be a villain and to bite everyone around him (I. iii. 32–6). The fact that Don Pedro's forgiveness of his brother is complete removes any dramatic tension between the brothers (as well as enabling Don John's plot to succeed). Indeed, the bastard's anger is with Claudio, the Prince's new friend who has the glory of Don John's overthrow (I. iii. 66–7; II. ii. 5–6). We might then infer that this revenge is based on a brother's desire to defeat a friend. Friendship wins in this play; it is Benedick, the third friend, who will 'devise brave punishments' for Don John (v. iv. 128); and it is Benedick who gains the greatest self-assertion and dramatic prominence. The bastard brother has a very minor role in the play: he is on stage very little, is not brought on at the end, and doesn't even devise his own plot – most of which comes from Borachio. The brother is simply superseded.

As You Like It examines the problem of brothers from two directions: in the case of the dukes it is the younger brother who is the usurping villain; in the case of the de Boys family the maltreated younger brother is the hero. The implication, then, is that primogeniture is more important in ruling families than in private ones. Given its premise, we might expect the play to make much of fraternal tension, but the theme is handled very lightly. Oliver's character and motivation are given less attention even than Don John's. His decision to become a shepherd is based on love for 'Aliena'/Celia, and on his brother saving him from a lioness and a snake. In Erasmus's Colloquy *Amicitia*, Ephorinus tells of lizards saving men from snakes in very similar circumstances – being about to crawl down men's throats.[13] Shakespeare's use of this suggests a natural sympathy between brothers similar to the natural sympathy between men and lizards that Erasmus is arguing for. Duke Frederick's *volte-face* is still less motivated: he undergoes an off-stage religious conversion that is stag-geringly casual in its abandonment of the expected plotline. These miracles of conciliation give some credibility to Rosalind's claim to be a magician (v. ii. 59–61); although that claim is made with regard to her ability to resolve the love plots, it may also extend to the resolution of the larger plot. Shakespeare seems to take fraternal enmity for granted and then to solve it as magically as Spenser's Cambina solves the conflict between Cambell and the Triamond brothers, but without representing the same level of violence that Spenser's heroes must go through. The conciliatory *if*s of this play suggest that it is a conditional fantasy, and that its reconciliations must be treated as such, but the initial problem is a grave one. Orlando sees nothing natural about primogeniture, telling his brother that it is a cultural construct: 'The courtesy of nations allows you my better, in that you are the first-born, but the same tradition takes not away my blood, were there twenty brothers betwixt us' (i. i. 46–9). The end of the play, restoring Duke Senior to his rights, endorses primo-geniture in the ruling family, but allows Orlando to trump his brother (without rebellion). William Kerrigan argues that hatred between men is 'an almost impersonal force' in the play, resolved by the friendly Rosa-lind, who, as an example of the good female, mitigates the complex of sibling rivalry and Oedipal anxiety amongst the men.[14] It is our impression that the Duke's daughter Rosalind (however obscurely) brings about the happy conclusion through her love. As the basis for this love is (she says) the fact that 'The Duke my father loved his father dearly'

(i. iii. 29–30), we might infer that Orlando's ability to take his brother's birthright is based on a chain of affiliation to the Duke: loyalty to one's father and to authority allows a younger brother to buck the system through marriage. Friendship, bound by marriage in a second generation, defeats or resolves the hierarchy of brothers.

Very different from the colourless brothers of *As You Like It*, Edmund and Edgar in *King Lear* are the most complex pair of brothers in Shakespeare: everything about each of them is shaped by the other. Their plot is more dramatic than that of any other brothers in the oeuvre, and yet it takes place in what is essentially a subplot, subordinated to the grander drama of Lear's royal family. Edmund, the downtrodden bastard soliloquizer, gets our attention and therefore sympathies first. Like Orlando, Edmund is a believer in nature rather than custom. Thomas Kelly argues that by failing to educate Orlando, Oliver has made him a natural; but this does not make him a fool – rather, it connects him to natural virtue.[15] This is not the case with Edmund, devotee as he is of a more sinister conception of the goddess Nature. He thinks his father a fop for believing in portents, and his brother appears to him as confined to his plots, 'like the catastrophe in the old comedy' (i. ii. 134). As the brothers meet for the first time in the play, Edmund takes on the role of 'Tom o'Bedlam' (line 136), anticipating Edgar's later role-playing, as if the legitimate brother were a puppet on the bastard's string. As Harold Bloom says, 'Edmund is brilliant and resourceful, but his prime, initial advantage over everyone else is his total freedom from all familial affect.'[16] Edgar, however bound he is by familial bonds, turns out to be a strange and individual character, playing many roles: he stands for natural feeling as the broken courtier mad Tom, and for generous friendship as the consoler of Gloucester; he stands for sexual morals, legitimacy and primogeniture in his chivalric defeat of Edmund. In killing Oswald he stands for the poor man he will later tell Albany he is (v. i. 38), behaving as a bumpkin to enrage the foppish courtier. It is as if his brother's treachery and his father's anger have radically unsettled his identity. This makes him one of Shakespeare's most baffling characters, constantly improvising his own motivation.[17] The similarity of the brothers' names intimates a confusion between them, as if nature abhors an excess brother. As in *Titus Andronicus*, where Titus's excess sons are trimmed back to one, *Lear* enacts a tidying process, allowing the multi-faceted Edgar to survive. He is hard to pin down: Regan, hearing of his supposed treachery to his father, alleges that he was one of Lear's riotous knights, as well as bringing up the fact that he is Lear's godson (ii. i. 91–5), but such association will not tie him to a particular affiliation. Whilst Nahum Tate would give him the motive of love for Cordelia to explain his remaining in the vicinity of his father's house, Shakespeare has him only wanting to 'preserve' himself (II. iii. 6), even if he regards himself as 'nothing' (line 21). Gloucester calls the disguised Edgar 'friend' in the scene where he leads him to the supposed cliff (IV. vi. 28), but Edgar is friend to no one. In the final act he takes on a chivalric role as the disguised knight prepared to prove to Albany his wife's dishonour. One might suppose that in acting as Albany's champion he is showing allegiance to that lord, but in truth he mainly wants to prove that he is 'noble as the adversary' his brother (V. iii. 123), repeating when he has killed him 'I am no less in blood than thou art, Edmund; / If more, the more thou'st wronged me' (lines 168–9). This is not just a matter of revealing himself, but of asserting his identity – something that can only be properly effected by cancelling his brother's. It is significant that, as Edgar tells us, Gloucester also died at the moment Edgar revealed his identity – father and brother are purged in order to make way for the wronged successor. This asserts primogeniture, but it also enables Edgar's grafting onto the royal stock, not through marriage, as Tate would have it, but through friendship. At the end of the play Albany calls Kent and Edgar 'noble friends' (line 297) and 'friends of my soul' (line 320), and it is only through this connection that Edgar gets the final word (in the Folio at least) and is the true successor to the kingdom. As Lear's godson he gains the kingdom, thus allowing the only officially authorized cere- mony of friendship, godparenthood,[18] to provide a resolution for the whole kingdom. Yet Edgar remains an enigma, not shaped by any real connection to others. His character determined by conflict with a brother, Edgar's identity is less firmly grounded than those who are shaped by friendship.

Like *Lear*, *The Tempest* sees an elder brother returned to his rights. As so often, there is outrage here at fraternal treachery, but also an under- lying sense that there is natural enmity between brothers. We might think that Prospero, as an apparently negligent ruler, deserved to be driven from Milan by his more politically active brother, but the play insists on restoring the order of primogeniture. Alonso's support of this usurpation is nearly requited by his own brother's rebellion against him in the play's direct action, but Prospero's magic brings peace, and a new alliance between Milan and Naples is created in the marriage of Miranda and Ferdinand. In Prospero's tale of his banishment, Shakespeare sets up a deeper relationship between the brothers than in the other plays we have been examining: Prospero 'lov'd' Antonio second only to Miranda

(I. ii. 68–9). The entanglement of the brothers' state is presented in a metaphor more commonly used of royal favourites or parasites:

> now he was
> The ivy which had hid my princely trunk,
> And suck'd my verdure out on't. (lines 85–7)

Prospero describes himself as a betrayed 'good parent' to his brother (line 94). In the dialogue with Miranda he shows rage that such a brother can exist. After all this, though, the interaction of the brothers in the play is curiously muted. Antonio's success in ousting his brother gives 'precedent' (II. i. 291) and encouragement to Sebastian's attempt against Alonso, but even though neither younger brother has a conscience, its role is taken by Ariel, who prevents them from murdering the king: their treacherous friendship can have no success. Prospero's careful magical arrangement of the groupings on stage metatheatrically highlights one of Shakespeare's chief methods of developing our sense of alliance – simply by putting people together, as when Antonio and Sebastian plot against the sleeping Alonso. Such an alliance is presented as opportunistic and circumstantial. Prospero's forgiveness is superhuman and godlike, as befits one who arranges relationships thus, but after his first scene he pays little mind to his brother. All is resolved in two speeches – first an aside to Sebastian and Antonio:

> But you, my brace of lords, were I so minded,
> I here could pluck his Highness' frown upon you
> And justify you traitors. At this time
> I will tell no tales. (v. i. 126–9)

There is a clear fraternal threat here (like a promise to tell daddy) that in the future he may do so. Then he turns publicly on his brother with a forgiveness that is hardly heartfelt:

> For you, most wicked sir, whom to call brother
> Would even infect my mouth, I do forgive
> Thy rankest fault–all of them (lines 130–2)

and demands his dukedom back. Antonio speaks no more in the play (except to contemplate a career exploiting Caliban): the brother has been cancelled. The true enactment of forgiveness has come when Prospero called the penitent lords 'friends all' (line 125), having led up to this with truly friendly addresses to his only true friend among the group, Gonzalo. Through magic and the marriage of Ferdinand and Miranda, a friendly union between all the characters has emerged; but the brother, though not punished, is not even acknowledged as much as Caliban is.

The Comedy of Errors is Shakespeare's only play that takes the relationship of brothers as its major theme. Its central premise presents a simple but delicious irony about human relationships: Egeon will die unless his 'friends' help him (I. i. 152); the friend who has the money turns out to be his son. Rather than insisting on the virtues of friendship, this play recovers family as the truest form of friendship. On the other hand, there is some unease about the recovery of brothers. The two Antipholuses, identical in face as in name, are confusing and therefore almost unnatural in their similarity. Yet their personalities are dissimilar and there is little joy in their greeting; they lack the congeniality to one another that Plato saw as central to friendship. Antipholus of Syracuse must marry his brother's sister-in-law in order to cement their relationship. This resembles the bonding of friends rather than of brothers: in a sense they have to become brothers through marriage, as friends like Cambell and Triamond do. That Shakespeare has added an extra pair of twins to his source (Plautus's *Menaechmi*) not only enhances the comic pleasure of the plot but also suggests an excess in the very idea of brotherhood. The play's context is enmity between Syracuse and Ephesus, and the rejoining of the family here does not reconcile these two states as friendship might. At the play's opening, Antipholus of Syracuse says 'I will go lose myself' in the town (I. ii. 30), and it is hard to say that he has really found himself at the end: the Antipholus brothers are more concerned with unravelling the material plot than with rapturous reunions. Their recognition feels more like a loss than a recovery. Antipholus of Syracuse soliloquizes about being

> like a drop of water,
> That in the ocean seeks another drop,
> Who, falling there to find his fellow forth
> (Unseen, inquisitive) confounds himself. (lines 35–8)

It is hard to see the end of the play as an unconfounding, precisely because his brother is not really a fellow to him, let alone another self. The idea of a second self is a fantasy – one which is, paradoxically, only sustained during the confusion of the play's middle. Patricia Parker has argued that the emphasis on the question of which Antipholus is older in the play's first scene and what she calls 'crossing' of parental attention is an attempt to drive out concern about primogeniture,[19] but the issue is only mutedly resolved, and in the case of the servants not the masters. The servants may go off hand-in-hand, unconcerned as to which is the elder, but the issue of primogeniture for higher-born families is more important, and the Antipholuses do not get on as easily as their servants: it is hard to imagine that they go off hand-in-hand, and one of them must therefore take precedence. The idea of things being 'out of season' (I. ii. 68) runs through the play, and although it is not a *Hamlet*-like sense of time being out of joint, it suggests the dissonance of this 'fairy land' (II. ii. 189). Given that Antipholus of Syracuse is actually looking for his brother, there is a comic irony in the fact that it never occurs to him that the confusion may be caused by the presence of that brother; he is ready to attribute it all to supernatural agency. This reflects his inability to step outside the confusion his double identity causes. When the Duke says that 'one of these men is genius to the other' (v. i. 333), he suggests how closely they sit in each other's place, that one of them is excessive. There is a fear here that brothers may cancel each other out; a fear which can only be mitigated by the Abbess's maternal description of 'this sympathized one day's error' (line 398). Fellow-feeling of confusion binds the family together: but we may wonder whether clarity will unbind. In any case, the brothers have no special bond. The parental guarantee is required and it is the family unit rather than the fraternal pair that is rejoined.

The recovery of family is the major romance theme of Shakespeare's late plays, and in *Cymbeline* we see perhaps the happiest pair of brothers in the oeuvre. The play shows considerable scepticism about friendship: Posthumus's male milieu at Rome, which insists on the ideal of friendship, causes his distrust of Imogen through Iachimo's treachery; his letter of credit for Iachimo gives countenance to one who is not really a friend, but rather a motiveless mischief-maker like Don John. He is, as it were, a bastard friend, and he is disowned by Posthumus when the latter thinks his trial of Imogen's virtue has been successful (II. iv. 48–9). The political friendships of the play are similarly disjunctive, as in this exchange:

> LUCIUS.   Your hand, my lord.
> CLOTEN. Receive it friendly; but from this time forth
> I wear it as your enemy. (III. v. 12–14)

Friendship and enmity are confused throughout the play, as in Posthumus's changes of side in the wars, and when Britain defeats Rome but then submits to her yoke. The pure, pastoral friendship of Guiderius and Arviragus for the disguised Imogen provides a real and redemptive contrast. This friendship springs up naturally, spontaneously, and with a definite tinge of homoeroticism:

> GUIDERIUS.   Were you a woman, youth,
> I should woo hard but be your groom in honesty:
> I bid for you as I do buy.
> ARVIRAGUS.   I'll make't my comfort
> He is a man. I'll love him as my brother. (III. vi. 68–71)

Brotherhood is here the model for friendship, but the obvious irony is that they really are brothers to this disguised woman. The irony is laid on thicker, and still more pleasurably:

> ARVIRAGUS.   ... Most welcome!
> Be sprightly, for you fall 'mongst friends.
> IMOGEN.   [*Aside*] 'Mongst friends?
> If brothers: would it had been so, that they
> Had been my father's sons, then had my prize
> Been less, and so more equal ballasting
> To thee, Posthumus. (lines 73–8)

In this wish, Imogen is hoping for the reassertion of male primogeniture: the natural friendship of brothers will solve her problems. Later, the brothers fight alongside their brother-in-law Posthumus to save their father Cymbeline; their martial alliance is the first step towards Shakespeare's longest and most elaborate recognition scene, which rejoins the royal family, reasserts primogeniture, and binds Posthumus into true friendship with the princes through the endorsement of his marriage to Imogen. Imogen (and her husband) may have 'lost by this a kingdom' (V. v. 374), but love and the royal order have been restored. And in the end, true friendship is also recognized, when Cymbeline tells Belarius, who has brought the princes up, 'Thou art my brother, so we'll hold thee ever' (line 399). One can become brothers through marriage, godparenting or fostering another man's son. The play finally resolves the claims of love, family and friendship, more radically even than *The Winter's Tale* and *The Tempest*. Juliana Lawrence argues that *Cymbeline*, in its 'multiplicity of recognition', displays an 'insistence upon the bonds of kinship' and that 'such recognition clarifies the psychological and ethical importance of human connectedness',[20] but the play can only achieve this by prioritizing family and by totally ignoring the Humanist ideal of friendship.

In this, *Cymbeline* is highly unusual, the most insistently familial of Shakespeare's plays (and one which gets rid of outriding step-family in the form of Cloten and the Queen). Brotherhood fares less well in the other literature of this period. In order to forge an identity, individuals must supersede their brothers and differentiate themselves from them. The self-assertion of fraternal conflict is more vigorous and violent than that in friendship, but not entirely different in kind. Humanist friendship, however, is conceived as an end in itself, valued as a liberation from the sometimes stifling bonds of family. Yet, as we shall see in the next chapter, friendship itself can involve stifling bonds; like brothers, perfect and equal friends can be too similar to one another, and stand too closely in one another's social and dramatic place.

CHAPTER 4

Love and friendship

Where friendship is a major and foregrounded theme in English Renaissance narrative and drama it tends to be put in competition with love. This is because the Humanist ideal of friendship bears some similarity to romantic love; the Humanist ideal in fact seems to want to displace love as a priority in men's lives. This tends towards an insistence that love and friendship are in some sense incompatible, and puts a great deal of pressure on friendship. The conflict between friendship and love is expressed in the narrative and dramatic form of the jealousy plot – in which two friends love the same woman – a plot that is sufficiently common in this period for us to call it a genre.[1] Through the test of jealousy, this genre allows an exploration of the nature of ideal friendship, which is ultimately shown to be a hollow rhetorical construct. When such friendship is taken seriously, however, it can cause an excessive sense of obligation which is often stifling, sometimes absurd. It also causes anxiety about the loss of identity, due to the similarity assumed between the friends. In characters' attempts to escape the stifling determinism of this genre, we can see the start of the kind of self-assertion we see in more differentiated friendly relationships.

Burton observes that sexual jealousy 'will make the nearest and dearest friends fall out; they will endure all other things to be common, goods, lands, moneys, participate of each [other's] pleasures, and take in good part any disgraces, injuries in another kind; but as Propertius well describes it in an elegy of his, in this they will suffer nothing, have no corrivals'.[2] Friends can share all things, but not a woman. To reconcile, either one friend must abandon the woman or they must fight to the death. Death, in fact, provides a form of reconciliation, by sublimating their past feeling into an ideal which can no longer be altered. More earthly reconciliation tends to leave the friendship compromised, and certainly the friends will no longer see each other as the most important thing in life. Love of women has in these cases superseded friendship. The friendship at the end is either dead and idealized or alive and compromised. This implies a recognition of friendship's limitations, but the genre in which it is expressed is in itself limited and cannot see beyond the ideal view of friendship. Shakespeare's use of the genre in plays like *The Two Gentlemen of Verona* and *The Two Noble Kinsmen* is constrained by what Pamela Mason calls 'the fierce demands of male bonding'.[3] A genre that focusses so much attention on friendship places too much pressure on the ideal and attends too little to the social world in which a friendship must exist, and to the basic and intuitively obvious priority of sexual love. The need to tell such moral tales of friendship's superiority to love shows that Humanists were using their rhetorical and narrative skills to fight against supposedly baser instincts in promoting male friendship over sexual desire for women.

Though narratives of friendship competing with love have a long history, the most influential version of the genre in the sixteenth century was Sir Thomas Elyot's tale of Titus and Gisippus in *The Boke Named the Governour* (1531). The tale, derived from Boccaccio, is a relatively simple one in which friendship is shown to be more valuable than love. Gisippus gives away his beloved to Titus and the favour is reciprocated when Titus later saves Gisippus from a false criminal charge. The narrative demonstrates some of the problems that later uses of the genre would highlight, such as the erosion of identity in ideal friendship and the question of whether tests and reciprocation are needed to establish a friendship or whether benevolence is enough. A couple of generations later, in *Euphues* (1578), John Lyly approaches friendship with more scepticism. Whilst he gives basic assent to Elyot's ideas about friendship he demonstrates that they are in practice a fiction, albeit a useful one.

Following Cicero, Elyot's Titus and Gisippus are an example of the central importance of similarity and virtue to true friendship. At the end of the narrative, Elyot also stresses the importance of 'longe deliberation and profe' (p. 163) for friendship. Love, his story has reckoned, can occur at first sight: indeed, it is more valid if it does. Gisippus, who has long developed his love for a lady through conversation, hands her over to his friend who falls for her at first sight: this is taken as a sign that the love is destined (of course, the woman's choice has no relevance here). This emphatically differentiates friendship from love. The long process of developing trust in friendship is crucial, but it is difficult to represent unless one puts the friendship to the test; tests and reciprocation therefore become essential components of friendship in narrative. Friendship is both the basis of the narrative and that which emerges from it.

Elyot is only able to make the tale of Titus and Gisippus a triumph for friendship by the use of a second narrative which balances the friendship.

Elyot finds that the only way to make friendship triumph is to present a model of friendship as reciprocation, albeit in different spheres. This would suggest that friendship needs testing, as what makes friendship here is Titus's recognition of obligation, more so than Gisippus's initial magnanimity in love, which only differentiates the friends – as Lorna Hutson puts it, 'Friendship here, for all its idealization, seems firmly rooted within an economics of liberality and timely reciprocity.'[4] The desirability of tests of friendship is a problem for Elyot, and he felt the need to add a qualification of it in his second edition:

Perchaunce some will saye that frendshyppe is nat knowen but by receyuinge of benefites. Here what Seneca sayeth [in *de Beneficiis*]. Like as all other vertues, semblably of frendship, the estimation is referred to the mynde of a man. For if a frende persist in his office and duetie, what so euer lacketh in benefite, the blame is in fortune. Like as a man may be a good syngingeman, thoughe the noyse of the standers aboute letteth him to be harde . . . So kyndenesse may be in wille, all thoughe there lacketh powar to declare it.[5]

There is havering here. The opportunity to confer benefits is desirable but not necessary. He goes on to argue that the assurance of a friend's virtue, along with familiarity, may be enough to promote friendship. Benevolence should be enough, and is certainly the key feature of friendship, but overall this suggests the ultimate uncertainty of friendship without narrative testing.

The use of exemplary stories, far from affirming friendship's universality, tends to make it seem exceptional, and in 'Titus and Gisippus' that exceptionality is based on the similarity of the friends, which is the central factor of the story: its moral import, its difficulties and resolutions, as well as some of its ambiguities, are all based on the friends being alike. Elyot is particularly emphatic about their similarity, which is expressed as physical resemblance. This resemblance is only partly metaphorical: at the story's opening we are told of 'Gisippus, who nat onely was equall to the said yonge Titus in yeres, but also in stature, proporcion of body, fauour, and colour of visage, countenaunce and speche. The two children were so like, that without moche difficultie it coulde nat be discerned of their propre parentes, whiche was Titus from Gysippus, or Gysippus from Titus' (p. 134). At first, this seems only a physical expression of Elyot's view that friends should be similar, but it has significant implications for the plot in that Gisippus is able to substitute his friend for himself in the marital bed owing to the fact that they look so alike. Gisippus also believes that the reason Titus fell in love with his (Gisippus's) betrothed in the first place was that they have such similarity of desire. Laurie Shannon sees this literalizing of the Ciceronian paradigm of likeness as crucial to the development of the friendship tradition in England,[6] but there are some complications even here. The second half of the story relies on subtler manifestations and reversals of this key aspect of their friendship. Titus fails to recognize Gisippus because the latter is in poor apparel, implying that the men's resemblance is only superficial and is dependent on their similarity of status. Gisippus had in fact earlier stated that the bed trick would only work if they wore the same clothes. This suggests that it is nurture, education and status, not nature, that make them the same. At another stage, Titus says that it was only different 'neckes lacis' that told them apart, by their own 'insignement or showinge' of identity (pp. 146–7). The signs of identity, once Elyot has insisted on similarity, become complicated. Perhaps the point here is that having been similar in their youth, the disparity of obligation provoked by Gisippus's generosity has created a differentiation between them. When Gisippus is on trial, Titus only recognizes his friend owing to 'a litle signe in his visage, whiche he knewe' (p. 157). This recognition is a recognition of the possibility of setting the record straight, and therefore of returning the pair to parity.

The presentation of equal friendship in narrative tends to remove *character* from the friends. In order to make Titus and Gisippus similar, Elyot turns his young men into virtuous ciphers. In order to be apt for idealized friendship, a young man must be as faceless as possible. This relates to his virtue: absolute virtue is rather blank and is always a problem for narrators to represent. Only in the crises of their friendship are Titus and Gisippus differentiated, and circumstances rather than character make the difference. Lyly, in *Euphues*, recognizes this problem, and presents a critique of the sort of smooth young man who is supposed to be adept at making friends. Whilst *Euphues* is not a wholesale debunking of 'Titus and Gisippus', its narrative and characterization provide a counterexample to Elyot's work, showing how fragile idealized friendship can be. The ironies of this text suggest the absurdity of trying to apply Elyot's theories of idealized friendship.

Whereas in 'Titus and Gisippus' the plasticity of the young men only emerges in the course of the plot, Lyly from the first emphasizes this aspect of his main character:

Euphues, whose witte beeinge lyke waxe apte to receiue any impression, and hauinge the brydle in hys owne handes, either to vse the raine or the spurre, disdayning counsayle, leauinge his countrey, loathinge his old acquaintance, thought either by wytte to obteyne some conquest, or by shame to abyde some conflicte, and leauing the rule of reason, rashly ranne vnto destruction. who preferring fancy before friends, & his present humor, before honour to come, laid reason in water being to salt for his tast, and followed vnbrideled affection, most pleasant for his tooth.[7]

This frank but elegant condemnation of our hero differentiates him in many respects from Titus, but he occupies Titus's structural position in the narrative. Both are visitors (though Euphues is from Athens, rather than a visitor to Athens), who fall in love with their friend's betrothed. Euphues' easily adaptable personality is a sophistication of Titus's blankness. Lyly's characters are acting out roles based on a consciously literary tradition; *Euphues* presents a version of the Titus and Gisippus story with more sophisticated characters for a more sophisticated and cynical age.

One important difference between the narratives is that Euphues, unlike Titus, has a history before he meets his friend Philautus. Titus and Gisippus were brought up together from childhood and have no other friends, but Euphues has already repudiated earlier friendships by the time he arrives in Naples as an adult. This avoids the long acquaintance that Elyot thought a precondition for friendship. Lyly's sophisticated and ironic narratorial stance relies upon his fundamental agreement with Elyot's position. The narrator describes the origins of the friendship between Euphues and Philautus with considerable scepticism, largely because it is a first-sight friendship that short-circuits Elyot's rule requiring the slow development of the ideal friendship. Laurens J. Mills sees them as 'persons relying on the classical theory but lacking constancy. It is a laboratory exercise in friendship with one element lacking.'[8] Euphues tries to make his wit substitute for long acquaintance, deceiving both himself and his friend. The function of wit here is that it pre-supposes a knowledge of Elyot's rules of friendship, and supposes that it knows also how they can be broken or subverted. Having wit rather than virtue, Euphues thinks he can avoid the tedious preliminaries of a friendship of virtue, for wit is quicker than virtue: 'a fine wytte, a sharp sence, a quicke vnderstanding, is able to atteine to more in a moment or a very little space, then a dull and blockish heade in a month' (p. 196). Just as 'these nouises' (young wits) 'thincke to have learning without labour and treasure without trauayle' (p. 196), such wits also think they can get friendship cheap. The friendship in *Euphues* is based on similarity, but not virtue, a fact that Lyly signals with his condemnation of wit's self-sufficiency:

Heereoff commeth suche great familyaritie betweene the rypest wittes, when they shall see the dysposition the one of the other, the *Sympathia* of affections and as it were but a payre of sheeres to goe between their natures. (p. 195)

In Cicero's (and Elyot's) terms this is a friendship of pleasure despite the ironic nod to the ideal of similarity. The paragraph goes on to describe such friendship in terms which firmly distinguish it from friendship of virtue:

one flattereth an other in hys own folly, and layeth cushions vnder the elbowe of his fellowe when he seeth him take a nappe with fancie, and as theire witte wresteth them to vice, so it forgeth them some feate excuse to cloake their vanitie. (p. 195)

This is a friendship of fancy, of fine words rather than of deeds, of rhetoric disconnected from virtue, as Richard A. McCabe puts it.[9] In the narrative that follows his moralizing, the relation of the text to *The Governour* becomes complicated, because it is the witty understanding of Elyot's doctrines that Euphues uses to cloak his vanity, concealing it from himself and from his friend. If, as Theodore L. Steinberg concludes, *Euphues* is 'an "anti-courtesy book", a parody on the usual works of the genre and a guide which should not be followed',[10] it is also one in which the characters are wittily *au fait* with conduct books like Elyot's. Having decided for one reason or another that he approves of Philautus, Euphues determines 'to enter into such an inuiolable league of friendship with him, as neyther time by peecemeale should empaire, neither fancie vtterly dissolue, nor any suspition infringe' (p. 197). This sense that he can get timeless friendship without the expense of time shows his failure to accept Elyot's economy of friendship, but he still reckons that he can get the benefits: he has *read* that 'a friend is in prosperitie a pleasure, a solace in aduersitie, in griefe a comfort, in ioy a merrye companion, at all times an other I, in all places the expresse image of mine owne person' (*ibid.*). This textualizing of ideal friendship, as Hutson puts it,[11] suggests the way in which books like Elyot's subvert themselves: the text is seen as a shortcut through reality and its time-based conditions. Euphues draws on Elyot's demonstration that tests are needed for true friendship by deliberately seeking them out, against Elyot's advice – 'Haue I not also learned that one shoulde eat a bushell of salt with him whom he meaneth to make his friend? that tryall maketh trust, that there is falshood in fellowship?' (*ibid.*). For Euphues, falsehood has paradoxically come to be a demonstration of friendship.

Given the false basis of the friendship, the love-triangle plot that ensues is doomed to a different outcome from that of 'Titus and Gisippus'. The woman involved, Lucilla, is much less of a cipher, and provides much more conflict with friendship than Elyot's Sophronia (who isn't even named until she has been handed over to Titus).[12] Lyly's narrator is as sceptical about the sudden love as he is about the sudden friendship: neither emotion is taken very seriously, and the characters' own moralizing platitudes serve to distance any sense of feeling, placing themselves self-consciously within a plot structure that is already conventionalized. When Euphues says 'where loue beareth sway friendshippe can haue no shew' (p. 209), he is justifying himself with an adage rather than exhibiting real thought about his emotions or situation. The idea that he is refusing to *show* friendship suggests that he is ironizing Elyot's view that friendship can exist without showing itself, turning friendship into a matter of more vague goodwill or Elyot's 'beneuolence', without the deeds to back it up. In justifying his breach of faith to Philautus, Euphues quotes from Euripides to the effect that love conquers all other obligations. He also tells Philautus that he should accept the betrayal, perhaps suggesting that Philautus should behave like Gisippus and give up his claims to the woman: 'The friendshippe betweene man and man as it is common so it is of course, betweene man and woman, as it is seldome, so is it sincere, the one proceedeth of the similitude of manners, the other of the sinceritie of the heart' (pp. 235–6). This piece of rhetoric (contained in a letter – thus demonstrating the distancing tactics of textualization) runs very much counter to Elyot's spirit: unlike Titus, Euphues has deceived his friend about his love (pretending to be in love with Lucilla's friend Livia), and only revealed it when he has won Lucilla. The insistence here on the commonness of friendship contradicts Euphues' own earlier assertions as well as Elyot's views. The way in which friendship and love are elided here by zeugma, implying that he and Lucilla are *friends*, further undercuts the significance of masculine friendship. In fact, the word 'friend' is used continually of the relationship between Euphues and Lucilla after they have become lovers, providing an ironic undercutting of all the earlier friendship discourse in the book. Love and friendship are thus elided, subverting the careful differentiation made in Elyot's work.

By a further irony, however, Lucilla's infidelity to Euphues (anticipated in her earlier reflections) allows something of a restoration of friendship between the men. As she casts him off, Euphues' anxiety is based not on lost love but on his relation to Philautus, who will now, he fears, laugh him to scorn. The friendship, however attenuated and based on a sense of intermasculine selfish dignity, is the basis of Euphues' feelings about himself. Lucilla consoles him on this score, again with a sense of distance in her aphorism: 'you have both druncke of one cup, in miserie *Euphues*, it is a great comfort to haue a companion' (p. 238). This harks back ironically to Euphues' earlier sense of trial being necessary to friendship, for even though Euphues has failed the test in Elyot's terms, there is some recovery of friendship. Their similarity now is based on hatred of Lucilla. This provides a sense of progress in friendship, on the surface at least; but Lyly's irony allows the discourse of friendship to be emptied of meaning:

> *Euphues* and *Philautus* hauing conference betweene themselves, castinge discourtesie in the teeth each of the other, but chiefly noting disloyaltie in the demeanor of *Lucilla*, after much talke renewed their olde friendship both abandoning *Lucilla* as most abhominable. *Philautus* was earnest to have *Euphues* tarrie in *Naples*, and Euphues desirous to haue *Philautus* to *Athens*, but the one was so addicted to the court, the other so wedded to the vniversitie, that each refused the offer of the other, yet this they agreed betweene themselves that though their bodyes were by distaunce of place seuered, yet the coniunction of their mindes shoulde neither be separated, by length of time, nor alienated by chaunge of soyle. (pp. 245–6)

The standard doctrine that friends can never be truly apart is also used by Elyot when Titus and Gisippus are separated, but Lyly's version is subtly different. Titus and Gisippus are only separated by their duties to their countries, whereas Euphues and Philautus are separated by differences of taste. In such a situation it is absurd to argue that their minds are the same. The principles that guide their minds are different and are themselves the reason for the physical separation. Thus the rhetoric of Elyot's ideal friendship is used to bolster an agreement that is simply a denial of enmity rather than a declaration of friendship. The ideal of friendship may not hold good in reality, but it can be *used*, not least as a way of saving face. As Lyly's irony so clearly demonstrates, ideal friendship can motivate and justify without being real or even possible. What the characters here desperately want is the reputation of being a good friend, not friendship itself. Friends do not so much increase each other's Aristotelian *eudaimonia* as the reputation for it.

This ironic and pragmatic position is the starting point for *The Two Gentlemen of Verona*, which does not go much beyond Lyly, despite a few incidental elaborations of plot. Proteus has a love of his own and deliberately rather than accidentally sets out to woo Valentine's beloved. These alterations are not true subversion, and serve to put the focus more on Proteus's untrustworthiness than the woman's. William Rosky points out that 'In *Euphues* there is finally no love to sacrifice to friendship, since the lady is simply faithless to both friends, a conclusion which *may* be used to prove that friendship is stronger than love but is more likely to prove that friendship is superior to a faithless love.'[13] Central to Lorna Hutson's argument is the idea that distrust in male friendship was often projected onto women, the exchange of whom in marriage was crucial to the establishment of friendship networks.[14] Shakespeare's plays present few unfaithful women – and those that are (Cressida, Goneril and Regan) are not the subject of desperate conflict between friends. By removing any genuine anxieties about women's sexual conduct from *The Two Gentlemen of Verona* Shakespeare forces the focus onto Proteus. One man's vice – symbolized most forcefully in Proteus's willingness to rape Silvia – dominates the play, and he can either be punished or forgiven arbitrarily. Valentine, Silvia and Julia all decide to forgive him, and so the play comes to its flat conclusion. The unexamined and naturalized theory on which this is based is that friends always forgive each other in the end. All this idea serves to demonstrate is that friendship is not really a very serious business. Its rhetoric is merely used to establish the peace of the comic ending.

The initial problem is that the emotions in this play are too easy to understand. Proteus, by far the play's most developed character, is regarded as a monster according to the conventional discourses of love and friendship, whereas in fact he is a perfectly ordinary and simple young man. Dropped into a plot where he is expected to behave like Titus or Gisippus, he simply acts as the average young man would. There may be a certain sub-Marlovianism in his line 'I to myself am dearer than a friend' (II. vi. 23), but unless an audience has its brains actually addled by books like *The Governour* it has no real shock value. When he says, 'I cannot now prove constant to myself, / Without some treachery us'd to Valentine' (lines 31–2), he is almost punning on the idea of a friend as a second self, and the buried nature of this idea for once gives life to the lines. The idea of the friend as second self is itself paradoxical, but its subversion has come to seem a paradox to Proteus. He is not just in a conventional plot, but his mind has been conventionalized. Stating the obvious has come to seem Marlovian to him.

This conventionalization lies behind Valentine's absurd and arbitrary forgiveness of Proteus. Valentine is simply acting here in accordance with the *rules* of friendship. Yet, as Aristotle pointed out, friendship is different from justice in that it does not have such rules. Even though he uses the phrase when he is betraying it, 'the law of friendship' (III. i. 5) clearly has an actual meaning for Proteus, and the idea of there being laws in friendship derives from chapter 12 of the crucial Humanist text on friendship, Cicero's *de Amicitia*. When friendship operates according to such a law it loses all its affective power and becomes a dead letter, at best a way of restraining bad impulses rather than encouraging good ones. It becomes equated with justice and thus has no real reference to individuals; it no longer provides the rules by which, as Laurie Shannon puts it, the individual can 'shape himself'.[15] Friendship can only be genuinely productive of strong, individualized selfhood once it is taken out of such a context. Proteus and Valentine are a classic instance of two young men brought up together, as if this were the only way in which friendship could develop. Shakespeare will from henceforth avoid such pairings, freeing himself from the law of friendship. When Hamlet shuns his schoolfellows Rosencrantz and Guildenstern he signals that he is freeing himself from that law, as well as from the law as imposed by Claudius (who has brought them to spy on him). Only very late in his career does Shakespeare return to such a pairing of cofostered men, and in *The Winter's Tale* he handles such characters very differently.

The question of forgiveness, and its dramatic representation – so unsatisfactorily handled in *The Two Gentlemen of Verona* – will again be a central concern of *The Winter's Tale*. This play contains Shakespeare's most mature version of friendship in two senses – that it comes very late in his career, and that the friendship in question, between Leontes and Polixenes, is the longest-standing in all the plays. In *The Two Gentlemen of Verona*, Valentine, still very much a young man, reflects on his upbringing with Proteus thus:

> I knew him as myself: for from our infancy
> We have convers'd, and spent our hours together,
> And though myself have been an idle truant,
> Omitting the sweet benefit of time
> To clothe mine age with angel-like perfection,
> Yet hath Sir Proteus (for that's his name)
> Made use and fair advantage of his days. (II. iv. 62–8)

The passage goes on in terms flattering to Proteus, whom Valentine is commending to the Duke. In essence, Valentine is commending himself to Silvia's father by insisting that he has reputable friends. The hollow conventionality of these lines suggests that he is a naive boy, still in need of further education, trying to impress his elders with the expected virtues – one of which is friendship; it is to this same Duke that Proteus mentions the laws of friendship. These boys are trying to live by standards that they think adults expect of them. As a result they are an odious and emotionally vapid pair, and their reconciliation seems like an adult-imposed kiss-and-make-up.

Nostalgic and rose-tinted though they be, the lines on youthful friendship in *The Winter's Tale* are a complete contrast to this. They present the childhood friendship as valuable in itself rather than as a mere preparation for adult friendship, as Polixenes' first lines on the subject make clear:

> We were, fair queen,
> Two lads that thought there was no more behind
> But such a day to-morrow as to-day,
> And to be boy eternal. (1. ii. 62–5)

This is a vision of friendship which is outside time and therefore outside the economy of obligations, allowing pure goodwill.[16] The pastoral, prelapsarian imagery that follows brings in the idea – crucial to the play's movement – of male friendship being only perfect before the intrusion of sexual desire and of women. Hermione's question 'Was not my lord / The verier wag o' th' two?' (lines 65–6) suggests that she wishes to differentiate them, and it is appropriate that she should, for the choice of wife must differentiate between the 'twinn'd lambs' (line 67) they once were. Polixenes admits that (in Hermione's words) they 'have tripp'd since' (line 76); they have fallen into their differentiated identities. Early in the play Camillo insisted that their friendship had developed, but his words contain a clear ironic ambiguity: 'They were trained together in their childhoods; and there rooted betwixt them such an affection, which cannot choose but branch now' (1. i. 22–4). The word 'branch' is meant as *flourish*, but more insistently suggests *separate*, and the double meaning suggests an inevitable relationship between growth and separation in friendship. This runs counter to the Humanist insistence on friendship's permanence. The two boys separated in or before adulthood; and now there is another separation, equally inevitable, but one which pulls Leontes back to the state of mind associated with the first separation – a separation which was conceived in childhood/adolescence as a fall from grace. However insistent Leontes is on sustaining the friendship by his invitations now, the past cannot be recalled (though this is something that the play's conclusion will seemingly refute). Aristotle observed that friends ought to live together, but it is obviously not possible to insist on it, even if separation means an inevitable erosion of the bonds of friendship. That friendship means so much to one's identity but confers so little real obligation is a paradox that may account for Leontes' madness.

Leontes' failure to persuade Polixenes to stay agitates him. Longing to call back the past, he can only call back immature feelings, and immaturely refuses an inevitable separation. Nora Johnson argues rather unconvincingly for the eroticism of the kings' childhood friendship on the basis that boyhood and play were associated with sexual instability, as well as instability of identity.[17] The stabilization of identity in adulthood is certainly one reason for the tension in the men's friendship, but there is no need to project a sexual side to this. As Stanley Wells points out, it is hard to present Leontes' jealousy in this direction on stage.[18] The jealousy may rather stem from a confusion of identities, from Leontes taking seriously the idea of one soul in bodies twain, and his recollection of the identity between the twinned lambs. The movement of sudden jealous rage comes just after Hermione announces her success:

> I have spoken to th' purpose twice:
> The one for ever earn'd a royal husband;
> Th' other for some while a friend. [*Gives her hand to Polixenes*.] – {Capell's S. D.}
> LEONTES. [*Aside*] Too hot, too hot!
> To mingle friendship far is mingling bodies. (1. ii. 106–9)

There are many other psychological elements in this scene, but the confusion and conflict over the idea of friendship here is surely the crucial one. The jealousy comes as she says Polixenes is *her* 'friend', which of course might also imply *lover*. Linguistic confusion, the mingling of separate senses of the word *friend*, is responsible for the whole situation, as Leontes' emotions get mixed up. Friendship and sexual love are not the same thing, but the rhetoric of idealized friendship has persuaded Leontes that they are equivalent, that his wife's friendship for Polixenes must mean that both are betraying him. His jealousy over his exclusive relationship with Polixenes gathers up associations and snowballs into his destructive and motiveless rage. Really, this is a rage against time's irreversibility, the infantile rage of a tyrant against the one aspect of life he cannot control. It may even be the phrase 'for some while' that really provokes him; he cannot bear the idea of impermanence. Such a rage can only be finally assuaged by the impossible recovery of Hermione at the play's ending. The recovery, as Shannon convincingly argues, is brought about not from within the equal friendship of the kings, but by lower-status counsellors.[19]

A crucial element in this conclusion is that sexual love, through Perdita and Florizell, can be a renewing force, and Hermione's recovery is a symbol of the continuity provided by womankind. The friendships of youth, though, cannot be renewed and brought back. They exist in and for themselves, but they are not permanent, despite the Humanist dream. The death of the boy Mamillius – in whom Leontes sees himself as a boy – symbolizes this irreversibility. He and Florizell will not renew their fathers' friendship. Male friendship is more fragile, less self-healing than the love of women. Once Leontes has sinned against friendship, he makes free with himself, telling Camillo that if he murders Polixenes, 'thou hast the one half of my heart' (1. ii. 348), but this profligacy of affection brings no new bonds. Leontes' insane process of rebellion against himself and against time leaves him isolated, without son, daughter, wife or friend, but it is the corruption of the spirit of friendship that begins the process, for it is his key anchor in human affections and society. In the sort of relationship that Polixenes and Leontes have, the corruption extends even to their memories. After the prolonged crisis of the first acts the friendship is killed and neither even thinks about it again. Their mutual forgiveness is therefore as perfunctory as Valentine's of Proteus. To keep society going (or keep the peace between states) one might as well forgive, but if this also involves forgetting, then the whole relationship has lost its basis, which is memory. There are perhaps intimations of this in *The Two Gentlemen of Verona*, but only in *The Winter's Tale* does Shakespeare give these ideas real force, through a rigorous and carefully worked-out representation of the effects of time on friendship.

In *The Two Noble Kinsmen* only death can breed forgiveness. The heroes are too trapped within the conventions of friendship to survive in life. Love for Emilia immediately destroys the friendship between Palamon and Arcite and neither of them is prepared to be truly magnanimous and cede her to the other. Although the friendship is expressed in Renaissance Humanist terms, it also harks back to a medieval chivalric context in which neither man is prepared to compromise his honour.

This, along with the stress on their kinship indicated in the play's title, means that death is the only end for them.

Given that Shakespeare had recently played fast and loose with a source (albeit a less canonical one) in the ending to *The Winter's Tale*, an audience might have suspected that he would make a similar alteration to Chaucer's *Knight's Tale*, perhaps by providing another woman for one friend to marry, but as William Carroll observes, 'The authors of *The Two Noble Kinsmen* do not . . . combine their tale with a romance story supplying a plot-convenient second female.'[20] Although they do not do so, the play offers hints that it might be so. Three linked features of *The Two Noble Kinsmen* are crucial for the recognition of the possibility of happy resolution: Emilia's lament for the lost friend of her youth, the friendship between Theseus and Pirithous, and the presence of the Jailer's Daughter. These features suggest how limited the love-triangle plot is, and how confining idealized friendship is.

It has been noted that *The Two Noble Kinsmen*'s rhetoric subtly but insistently presses the claims of friendship over love even whilst its plot makes married love the winner,[21] and this is because the friendships that are most valorized are dead ones, viewed nostalgically, whereas present friendship is much more problematic. Alan Stewart argues that 'rather than being a failed attempt at a play about idealised male friendship, *The Two Noble Kinsmen* is rather a play about a failed attempt at idealised friendship', and suggests that the establishment of their friendship is merely a device to while away the long hours of imprisonment.[22] Stewart is right to emphasize the importance of the men's kinship over their friendship, and it is clear that the latter is not a simple matter. It has been undermined previously, in the very first scene we saw them. The two young men have conflicting loyalties in their decision to fight for Thebes, given that the city is a den of vice. They agree that they should do so out of patriotism but recognize that they 'third' their worth in fighting for a bad cause (I. ii. 96). Their friendship for each other is not able to get them out of this double bind: it promotes only martial virtue rather than clear reasoning about choice of conduct. Palamon replies to Arcite's doubts by saying 'Leave that unreason'd' (line 98). Friendship here – between two men who too exactly mirror one another – allows a refusal of the reflection that it ought to be able to promote. Thus these virtuous men are set up against the virtuous Theseus (himself a notable friend), demonstrating that friendship, national ties and kinship can set virtuous men against one another, and bringing the compatibility of loyalty and virtue into question. Palamon recognizes this inner conflict in his anger at being corrupted by blood ties with Creon:

> Let
> The blood of mine that's sib to him be suck'd
> From me with leeches! let them break and fall
> Off me with that corruption! (lines 71–4)

This looks forward to his later disclaiming of blood relationship with Arcite (II. ii. 171–6). There is a bloody taint to their relationship from the first, and it can only be purged by the death of one of them.

There is a clear contrast with the purity of Emilia's former friendship with Flavina. She tells her sister Hippolyta:

> You talk of Pirithous' and Theseus' love:
> Theirs has more ground, is more maturely season'd,
> More buckled with strong judgement, and their needs
> The one of th' other may be said to water
> Their intertangled roots of love, but I
> And she (I sigh and spoke of) were things innocent,
> Lov'd for we did, and like the elements
> That know not what or why, yet do effect
> Rare issues by their operance, our souls
> Did so to one another. What she liked
> Was then of me approv'd, what not, condemn'd,
> No more arraignment. The flow'r that I would pluck
> And put between my breasts (O then but beginning
> To swell about the blossom), she would long
> Till she had such another, and commit it
> To the like innocent cradle, where phoenix-like
> They died in perfume. (I. iii. 55–71)

This lovely speech contains some ironic anticipations that point up the contrast with Palamon and Arcite. The girls' shared desires, particularly as exemplified by what looks like an innocent form of envy over the flower, could easily ripen (with the growing breasts) into rivalry in love such as we are to see in Palamon and Arcite's relationship. Only the girls' youth when one of them died has prevented this possibility. Not being rationally based (in contrast to the friendship between Theseus and Pirithous), their friendship was so evanescent that it can only be seen as beautiful in retrospect.[23] The friendship has also convinced Emilia that she can never love a man – indeed she almost talks Hippolyta out of love with Theseus. Such an idealization is a challenge to real and present relationships. As we shall see, the idealization that challenges Palamon and Arcite's friendship is twofold, idealizing both their own relationship and the distant figure of Emilia. Emilia's speech, though, doesn't point entirely at the play's unhappy ending for friendship; it also offers the possibility of a joyful resolution. Barry Weller points out that this friendship is presented on a higher level of poetry than that between Palamon and Arcite,[24] but this is because the men's friendship is dialogic and cannot find such a lyrical resolution. The association of the girls with the phoenix hints that Flavina might miraculously reappear to alter the Chaucerian ending. After all, Shakespeare had quite recently altered a source in order to affect a miraculous recovery of one thought dead – in *The Winter's Tale*'s shocking alteration to Greene's *Pandosto*. That Shakespeare does not take up this possibility shows that friendship, unlike familial relations, cannot be recovered – because its truest preservation is through death.

Emilia's early friendship is more explicitly contrasted with Theseus's friendship with Pirithous, which is itself clearly designed as a contrast with the friendship of Palamon and Arcite. Other than contributing to the idea of friendship as a key context for the action, Pirithous's role is small. His affection for Theseus prompts Emilia's reflections on her childhood playfellow; the fact that he is so eager to follow Theseus into battle (and has fought alongside him before) establishes the chivalric nature of friendship in the play; and Hippolyta's shaky assurance that Theseus loves her better than Pirithous establishes the conflict between love and friendship. In the rest of the play he seems like merely a convenient extra hand: it is he who gets Arcite freed from prison (with no explanation – ii. ii), and who gives the disguised Arcite to Emilia as a servant (ii. v); later (iii. vi), he joins with Emilia and Hippolyta in begging Theseus for mercy on Palamon and Arcite; and at the end (v. iv) he brings Palamon news of Arcite's death. His part is that of an attendant lord. Despite being regularly seen as part of a foursome with Theseus, Hippolyta and Emilia (and calling Emilia 'My precious maid', i. iii. 8), he is not a rival with the young heroes for Emilia's affections. Not being in conflict with any of the play's other characters, his friendship with Theseus is merely one of the play's givens, not a cardinal point of interest in the action. Donald K. Kendrick argues that 'Friendship, a given in Chaucer, is the subject under investigation by *The Two Noble Kinsmen*', but the friendship of Theseus and Pirithous *is* a given, harking back perhaps to an older, less problematic model of friendship.[25] Any opportunity for him to be seen siding with one of the young men is

skipped over: no use is made of his apparent support for Arcite (mani-
fested in getting him freed); his functional roles are deliberately under-
motivated so that he never comes into any actual conflict with Theseus
over the treatment of the young men. His role in foregrounding the
theme of friendship is decidedly muted; at most this friendship proves
that Theseus isn't a tyrant – because tyrants don't traditionally have
friends. Derrida argues that 'There is no friendship for the father, one is
not the friend of the one who makes friendship possible.'[26] This also
applies to the King. In this case, Theseus does have a friend, but the play
makes him little more than a token one. There is something stale about
Theseus's friendship, suggesting the problems of a friendship that has
gone on too long and has nowhere to go. Hippolyta's description of
Theseus and Pirithous is vigorous enough, though rather conventional:

> They two have cabin'd
> In many as dangerous as poor a corner,
> Peril and want contending, they have skiff'd
> Torrents whose roaring tyranny and power
> I' th' least of these was dreadful, and they have
> Fought [or sought?] out together where death's self was lodg'd;
> Yet fate hath brought them off. Their knot of love
> Tied, weaved, entangled, with so true, so long,
> And with a finger of so deep a cunning,
> May be outworn, never undone. (1. iii. 35–44)

The past tense here is revealing. Conflict, albeit with others, has been
necessary to give life to the men's friendship. Death must be risked in
order to bind men together, and fate plays a notable part (it saved them,
but will be against Palamon and Arcite). The knot of their mutual
affection here is an ambiguous symbol: piled up with descriptive parti-
ciples 'Tied, weaved, entangled', they seem over-obligated to one another,
and there is a strong suggestion that the bond can and should be worn out
(at least as far as Hippolyta is concerned), so much of a net does it seem.
The women, we feel, may want to cut this Gordian knot. Successful
friendship, it appears, can be as much burden as boon. Just as Palamon
and Arcite in the previous scene desire war in order to purge the vices
of Thebes, this scene shows a nostalgia for the conflicts that are the
foundations of friendship, because amicable stasis creates stagnation.
Aesthetically, friendship only has power through some form of conflict,
either between the friends or with others: having no consummation, its
success can only be entanglement.

The scene which begins the conflict between Palamon and Arcite, despite (or because of?) its high-flown language, develops through cynical irony that recalls *The Two Gentlemen of Verona*. Their laments in prison and assurances of friendship are highly conventional to the point of being stifling:

> ARCITE. While Palamon is with me, let me perish
> If I think this our prison!
> PALAMON.   Certainly,
> 'Tis a main goodness, cousin, that our fortunes
> Were twin'd together. 'Tis most true, two souls
> Put in two bodies, let 'em suffer
> The gall of hazard, so they grow together,
> Will never sink. (II. ii. 61–7)

The imagery here does not suggest joy in their relationship, only its fated and doomed quality – their *twining* (with a suggestion of twinning?) being more about obligatory ties than feeling. Arcite goes on:

>   here being thus together,
> We are an endless mine to one another;
> We are one another's wife, ever begetting
> New births of love; we are father, friends, acquaintance;
> We are, in one another, families;
> I am your heir, and you are mine. (lines 78–83)

There is a distinct aura of homoeroticism here, but of a desperate kind. The mutual narcissism (picked up on Emilia's entrance as she and her woman talk about the narcissus flower), the grim sense of eternity, the possessive pun on mine/mine, and the extravagant overdetermination here makes the endlessness of friendship seem a deeply unwelcoming bottomless pit (one is reminded of Sartre's *Huis Clos*). As Weller puts it, 'The dream of intimacy turns into a nightmare of claustrophobia.'[27] The dramatic rhythm of the scene develops their imprisoned entanglement until the inevitable collapse brought about by the sight of Emilia. The rise of conflict comes as a dramatic relief or release, which can provoke only laughter in an audience. So histrionic are all the feelings in this scene that we cannot take them at all seriously. The playwrights' genius though is in ratcheting this up further in the succeeding acts until the young men come to seem tragically trapped in conventional dramatic and chivalric roles. The absurdity of their considerate conduct to one another as they prepare to fight (III. vi) is peculiarly poignant in that respect; the nostalgia they show for fights when they were on the same side shows that a deeper form of friendship is already emerging. Here Palamon says, 'Only a little let him fall before me, / That I may tell my soul he shall not have her' (lines 178–9). The extravagance of conflict in such an excessively virtuous friendship leads to absurd paradoxes. Its basis cannot therefore be sound.

One of the great critical problems with regard to *The Two Noble Kinsmen* is whether the two heroes are really differentiated.[28] The first twentieth-century revival of the play apparently attempted to distinguish between them by playing Palamon comically, in a red wig.[29] We might argue that both playwrights wanted to distinguish them, but pulled in different directions and ended up confusing those distinctions. Rather than trying to distinguish between them through the whole play it is worth isolating distinctions in individual scenes to show how the play's economy of friendship works. When we first see them, Palamon and Arcite finish each other's sentences and are absolutely of one mind that they disdain Creon, but must fight for him. Later, a distinction is made when one of them is freed from gaol, but because the love plot has become tangled with the justice plot, rather than the two occurring serially as in 'Titus and Gisippus', there can be no evening out of friendly favours. The differentiation is accidental in this case, caused by Arcite being the one who is (very arbitrarily) released. It is also fairly arbitrary that Palamon is the one to see Emilia first, and thus has some sort of spurious claim on her, later endorsed by both Theseus and even the dying Arcite (v. iv. 116–18). Yet the Jailer's Daughter (an addition to the Chaucerian narrative) has already shown that she can tell the difference between them, even if the Jailer can't (ii. i. 50–3) and it is Palamon she loves. Though her choice of Palamon is later undermined by her madly taking the Wooer for Palamon, she offers the possibility of a way out of the play's impasse. In Davenant's version of *The Two Noble Kinsmen, The Rivals* (1668), her equivalent (suitably raised in status) provides a love option for one friend and thus obviates the tragic ending. The woman's less arbitrary love-choice offers a way out of the knots of tangled male friendship, and suggests differentiated identity for the men. Ideal friendship tries to make men the same; women's love tries to differentiate them.

The greatest difference is that it is Palamon who is ultimately successful, and he is the one who engages our sympathies rather more during the action. This is perhaps in part due to an audience's superstitious belief that his first-sight claim on Emilia gives him rights, but the progress of the characters' dynamic further reinforces this. Firstly, we are sympathetic to Palamon's condition left behind in gaol – a gaol Arcite had envisaged as a paradise for the two of them until he saw Emilia, but to which he now shows no inclination to return. Secondly, this gives Palamon the opportunity to soliloquize, a surefire way of getting an audience on side. When Arcite soliloquizes (ii. iii) it is to express envy at Palamon's closeness to Emilia, something with which we have little sympathy as we have just seen Palamon taken away from the window through which he could see Emilia. These apparent incidentals lead up to a major differentiation in the manner of the friends when they next meet. Arcite, thinking himself alone, seems almost to crow of his good fortune in entering Emilia's service and to delight in Palamon's envy were he to know of it:

> Alas, alas
> Poor cousin Palamon, poor prisoner, thou
> So little dream'st upon my fortune that
> Thou think'st thyself the happier thing, to be
> So near Emilia. (iii. i. 22–6)

The alliterative *p*s here are spat out as if in contempt, and the thought of his kinsman as a 'thing' is far from noble. Palamon overhears this and is understandably enraged, so that when Arcite tries to behave magnanimously in this scene, we see it as affectation, and Palamon's irate response as appropriate and justified. Much of this rage is in any case precisely directed at Arcite's magnanimity, which looks like crowing condescension:

> Oh you heavens, dares any
> So nobly bear a guilty business? None
> But only Arcite; therefore none but Arcite
> In this kind is so bold. (lines 89–92)

This is very similar to the insistence on the uniqueness of Proteus's treachery in *The Two Gentlemen of Verona*:

> PROTEUS.   In love
> Who respects friend?
> SILVIA.   All men but Proteus. (v. iv. 53–4)

Whilst idealizations of friendship such as Elyot's acknowledge that ideal friendship is rare, dramatic presentations of ideal friendship tend to take for granted that it is the norm, ironically suggesting that treachery makes men egregious – despite the proliferation of such plots.

Arcite's superiority (or superior manner) is an attenuation of friendship as far as Palamon is concerned:

> Most certain
> You love me not; be rough with me, and pour
> This oil out of your language. (lines 101–3)

Arcite's refusal to use 'hard language' (line 106) is a disdainful response – he is vain like Euphues, lacking passion. This mode of differentiation continues in the arming scene, though now Palamon, having been fed, is grateful and tries to be magnanimous too, if less successfully. It is Arcite's lack of passion that is striking, though:

> Your person I am friends with,
> And I could wish I had not said I lov'd her,
> Though I had died; but, loving such a lady
> And justifying my love, I must not fly from't. (III. vi. 39–42)

The implication is that Arcite is standing on his chivalric pride in being entitled to love Emilia, not that he really loves her.[30] Magnanimity is again a problem between the friends rather than (as it should be) a mode of resolution. It provokes stubborn pride rather than generosity, and provokes Palamon's resentment again when Arcite insists that Palamon should have choice of weapons:

> Wilt thou exceed in all, or dost thou do it
> To make me spare thee? (lines 46–7)

Palamon's confusion is signalled by his veering out of their normal use of *you* to *thou* (which he used in soliloquy to express his gratitude at the scene's beginning). This may be rage, gratitude, or a curious mixture of both; but the overall impression he gives is of a desire to assert himself against his friend's stance of magnanimity. In any case, the problem with all this magnanimity is that it doesn't cover the main issue. To be like Titus and Gisippus, Palamon should have given the girl to Arcite and Arcite should have rescued Palamon, rather than leaving this to the Jailer's Daughter. We see a form of Aristotelian moral competition here, but it is not self-sacrifice; thus even that competition can be seen as destructive.

Emilia's differentiation between the two men (IV. ii) identifies a blithe, loveable disposition in Arcite and what Weller aptly calls a 'Byronic sulkiness' in Palamon.[31] Romantically, this is the signal of a greater passion in Palamon, but because Emilia cannot choose, and because the friends cannot come to an accommodation, one of them must die, not through battle or judicial murder on Theseus's part, but through the caprice of fate. When Theseus tells Palamon:

> Your kinsman hath confessed the right o' th' lady
> Did lie in you, for you first saw her and
> Even then proclaimed your fancy (v. iv. 116–18)

the arbitrariness and simplicity of this conclusion is the essence of tragicomic absurdity. All the men's claims to honour, friendship and nobility come down to this judgement, in which one of the friends must die to prove the fact of Palamon's priority. The recognition here is not of the true nature of individuals, but of fact – a kind of recognition that Aristotle saw as dramatically inferior.[32] That this fact is self-evident and was never denied makes it absurdly hollow. The assertion of Palamon's priority resembles the assertion of primogeniture between brothers, and the conflict between Palamon and Arcite takes on some of the stifling qualities of fraternal conflict that we saw in the previous chapter. Friendship, then, in a chivalric society, is utterly inflexible, even if it is, as the play's title suggests, nobler than more modern modes of friendship. Judgement in *The Two Noble Kinsmen* emerges not from the dialogic interaction of autonomous individuals but from the final authority of Theseus, asserting a feudal priority in love. Even though he is not a tyrant, the king here has absolute power and consequently stands as the representative of fate. In such a context friendship – a democratic emotion, as Aristotle implies – is limited and imprisoned. In a sense Palamon and Arcite never escape from the gaol which tangles up their friendship, and which is Shakespeare's ultimate symbol for the Humanist ideal of friendship.

Despite Shakespeare's demonstration of both the hollowness and the self-thwarting of ideal friendship, its rhetoric could still be used to motivate plots, partly because the inherent contradiction between the natural desire for a sexual partner and the absurd overvaluation of one-on-one friendship requires a good deal of plot untangling. Webster and Rowley's *A Cure for a Cuckold* (1624/5) is a late example of a friendship versus love play which, typically for its time, overelaborates its plot in a desperate effort to find some proper balance between friendship and love. Lessingham's beloved Clare is in love with his friend Bonvile, who has just married. Refusing Lessingham's proposal, she says that she will consent if he kills 'that friend that loves thee dearest' (I. i. 98). By *friend*, she really means herself, but he takes this as meaning a male friend. (In fact, this is a serious plot hole, for when she reveals what she meant, she talks of herself as 'the best esteemed friend' (IV. ii. 16): there is surely a major difference between her loving him and vice versa.) This demonstrates the perceived problem of taking women at face value, but it also shows the category confusions of the play, particularly between love and friendship. Lessingham indulges in a bookish soliloquy debate about whether he should destroy friendship – which is, as he paraphrases from Cicero, the rarest and greatest thing in nature (I. ii. I). He tries to excuse Clare's demand with the argument that friendship has disappeared from the world, revealingly connecting it with the decline of traditional society and royal legitimacy: he wonders if she thinks that 'as kindred / And claims to crowns are worn out of the world, / So the name friend?' (lines 14–16). Therefore, he argues, she means him to kill no one, as there are no true friends in the world. Having found Bonvile to be a true friend (because he is prepared to delay the consummation of his marriage in order to second Lessingham in a supposed duel), he engages in an absurdly complicated debate with him. Bonvile is first willing to be killed for his friend's sake, but then concludes that in being prepared to kill him Lessingham has already killed him as a friend. There are other complications here, and it all seems to be satirizing earlier friendship plots with its overelaboration, but the character of Bonvile is a fascinating portrait of a certain type of friend. He is motivated less by particular affection for Lessingham than by a generalized sense of chivalric honour, or, as his name suggests, *good will*. He seems an anachronism in a play whose subplot presents the unjealous compromises of a lower-status man who is prepared to accept his wife's child by another man as his own. The play foregrounds friendship as the social glue, and condemns women's demands for love's pre-eminence and the destruction of male friendship. Clare admits that her love for Bonvile was 'beyond reason' (IV. ii. 56). The dialogue between Bonvile and Clare is absurdly full of twists and turns, but it shows the ability of reasonable (male) friendship to solve the problems caused by unreasonable (female) passion. This is based, however, on the fact that Bonvile is not really making a sacrifice for Lessingham, as he has never loved Clare. He tells Clare to love Lessingham; she argues that this is strange, as it seems a friendly office for one who is now an enemy to Lessingham; he retorts that it is an act of enmity to wish such a whore upon the other man (she's a whore for loving Bonvile after he has married another); she says that she would not do Lessingham such ill; her refusal makes her good in Bonvile's eyes and therefore a fit companion for Lessingham, for whom he still essentially has goodwill. Even this does not quite resolve the plot. Lessingham tries to get revenge on Bonvile for his being loved by Clare in sowing seeds of suspicion about Bonvile's wife Annabel and the highwayman Rochfield. This fails, and all live happily ever after: a general atmosphere of forgiving goodwill is all that is required.

As at the end of *The Two Gentlemen of Verona* and *The Two Noble Kinsmen* we feel that particular friendship has been severely compromised, but a general desire for friendly peace has prevailed. Bonvile represents a sane attitude to friendship, using the rhetoric of idealization, but with a firm sense of its real importance as a social glue. His skilful manipulation of tropes of idealized friendship talks Lessingham down from his belief in unitary friendship and persuades Clare to accept the lesser lover Lessingham. In essence, he makes them compromise their overblown ideals of perfect love and friendship, something that was not possible for the noble – and therefore uncompromising – kinsmen. Bonvile, the perfect man, does not need friendship, but he can move others. All this is founded on the fact that the friends are obviously not equal; Lessingham is the lesser man.

In Beaumont and Fletcher's *The Maid's Tragedy* friendship's true valuation of male worth is set up against royal tyranny and romantic love – both of which are seen as irrational. Amintor, whom the older soldier Melantius values for his worth, is married off to Evadne, Melantius's sister, the marriage taking place through the command of the King and without Melantius's involvement, as the King is really using the marriage as a screen for his own affair with Evadne. Amintor's private if reluctant acceptance of the arrangement means that he can no longer be open with his friend; their becoming brothers-in-law, then, reduces rather than increases their friendship, putting an element of irony into Melantius's comment that their friendship is more important than their new relationship by marriage:

> to me the name
> Of brother is too distant, we are friends,
> And that is nearer. (III. i. 41–3)[33]

This eventually leads to an extraordinary (though typically Fletcherian) scene in which Melantius rages at Amintor, demanding the restoration of their intimacy; yet when Amintor reveals the truth Melantius is for the moment angry at the slur on his sister:

> shall the name of friend
> Blot all our family, and stick the brand
> Of whore upon my sister unreveng'd? (III. ii. 135–7)

Amintor's despair is such that he is willing to be killed, leading Melantius to decide again that 'The name of friend, is more than familie/ Or all the world besides' (lines 168–9). The friends agree to league against the King, but not before Amintor has threatened to fight, concerned about the slur on *his* honour that would be involved in acknowledging his wife's treachery. The scene is both intense and slightly absurd, with various codes of honour and friendship put in opposition, but its overall tendency is to insist on the priority of friendship over all other codes, either of loyalty to the monarch, or of family as represented through women; the bond between men transcends any bond involving women. Melantius and Amintor resolve their moral scruples against regicide by persuading the repentant Evadne to do their dirty work and kill the King; tainted already by the sin of sexual infidelity, she is able to make two wrongs a right, thus allowing the friends to avoid any taint to their honour. Although the play moves into further tragedy as Amintor kills his true love Aspatia, it is a remarkable example of how friendship enables men to preserve their honour whilst displacing sinfulness onto women and tyrants. The friends' ultimate fate – Amintor committing suicide and Melantius promising to starve himself – proves that finally one cannot escape the irrational forces that are brought about by tyranny and female sexuality, even if one can preserve oneself from their taint.

The Humanist ideal of friendship, then, is ultimately compromised in the drama of the period; it may have great rhetorical intensities, but those intensities cannot survive confrontation with larger forces like time, tyranny and (female) sexuality; it also cannot provide a satisfactory conclusion to a plot as love does. Attempts to make ideal friendship exist in time, to have the permanence sought in the Humanist ideal, end up producing extraordinary and destructive tensions in the friendship, as in *The Winter's Tale* and *The Two Noble Kinsmen*. Leontes and Palamon, at their plays' end, may have recovered and gained a wife respectively (and even Proteus has got a better woman than he deserves), but because these characters are so rooted in an ideal of friendship, they are left with no real selves. Truer versions of friendly sympathy, in Erasmus's terms, which exist between differentiated men, can be found in other forms of male relationships. These relationships stand the test of time and dramatic plot much better, but have their own tensions. Of these, service is perhaps the most obviously unequal yet intimate.

CHAPTER 5

Servants

The idealizing Humanist tradition, with its insistence on equality between friends, cannot regard the relationship between masters and servants as friendship, but service necessarily provides a form of intimacy that is at least as great as friendship. Service is of course very similar to instrumental friendship, the imperfect friendship accepted by Aristotle but condemned by Cicero. The Humanist insistence on equal friendship is precisely an attempt to do away with a model of friendship as involving service. At the top of the social hierarchy, semi-feudal service persisted, particularly in aristocratic bodily attendance on the monarch, which was an honour and gave evidence of royal 'countenance'.[1] This sense of service as providing friendly access to and intimacy with the powerful still extended down the social ladder, but the nature of the bonds between masters and servants was deeply problematic in the early modern period. The old assumption that a gentleman's or an aristocrat's servants were of roughly similar status to their master no longer held. Consequently, it was increasingly hard to regard servants as part of the family. What had until recently been a semi-feudal, familial arrangement was transforming into a more financial and temporary arrangement, to the affective detriment of both masters and servants.[2] Thomas Moisan notes that service was a troublesome category in Renaissance England: 'the social identity of the servingman in particular seems often to have eluded neat taxonomies and to have been assessed in patriarchalist terms as an extension of the master or house served'.[3] Service was rarely a permanent condition, but a transitional one; as Frances Dolan puts it, service 'was considered a developmental phase more than a social status'.[4] Young people of both sexes and most classes were frequently sent into service in another family, and this was regarded as providing experience, friendly connections and marital opportunities. The representation of service in drama tends to be as a one-to-one relationship rather than as part of a larger familial structure; it therefore has more opportunities to shade over into friendship. Its natural impermanence and provisionality contrasts with ideal friendship's supposed freedom and permanence; these very features, however, make it a more realistic model for friendship. This chapter will demonstrate that feelings of friendship, with all their capacity for dramatic complication, have a tendency to emerge through intimacy, even when that intimacy is frankly instrumental as in a master–servant relationship. As the servant must carry out the master's will, service provides a truer version than friendship of the idea of 'one soul in bodies twain', although it is assumed that the one soul is the master's. In a hierarchical society such as early modern England, almost all relationships are likely to involve a social gradient, but it is clearest and most focussed in the master–servant relationship. Whilst affective loyalty may emerge in such a relationship, so may recalcitrant individualism which shapes the dramatic identity of both master and servant. The limited loyalties of service allow the proper boundaries of selfhood to be respected.

A play which denies the value of friendship among the wealthy bourgeoisie (see chapter 7, below), *Timon of Athens* presents a nostalgic image of loyal and friendly service. When Flavius comes to try to help him in the wilderness, Timon decides that he is the only honest man in the world:

> I do proclaim
> One honest man – mistake me not, but one;
> No more, I pray – and he's a steward.
> How fain would I have hated all mankind,
> And thou redeem'st thyself. But all, save thee,
> I fell with curses. (IV. iii. 496–501)

He is somewhat disappointed at Flavius's honesty, and tries to account for it by wondering if Flavius's kindness is 'usuring' (line 509); on the basis of his experience in friendship he has come to acknowledge that all human relationships work in expectation of gain. It may be moral nit-picking to observe that Flavius does (if reluctantly) accept gold: but then he can't refuse, as he is presumably taking it for the other servants as much as for himself. It is Timon who is being instrumental here as he buys Flavius off, clearing his conscience in getting rid of him. The play insists on a deeper, if qualified, loyalty that Timon cannot see. The servants have, throughout, been the most loyal friends to Timon, and the steward is obviously their representative. Even if one agrees with A. D. Nuttall's view that 'one's credulity is stretched by these patholo-gically loyal persons',[5] it is clear that Timon's relations with them are the healthiest thing in the play. Starting with his marriage-portion to Lucilius (i. i), he consistently shows them kindness, which is reciprocated, and which gives the audience the best guarantee that Timon is a good man and not just a profligate fool; the judgements of a man's servants might be regarded as the best guide to his moral character. Flavius's pity for his foolish master – 'I bleed inwardly for my lord' (i. ii. 205) – trumps Apemantus's cynicism and engages our sympathies, not least because it is spoken as one of the play's few reflective asides. When Timon sends his servants out to get money, he calls them his 'friends' (ii. ii. 44), and although this is a formula of his overgeneralized friendship, it ironically suggests that his true friends are to be found in his household. The servants are eloquent (if unnecessary) commentators on the venality of the supposed friends in act iii, but they really come into their own in act iv scene ii, where they show their persistent loyalty, despite their master's fall. This may be absurd, and it may also make us wonder rather seriously how we are to judge a man who can so easily abandon such loyal servants, but it makes it quite clear that even if friends are untrustworthy, the household is an environment of secure virtue. The baby should not have been thrown out with the bathwater. The responsibilities of the patriarchal family seem more reliable than the pleasures of friendship. Timon's remembered goodness holds the servants together: as Flavius says, 'for Timon's sake / Let's yet be fellows' (iv. ii. 24–5). This is nostalgic for an older ideal of service (which may never have actually existed), but the nostalgia is nicely tinged with realism. Flavius concludes:

> I'll ever serve his mind with my best will;
> Whilst I have gold, I'll be his servant still (iv. ii. 49–50)

This balance between practicality (*gold* not *life* is Flavius's limit) and affection is just right, setting proper and sensible limitations on this form of friendship. It deserves the name of honesty in its fullest sense. That Timon ultimately has no use for it is owing to the crazed nature of his ideal, and of the ideal of pure and true friendship in general.

Whereas ideal friendship is all-or-nothing, resulting in such irresolvable conflicts as we have seen in *The Two Noble Kinsmen*, service opens up rich possibilities for admittedly limited, but ultimately dynamic and developing relationships between men, putting human connections to the test of reality. In *Damon and Pythias*, a play that extols an excessively smooth ideal friendship, Richard Edwards does provide one interesting potential source of tension between the friends, although he keeps it rather muted: that is, the fact that the friends share a servant. In the first place this enables Edwards to point up the contrast between our heroes as friends and the false friendship between Aristippus and Carisophus. The latter pair, normal in their imperfection, each has his own servant, and we see those servants quarrelling in some of the play's livelier scenes. Sharing a servant is perhaps as difficult as a sharing a woman – though less morally dubious – and the oddity of their doing so adds to the sense of Damon and Pythias's exceptional relationship. Stephano himself is impressed by the strangeness of his position:

> Oft-times I have heard, before I came hither,
> That no man can serve two masters together –
> A sentence so true as most men do take it,
> At any time false that no man can make it.
> And yet by their leave that first have it spoken
> How that may prove false, even here I shall open.
> For I, Stephano, lo, so named by my father,
> At this time serve two masters together,
> And love them alike. (v. 1–9)[6]

This rather typically diffuse speech goes on to describe the long growth and basis in virtue of his masters' friendship, and to sum up his thoughts: 'Serve one, serve both' (line 31). The biblical aphorism (Matthew vi 24) about serving two masters is lengthily refuted, in the process presenting us with the first picture of their ideal friendship. The servant is therefore the validator of their friendship, whereas a woman would be a source of tension. His servile love for them also serves to validate their virtue in contrast to the evil mastery of Dionysius, whose subjects only fear and hate him.

Yet Stephano's function in the play is not limited to endorsing the ideality of his masters' friendship. He is also a character with more down-to-earth needs, which indirectly lead to the friends' crisis. He is a more practical figure than his masters. Unlike them, he sees the dangers of the city they have come to, and he is not so philosophical. As they are viewing the city he complains that 'Your philosophical diet is so fine and small / That you may eat your dinner and supper at once, and not surfeit at all' (viii. 15–16). His insistence on eating leads to Damon being left alone, and this will lead to Damon's arrest. The servant's less perfect and philosophical disposition ensures that there is a narrative for the play to present. Damon, sending him off to eat with Pythias, tells him, 'So doing, you wait upon me also' (line 36). Damon's philosophical doctrine of friendship has led him to some absurd positions: the belief that Pythias's 'company' can 'feed' him (lines 20–1), and that Pythias eating will be as good as eating for himself; we must detect a tinge of mockery here. Damon's absurdity leads to all his troubles in that his lack of a servant for himself – his trust that he and Pythias can share a servant – means that he has no one who could protect him against Carisophus's treachery by acting as a witness. Although the idealized ending of the play endorses ideal friendship, this aspect of the action demonstrates the absurdity of dogmatic adherence to friendship discourse. That the practical flaws in ideal friendship are partly exposed through the human needs of a loving servant is revealing: Damon and Pythias are too exceptional to live safely in a world where others have simpler needs and desires. Elliot Krieger observes that in Shakespeare's comedies servants or subordinates provide a 'residual presence of a primary-world consciousness' that roots aristocratic protagonists in reality.[7] In *Damon and Pythias* the servant is drawn up into the ideal second world of friendship when he is rewarded for his loyalty to them by his freedom, thus bringing him to the masters' level. Dionysius is told that he has to forget his royal status if he is to join in their friendship (xv. 238). All *status* needs to be erased for friendship to become the world's governing principle. This utopian egalitarianism is the only way that friendship can become general rather than exceptional. In Shakespeare, by contrast, characters with idealized views of human relations tend to be brought down to the lower level of pragmatic relationships, qualifying such ideals with a recognition of the realities of social hierarchy.

In Shakespeare's earliest comedies, the most dramatically interesting relationships are often those between masters and servants. Friendship between equals, love and brotherhood all have prominent positions in the plots of *The Two Gentlemen of Verona*, *The Taming of the Shrew* and *The Comedy of Errors*, but these relationships are colourless compared to the master–servant interactions, which are all the more striking for being peripheral to the plays' plots. Shakespeare's comic talents were first honed on the inherently absurd nature of service, which relies on an unsustainable assumption of one person's absolute superiority to another – in particular the superiority of his will. The tensions of such a relationship are inherently dramatic and the servant who is wittier and/or more intelligent than his master is a standard trope of comedy, from Aristophanes to Wodehouse. It highlights the absurdity of a hierarchical society, but also subtly endorses the pleasures of that society. As George Meredith's 'wise youth' Adrian Harley puts it:

I see now that the national love of a lord is less subservience than a form of self-love; putting a gold-lace hat on one's image, as it were, to bow to it. I see, too, the admirable wisdom of our system: – could there be a finer balance of power than in a community where men intellectually nil, have lawful vantage and a gold-lace hat on? How soothing it is to intellect – that noble rebel, as the Pilgrim has it – to stand, and bow, and know itself superior![8]

Shakespeare is engaged in something similar, though more serious, in the *Sonnets*, and his dramatic presentation of servants enables him to show the limitations of his characters at the same time as allowing them to assert themselves, however privately.

Mark Thornton Burnett has argued that, although Plautus and Terence provide the source for the dramatic type of the trickster servant, Elizabethan playwrights extended the type 'to meet a new variety of dramatic functions', and that this type has 'range of metaphorical uses': 'the representation of this type facilitated an exploration of a perceived crisis in service, as well as providing a means of addressing broader insecurities'.[9] This is borne out by Ben Jonson's use of the type (Brain-Worme and Mosca in particular). Burnett also notes that the trickster type and the faithful servant, which were one figure in the Roman comedy, tend to be separated on the Elizabethan and Jacobean stage.[10] If we see a Renaissance servant trick anyone, we suspect that he is likely to trick and betray his master eventually. Jonson's Mosca and Adam in *As You Like It* are poles apart, one tricky and treacherous, the other loyal to the point of simplicity. When Orlando bears his old servant on his back (*As You Like It*, II. vii), Shakespeare presents his most idealized and nostalgic image of mutuality in the master–servant relationship. As Burnett concedes (discussing Kent in *Lear*), however, Shakespeare more often places his characters somewhere between the poles. This is clearly the case in the early comedies, where servants are basically loyal but not wholly trustworthy – because they have independent personalities and desires. In *The Comedy of Errors*, Dromio of Syracuse says that 'servants must their masters' minds fulfill' (IV. i. 113), but the statement is made with reluctance and irony. The idea of a servant as no more than an extension of a master's will is similar to the friends' 'one soul in bodies twain' idea, and is similarly exposed as a limited and impractical ideal. It is neither true nor a good practical basis for action. As in friendship, the ideal is shown to be very limited, partly because of the individual's desire for recognition and self-assertion.

Tranio is clearly the main character of the Bianca plot in *The Taming of the Shrew*, as Tillyard points out,[11] and his relationship with his master Lucentio is perhaps the friendliest such relationship in Shakespeare. On his first entrance Lucentio asks him to 'Tell me thy mind' as to what they should do in Padua (1. i. 21), treating him as a tutor and friend, and it appears that the two men are going to study together. The relationship is almost one of equals: Lucentio pairs his father's 'good will' with Tranio's 'good company'; whilst he calls him 'My trusty servant', he does not exactly command him: 'Here let us breathe, and haply institute / A course of learning and ingenious studies' (1. i. 7–9). As well as the explicit statement of trust, Lucentio seems to be opening his heart here, and his use of *us* suggests that they are something like equal companions. Tranio may be a little older than his master, being able to give him advice (but not so old as to be implausible when he impersonates Lucentio), and is more intelligent. Yet he is no Mosca or Brain-Worme: Lucentio claims all his loyalty, and he takes no advantage when he is disguised. (In this, he resembles the classical servants identified by Burnett.) Indeed in his first speech his words 'I am, in all affected as yourself' (line 26), though containing a simple joke about Lucentio's affectation, seem literally meant, without even bringing up the conflicts that similarity in friendship narratives bring – usually the two men being so similar as to love the same woman. The whole inter-masculine plot of *The Shrew* attempts to avoid conflict. Bianca's suitors want to be, as Hortensio says, 'happy rivals' (1. i. 117). This is the main reason for a lack of tension and drama in the Bianca plot. What little wit and energy there is in that plot comes from Tranio, who is more learned than the buffoons around him (he quotes Latin and Italian gracefully and without pedantry), and is a cheerfully reluctant actor in the farce:

> I am tied to be obedient –
> For so your father charg'd me at our parting;
> 'Be serviceable to my son,' quoth he,
> Although I think 'twas in another sense –
> I am content to be Lucentio,
> Because so well I love Lucentio. (1. i. 213–17)

Tranio here enacts the idea of a servant as fulfiller of his master's will, but he has a clear sense of his own inherent superiority. He can include Lucentio but not vice versa.

Petruchio's blockish servant Grumio is a complete and deliberate contrast; recalcitrant for the sake of it, and only submitting when he is beaten by his master, he bears some similarity to Katherina (as Tranio perhaps does to Bianca). Like Katherina, Grumio thinks Petruchio 'mad' (iv. i. i). The roles of the servants in *The Taming of the Shrew* underpin the love plots, suggesting that the masters look for wives as similar to their servants as possible, and that the way a man interacts with his servants is an index of his character and therefore of the way he will treat his wife. In this, servants, individual in themselves, more fully bring out the indivi-duality of their masters than friends could.

As in *The Taming of the Shrew*, there is in *The Two Gentlemen of Verona* a continuity between a master's treatment of his servant and his treatment of women. There is also a continuity between service and friendship. Valentine treats friend, beloved and servant well; Proteus treats all badly – his quarrel with Speed in the play's first scene giving us the first hint of his untrustworthy nature. Service, love and friendship are shown to be similar relationships, all bound up together, and trans-forming one another. At the opening of the play, Valentine is chiding Proteus for being love-lorn; with deliberate parallelism, act ii begins with Speed mocking Valentine in a manner we might expect from a friend:

you have learned, like Proteus, to wreathe your arms, like a malcontent; to relish a love-song, like a robin-redbreast; to walk alone, like one that had the pesti-lence; to sigh, like a schoolboy that had lost his ABC; to weep, like a young wench that had buried her grandam; to fast, like one that takes diet; to watch, like one that fears robbing; to speak puling, like a beggar at Hallowmas. You were wont, when you laugh'd, to crow like a cock; when you walked, to walk like one of the lions; when you fasted, it was presently after dinner; when you look'd sadly, it was for want of money.

This seems to be a joke about the idea of friends being similar, for they have now become similar in becoming changeable, or protean. The speech ends on a slightly subversive note; mastery is attenuated by the master being in love: 'And now you are metamorphosed with a mistress, that when I look on you, I can hardly think you my master' (ii. i. 19–32). As in the case of Lucentio and Tranio, when the latter is disguised as the former, love has undermined the master's power, however little subversive effect this ultimately has.

It is indicative of the closeness of the two gentlemen at the play's opening that they appear to share a servant. Perhaps not trusting his own servant Launce to undertake a sensitive errand, Proteus suborns

Valentine's servant to take letters to Julia. Here, unlike in *Damon and Pithias*, sharing a servant is used to promote tension between the friends, suggesting the inherent absurdity of close friendship. This arrangement may be somewhat impractical, but it is a step lower than the impossibility of sharing a woman which will be the play's main plot. Service is further connected to love by the courtly trope, in which Valentine regards himself as Silvia's servant. The origins of Proteus's love for her are in the scene (II. iv) in which he is taken on as a 'fellow-servant' (line 105) and addressed by her as such. The actual servants, Launce and Speed, are then contrasted with the masters-as-servants. Proteus has kept up the façade of polite friendship with Valentine even as his thoughts turn to the betrayal of his friend, showing that higher-status men can hide conflict behind formal expression of affection. Launce and Speed by contrast have a frank friendship: they banter with each other about their masters' affairs, and then head off for a drink together. This simpler companionship between the servants shows how overwrought and artificial any relationship is that involves the gentlemen. Low-status servants may not be thought capable of any profound emotion, but supposedly profound emotions are treated with considerable scepticism in this play.

The late appearance of Launce has been plausibly seen as evidence of revision on Shakespeare's part,[12] but it can also be justified in terms of the growing division between the friends, in that the gentlemen now need separate servants. Launce's speeches reflect on the whole nature of the servile relationship. He has only one real function in the plot – to be sacked for failing to deliver a message to Silvia, and replaced by 'Sebastian' (i.e. Julia). In the first of his two major scenes as he prepares to depart from Verona with Proteus, he rails at his dog for not beweeping their separation, calling him a 'cruel-hearted cur' (II. iii. 9). Crab and Proteus, both master in a way to Launce, are parallel figures. The implication of this scene may be that it is as unreasonable to complain of Crab's bad nature as of Proteus's, yet it is also entirely fair for Launce to do so. Later, the dog has misbehaved – its soiling of a woman's petticoat a possible parallel with Proteus's infidelity. Launce, having saved the dog's life in its infancy, now saves it again, taking the blame for its indiscretion. He wistfully comments:

How many masters would do this for his servant? Nay, I'll be sworn, I have sat in the stocks for puddings he hath stolen, otherwise he had been executed; I have stood on the pillory for geese he hath killed, otherwise had suffer'd for 't. Thou think'st not of this now. Nay, I remember the trick you served me, when I took my leave of Madam Silvia. Did I not bid thee mark me, and do as I do? When didst thou see me heave up my leg and make water against a gentlewoman's farthingale? Didst thou ever see me do such a trick? (IV. iv. 29–39)

Though the incident shows that you can't make other people or dogs act as extensions of yourself, Launce's feeling for his dog here is truly other-directed, and such devotion seems all too rare in a play about love and friendship. Launce undermines the formal devotion of his superiors. His sacking shows the impermanence of service and, by extension, other human relationships. Only Julia approaches him in accepting humiliation for love's sake, and she may in this be as much a fool as Launce. True affection can only lead to servile humiliation, but only such humiliation can prove genuine affection. Despite the complex interactions of love, friendship and service in this play, no one apart from Launce and his dog seems to make much of a connection with anyone else, and this perhaps accounts for one's sense that it is Shakespeare's weakest play.

The servile relationships in *The Comedy of Errors* are much less complex than in *The Two Gentlemen of Verona*, partly because the farcical plot means that any complications are largely practical rather than emotional. Nonetheless, the play exhibits many of the familiar preoccupations with regard to servitude and status with great clarity, because the relationship is not contrasted here with friendship, but with brotherhood. At the end of the play, it is the Dromios who celebrate their discovery of each other with greater delight and openness. As in *The Two Gentlemen of Verona*, the gentlemen find it harder to be intimate than their servants do, and part of the contrast between the Antipholuses is presented in the different ways they treat their servants. The Dromios have to be similar so that their masters' difference may be brought out through operating on similar material. Maurice Hunt argues that 'the beating of the Dromios may represent Shakespeare's veiled criticism of certain Elizabethan social injustices', but the beatings also serve the purpose of differentiating the brothers.[13] Both Antipholuses beat the servants, but the terms of the relationship are clearly different. Dromio of Ephesus indicates that his master's beatings are customary and that no love is lost: 'I have serv'd him since the hour of my nativity to this instant, and have nothing at his hands for my service but blows' (IV. iv. 30–2). Ephesian Antipholus does trust his Dromio more than his wife when there is a dispute between them about money in act IV scene iv, but he is as harsh to his wife as to his servant. A man's man, who sees dining with his companions as more important than placating his wife, Ephesian Antipholus contrasts with his more romantic brother. The difference here is that between a man who has already married and needs to cultivate friends and one who is still seeking the first priority of marriage. He is more generally irascible and standoffish than Antipholus of Syracuse. When the latter rails at a confused Dromio of Syracuse in act II scene ii, Dromio thinks his master must be jesting – a sign that jests are common currency between the Syracusans. Antipholus (of Syracuse) justifies beating him as a way of preventing their familiar relationship from becoming too friendly:

> Because that I familiarly sometimes
> Do use you for my fool, and chat with you,
> Your sauciness will jest upon my love,
> And make a common of my serious hours. (II. ii. 26–9)

This illuminates the way the necessary intimacy between master and man sometimes steps over into friendship and needs to be driven back by violence. Something very similar happens when Hal repels Falstaff's desire to be too close to the future king. Friendship naturally emerges from other relationships and needs to be repressed in the interests of the social order. Whereas Launce has been sacked by the end of *The Two Gentlemen of Verona*, we can infer that Dromio of Syracuse will stay with his master permanently. Part of the reason for him telling his master about his encounter with the kitchen wench (III. ii) is that it further demonstrates master–servant friendliness, but his rejection of the lady in question also shows his complete devotion to Antipholus. The fact that Ephesian Dromio is betrothed to the woman and is nearly dismissed from his master's service suggests that he may not have such a settled future as his brother. Syracusan Antipholus and Dromio are exemplary of the master–servant relationship functioning well, just on the right side of friendship. The play ends, though, with the brother servants 'hand-in-hand': their fraternal relationship is more permanent than any service relationship, even one in which the servant has been brought up with the master, as an equal friend ought to be.

The relationship between Achilles and Patroclus in *Troilus and Cressida* is a fascinating case of the ambiguity of the roles of servant and friend. Whilst these men were famous examples of friendship shading into homoeroticism, Shakespeare does not exactly highlight the homoerotic aspect of the relationship between Achilles and Patroclus. The only real suggestion of homoeroticism comes from Thersites, ambiguously a slanderer or a sharp exposer of the realities that lie beneath pretensions of

honour. The use of the phrase 'masculine whore' to describe Patroclus
(v. i. 17) needs to be understood in its full context. The burden of
Thersites' attitude to Patroclus throughout the play has been to regard
him as a servant rather than a friend to Achilles. Thersites himself is in an
ambiguous position – as a 'privileg'd man' (II. iii. 57) he appears to be a
fool, giving him the status of a relatively free servant. Like Feste, he can
come and go between masters; he insists that he does not 'serve' Ajax, and
that he serves Achilles 'voluntary' (II. i. 94–6), though Achilles points out
that he had to endure beatings from Ajax, as a servant would, jokingly
calling that service 'suff'rance' (line 95) and insisting that none would
endure a beating voluntarily. Thersites, keen to assert himself, takes a
double-pronged approach to this refusal to recognize a servile status: on
the one hand, he denies that he is a servant; on the other, he insists that
Patroclus is a servant. Indeed, there is considerable similarity in their
roles: Ulysses tells us that Patroclus entertains Achilles with impersonations of the military leaders; Achilles employs Thersites as an entertaining
fool. Both men act as messengers for Achilles. In an age where enter-
tainers (actors, playwrights, fools) were all categorized as servants to great
men, there was an understandable desire to transmute the humiliating
servile relationship into the nobler one of friendship (the *Sonnets* are an
example of Shakespeare engaging in this process), and there was a natural
competitiveness involved. Achilles' own attitude to Patroclus is left
unclear. He treats him as a messenger, but he is such a lofty, self-absorbed
figure that it is clear his friend/servant is not the centre of his life. If we
understand Thersites as being engaged in such a competition with
Patroclus, the allegation of homosexual relations makes a new kind of
sense. Thersites prefaces the 'masculine whore' jibe by calling him
Achilles' 'male varlet' (v. i. 15), and the latter insult depends on the
former. If Patroclus is a servant, then his intimacy with Achilles verges on
the sodomitical, but only in the mind of the jealous Thersites.

   A man whose primary relationship is with his servant is not a genuinely sociable man. This selfish and untrustworthy aspect of the
master–servant relationship comes out most clearly in the work of
Shakespeare's greatest contemporary. Ben Jonson persisted with an
interest in the relationship well after Shakespeare had moved onto other
themes. Jonson is much more interested in presenting the New Comedy
trickster servant than Shakespeare. His Brain-Worme in *Every Man in
His Humour* (2nd version, 1616) is 'pardoned for the wit o' the offence'
(v. i. 177–8),[14] and Face in *The Alchemist* is forgiven by his aptly named
master Lovewit. In each case the servant procures a wife for his master,

though the fun of witty plotting and the motive of self-advancement is more important to the servant than the happy end he brings about. The forgiveness of masters, at least in drama, seems to have become proverbial, to the extent that Frank Thorney, in Rowley *et al.*'s *Witch of Edmonton*, can say 'Fathers are / Won by degrees, not bluntly, as our masters / Or wrong'd friends are' (1. i. 24–6), also perhaps reflecting on the easy forgiveness of such friends as Valentine.[15] Jonsonian comedy gives a certain licence to autonomous mischief on the part of servants which anticipates the ironic licence counselled in Swift's *Directions to Servants*. In these cases and in *Volpone* the servants' actions make them the plays' protagonists. There may be some doubt about whether Mosca is a servant or an aspirant friend,[16] and this reflects the permeability of the two conditions. In the end, for Mosca, service, far from being a route to power, is a route to the deepest servitude, as he is condemned to be a galley-slave. Such is the reward of activity. From the first, Mosca initiates all his master's schemes, is their organizer and driving force, and is the main actor in both the play's primary action and its resolution. He is the character who goes through the greatest transformation and at the end he is the one most severely punished – whipped and sent to the galleys for life, his most significant difference from Brain-Worme and Face. There is something Marlovian about his aspiration to power, and something almost tragic in his fall. His relationship with his master is of course the play's crucial dynamic. Mosca's ultimate betrayal makes a moral point about the dangerously untrustworthy servant. Shakespeare's nearest equivalent to him is Iago, as Brian Tyson suggests.[17] Mosca is *sympathetic* to Volpone, in Erasmus's terms (see chapter 1, above), but that very sympathy, which we might call symbiosis, is very close to dangerous parasitism.

For the first four acts Mosca is a perfectly loyal servant, but the fact that this loyalty is in pursuit of nefarious ends hints at its conditional nature. Although Mosca, as his name suggests, is a parasite who flatters his master, Volpone has a genuine affection for him. Their symbiotic relationship is reflected in the fact that Volpone hardly moves in the course of the play, using Mosca to carry out his will; but this is based on Volpone's mistaken assumption that Mosca's will is coterminous with his own. Although we delight in their interaction as Mosca bustles about the supposed invalid, it is also unsettling. It points up how much of himself and his capacities a master gives away when he relies too much on a servant, and perhaps how much a ruling class weakens itself by refusing to act for itself – as Shakespeare suggests when he makes the young man so passive in the *Sonnets* (see chapter 2, above). Mosca suggests something of this in his speech to Voltore:

> ... gentle sir,
> When you do come to swim in golden lard,
> Up to the arms in honey, that your chin
> Is borne up stiff with fatness of the flood,
> Think on your vassal; but remember me:
> I ha' not been your worst of clients. (I. iii. 69–74)[18]

This may also be directed to Volpone, playing on the pair's shared delight in gold, but such a friendship of pleasure is truly incapacitating to one party, who is imagined as unable to move because of his wealth. Mosca's desire to be remembered is a kind of threat, an insistence that the master (whoever he is) will always need him. The implicit assertion of self here reaches its fullest form in Mosca's soliloquy on his own role as parasite when he says 'I fear I shall begin to grow in love / With my dear self and my most prosp'rous parts, / They do so spring and burgeon' (III. i. 1–3). The irony here, that he claims he is only now beginning to love himself (as opposed to his master), is directed against the foolish assumption that a servant loves his master more than himself.

This is the springboard for Mosca's increasing boldness and self-assertion in the remainder of the play. His half-histrionic performance after Bonario thwarts Volpone's attempt on Celia's virtue shows a new stage of their relationship. Mosca has come to initiate even life-or-death plans for his master:

> VOLPONE. What shall we do?
> MOSCA.   I know not. If my heart
> Could expiate the mischance, I'd pluck it out.
> Will you be pleased to hang me, or cut my throat?
> And I'll requite you, sir. Let's die like Romans,
> Since we have lived like Grecians. (III. viii. 11–15)

Given the loving terms in which Volpone routinely addresses his man, this last line even hints at a sexual relationship between them, and certainly creates a strong sense of disorderly intimacy; the vague category of sodomy is invoked here, with all of its subversive associations.[19] The relationship between Volpone and Mosca has moved from sensual incapacitation of the master to an offer to kill him. Jonson sees a logical development from debauchery to death. Instead of killing himself and

Volpone, though, Mosca announces the master's death, and becomes his heir. The closely symbiotic relationship has allowed the absorption of host by parasite. Such closeness is, finally, doomed. Mosca's final pleasure comes in an insult to Volpone, after his plot has collapsed. He tells his master that he has been 'Bane to thy wolfish nature' (v. xii. 115). Even whilst trying to defeat him in the foregoing scenes Mosca had persisted in addressing Volpone as *you*. This final use of the intimate (or disrespectful) *thou* declares their closeness, and makes clear their symbiotic nature, initially implied in the concept of parasite. As an appropriate poison (*bane*), Mosca has a demonic relationship to his master, and these words constitute a belated recognition of an excessive intimacy whilst also asserting a special connection or affinity between them, however destructive it may be. A servant can be a man's greatest intimate, but that intimacy is ultimately destructive if there is no wider social connection.

The Jew of Malta provides the first great instance of the dangers of this kind of servile relationship in Ithamore's betrayal of Barabas, and significantly this betrayal can only take place after Barabas has made Ithamore his 'friend' and heir (III. iv. 42–3), as if only friendship can be so betrayed.[20] It is in *Doctor Faustus*, however, that Marlowe most powerfully explores the idea of dangerous familiarity. Ithamore and Mosca are examples of the servant as disorderly family: Mephistopheles is more truly a familiar. Faustus initially believes that Mephistopheles will be his servant, but there is of course another master. Faustus's love for Mephistopheles is as undisguised as Volpone's for Mosca, and it seems to have an even stronger sensual element. Laurie Maguire observes that 'Faustus's interest in Mephistopheles seems as much due to loneliness as to necromantic ambition.'[21] From the first, Faustus's language is that of a lover: 'Had I as many souls as there be stars, / I'd give them all for Mephistopheles' (I. iii. 104–5).[22] His chief request, for which he sells his soul, is that Mephistopheles serve him: Mephistopheles is quite clear that Faustus has bought his 'service' (II. i. 32), even that he is his 'slave' (line 46). The relationship we see, though, is much less hierarchical than this implies. Mephistopheles addresses Faustus as *thou* throughout – except when the contract requires legal formality. This contrasts strongly with the scene after the contract, in which Wagner, himself a servant, takes on Robin as a servant who respects him properly with *you*. Judith Weil sees continual parallels between the idea of service and the idea of demonic possession, and argues that 'Like Robin, Mephistophilis attaches himself to an employer in order to increase his own power',[23] but there is a clear contrast in terms of their confidence of success, as well as their effectiveness. Man and devil are very much equal companions on their travels, rather like Tranio and Lucentio, but Mephistopheles' priorities remain with Lucifer's rather than Faustus's interests; he entertains Faustus in order to distract him from thoughts of salvation. This manipulating role bears some similarities to Mosca's provision of entertainments for Volpone, and in both cases it emphasizes the passivity of the nominal master. Mephistopheles' initiatory power is as strong as Mosca's; it is he who suggests the tricks they play on the Pope and cardinals. Faustus is in fact Mephistopheles' possession: when Mephistopheles addresses him as 'my Faustus' (iii. i. 29), this term of endearment has sinister possessive overtones. From the very first, we are shown, gently but firmly, that Mephistopheles is in control, refusing to allow Faustus to marry, and forcing his opinion of that institution on him:

> How, a wife? I prithee, Faustus, talk not of a wife . . .
> Tut, Faustus, marriage is but a ceremonial toy. If thou lovest me,
>   think no more of it. (ii. i. 145–6, 154–5)

P. G. Wodehouse's Jeeves (an archetypal servant) continually thwarts Bertie Wooster's marriage plans, because he knows that a wife's first step is often to dismiss the manservant of bachelor days. The implication is that intimacy with servants is incompatible with marriage. Helen Gardner argues that the sacrament of marriage is incompatible with Faustus's damnation, and this is the theological side of the human drama,[24] but for dramatic reasons Faustus's relationship with Mephistopheles has to be exclusive. His friends are all kept away from him until the very end. Cornelius and Valdes, his initial assistants in necromancy, disappear. Like Mosca, Mephistopheles wants to monopolize his master. When the master–servant relationship is eroticized as it is in *Faustus*, it has a greater intensity than even ideal friendship. The fact that Mephistopheles' most powerful threat is the withdrawal of love shows the confusion of categories Faustus is engaged in. The end of the play drives home the social bonds that Faustus has been missing out on by showing several varities of friendly goodwill to him: Wagner, an unruly but honest servant, and Faustus's heir, is prepared to offer his life and service to his master; the scholars regret his passing; the Old Man tries to redeem him, and Faustus acknowledges him as a 'sweet friend' (v. i. 58); finally, Faustus expresses his regrets to the scholars, saying 'Ah, my sweet chamber-fellow! Had I lived with thee, then had I lived still, but now must die eternally' (v. ii. 3–4). Faustus has lost his soul primarily through his exclusive intimacy with Mephistopheles.

Shakespeare did not reflect on the Mephistopheles–Faustus relation-ship until his last single-authored play, but the complexity of the nature of service in *The Tempest*, and its powerful symbolic import, imply that the playwright remained fascinated by the way power and affection mingle in a master's dealings with his servants. David Lucking sees *The Tempest* as 'actualizing' ideas implicit in *Faustus*.[25] Servants are members of the *family*, in the Latin (and medieval) sense of household. By a further extension, they may be regarded as *friends*, because the word is often used for family members. Prospero's family is richly symbolic. Lacking the relative social realism of his own early comedies or the more grounded realism of Jonson's city comedies, *The Tempest* is Shakespeare's greatest exercise in experimental anthropology. Real people are placed in symbolic relation in an isolated spot in order to explore the fundamental nature of social relations, the magical element allowing a contrast between the ideal and the reality of service.

Prospero is a master with (initially) two servants. Or, to put it another way, Prospero is a ruler with two subjects. One of Prospero's subjects is idealized, perfectly obedient and capable – Ariel. The other – Caliban – is more inflexibly real. Neither is regarded as human (though Caliban is more so); but, though the relationship remains symbolic, Shakespeare is presenting the master–servant relationship as a figure for political dom-inance. Ariel presents himself as the ideal servant, but in doing so he reminds his master of his promised freedom:

> I prithee,
> Remember I have done thee worthy service,
> Told thee no lies, make no mistaking, serv'd
> Without or grudge or grumblings. Thou didst promise
> To bate me a full year. (1. ii. 246–50)

This is a device to tell the audience of their deal, but Ariel's constant repetitions of his reminders during the play suggest that, despite his loyalty, he is straining at the yoke, and his argument that he did not grudge or grumble in the past only serves to emphasize that he is doing so now. As Elliot Krieger points out, 'Ariel maintains a curious tension between enthusiastic service and the will to freedom.'[26] In addressing Prospero as *thou* he is doing three things: asserting his freedom as a spirit from the normal hierarchical forms of language, declaring an intimacy with Prospero, and addressing Prospero as his deity rather than merely his master. Prospero addresses him with terms of affection that recall Faustus's addresses to Mephistopheles: 'Fine apparition! My quaint Ariel'

(1. ii. 317). This is to be contrasted with the way he addresses Caliban immediately afterwards: 'Thou poisonous slave, got by the devil himself' (line 319). The word *slave* here is more than just an insult; it reflects Prospero's sense of Caliban's lower status as a possession rather than a free servant. In fact, Caliban's and Ariel's true positions are opposite to these linguistic constructions. The bonded deal with Ariel is truly slave-like, especially in that he has to earn his freedom like a Roman *liberus*.[27] Terence's comedies (e.g. *The Brothers*) often deal with a capable slave using his cunning to earn freedom, and this is the essence of *The Tempest*'s Ariel plot. Caliban is more like a Renaissance servant, with personal autonomy of thought, reflected in his insults to his master. His attempt on Miranda's virtue is the classic act of an ambitious servant (Malvolio, Antonio in *The Duchess of Malfi* and de Flores in *The Changeling*). His telling ability to taunt Prospero makes clear the mutual dependency implicit in the master–servant relationship: 'I am all the subjects that you have' (1. ii. 341). The symbolic action of the Caliban plot brings out an almost Hegelian discourse on political power. Certainly Caliban belittles Prospero's mastery of the airy spirits. Only the mastery of the hominoid and earthy Caliban counts as true power. Addressing Prospero as 'you' implies Caliban's respect for the master's power, but that power is based entirely on fear, not affection or loyalty.

When he transfers his allegiance to Stephano, it may be only for the sake of his wine and with a view to projected vengeance against Prospero, but this new relationship is at least based on something more positive than fear. His earlier rebuke to Prospero makes it clear that affection is a much better way of ruling him, and the audience is moved by his eloquence:

> When thou cam'st first
> Thou strok'st me and made much of me, wouldst give me
> Water with berries in't, and teach me how
> To name the bigger light, and how the less,
> That burn by day and night; and then I lov'd thee
> And show'd thee all the qualities o' th' isle,
> The fresh springs, brine-pits, barren place and fertile.
> Curs'd be I that did so! (1. ii. 332–9)

This earlier relationship may have been just as exploitative as the present fear-based one, but the sense of mutual give-and-take makes us forget its political aspects and see it as a form of friendship. It is a pure example of the pastoral relationship as articulated by William Empson, the sense of a 'beautiful relationship between rich and poor'.[28] Stephano, no aristocrat himself of course, does not define his relationship with Caliban as one of dominance: he says he is Caliban's 'friend' (ii. ii. 85). That Caliban chooses to regard him as a master in any case is a sign of his ingrained servility, but that Stephano uses the word indicates the possibility of more amicable social arrangements than Prospero is able to countenance. As in the early comedies, the lower social castes are more able to think in terms of friendship than the untrustworthy aristocrats, whose thoughts are of domination rather than sympathy.

The whole play enacts the shift to love and friendship amongst the Italians, but the rancorous relationships of the island society are less easily settled. Caliban cannot be converted from his hatred. Like the spirits, he drifts off from the conclusion rather than being integrated in it.[29] At one point, he draws a startling parallel between himself and the spirits who, he says, 'all do hate him [Prospero] / As rootedly as I' (iii. ii. 94–5). Most of Ariel's explicit behaviour does not endorse this, but Ariel, who is much given to asides, is present when Caliban speaks these words, and does not gainsay them. When we couple this with Ariel's impatient insistence on being released, we may infer that Caliban speaks true, and that Prospero is a man who provokes only hatred and grudging servitude. His instinct to be a master rather than a friend extends to enslaving Ferdinand and perhaps offers an additional reason why the people of Milan connived in Antonio's deposition of him. Gonzalo's loyalty to him militates against the last interpretation, but Prospero does come across as a peculiarly lonely man, wrapped up in his books, incapable of forming bonds without the use of his royal power or his art. Even his masterly power is eroded. Ferdinand, having agreed to serve Prospero, privately does not accept him as his master. Instead, he reconstructs the relationship by *volunteering* to be Miranda's servant, throwing off the feudal bond and replacing it with a courtly one. The resemblance of his role to that of Jacob serving Laban also hints at the possibilities for treachery. Prospero's proper respect for him and the real nature of their respective social positions are reflected in the fact that he addresses Ferdinand as *you* throughout the period of his servitude. Real social relationships are never far away in the idealized world of *The Tempest*. Ariel's desire to be free shows a basic inequality in his relationship with his master, who loves him. Until he is released, though, Ariel can say 'Thy thoughts I cleave to' (iv. i. 165), enacting the ideal stated by Dromio of Ephesus. This is the closest one can get to the one soul in bodies twain ideal, but Ariel, of course, has no body. The impenetrable physicality of other people prevents the ideal from being realized in normal life. It is Caliban, in the end, whom Prospero must 'acknowledge mine' (v. i. 276), implying a deeper symbiotic connection between them even if Caliban's service is as impermanent as Ariel's. The differing priorities of individuals prevent even service from being perfectible. If even beloved servants whose duty it is to fulfill one's mind cannot do so, how much less can a friend.

A further aspect of the power of service to promote intimacy can be seen in plays where people disguise themselves as servants. In *The Two Gentlemen of Verona, Twelfth Night* and Beaumont and Fletcher's *Philaster*, women do this in order to get close to the men they love, and show the loving nature of service: in *King Lear* Kent does so out of what can only be called friendship for the king (feudal though it be). The pretence of service can tell us something about both the nature of service and the nature of the feelings that emerge from it. Proteus and Orsino requite their servants with love, as their servants fortunately turn out to be women. In *Philaster*, when the eponymous hero has to ask Bellario forgiveness (v. ii), service has clearly given way to equal and idealized friendship. This might imply the breakdown of social hierarchy were it not for the revelation of Bellario's true identity as a gentlewoman who hopelessly loves Philaster. The emergence of such friendship between a master and a servant can only be obviated by such a reversal, and the introduction of this hopeless love removes the burden of gratitude to another man from the new king Philaster. Hopeless sexual love seems comprehensible, whereas the excessive loyal love of a servant might seem disorderly. The pure and disinterested motivation of a servant becomes problematic when the master becomes aware of the debt of gratitude and so a more interested motive has to be assigned.

There is no such problem in *King Lear*, because Lear is so used to mastery that he is incapable of so mean an emotion as gratitude. The King's much-vaunted development of human sympathy does not extend to recognizing the value of what others might do for him (with the possible exception of Cordelia). The conduct of Kent in *King Lear* is not only helpful for an understanding of Shakespeare's view of service but also illustrates the way in which the playwright uses the emotions of a relatively minor character to contribute to the grander passions of his overall dramatic scheme. Kent is one of the trio of peculiar characters that surround Lear at the centre of the play (the others being the Fool and Edgar). Their peculiarity comes from their lack of clear motivation and the fact that they are all playing roles. Kent and Edgar are in disguise, and the Fool's dual function as court jester and theatrical clown removes the question of true selfhood from him. In the presence of the King's egotistical drama, others' selves are qualified and attenuated, and have to force themselves to the fore.

Kent is one of the first characters we encounter in the play. He is introduced (to Edmund) as Gloucester's 'honourable friend' (1. i. 28), thus establishing his position as a man of friendship, before he goes on to take a crucial role in the first action of the play, resisting Lear's folly in banishing Cordelia. His address to Lear overdetermines his relationship to the King:

> Royal Lear,
> Whom I have ever honour'd as my king,
> Lov'd as my father, as my master follow'd,
> As my great patron thought on in my prayers – (1. i. 139–42)

He is servant, son and client, almost worshipper. This overdetermination perhaps leads him to express his good counsel in rather excessive terms. Claiming to be motivated by concern for the King's safety, he seems in fact to be motivated by anger and impatience.[30] He even goes so far as to call the King 'mad' (line 146). As well as introducing one of the play's great themes – the King's concern for his sanity – there is also an element of taunting Lear here, for he surely cannot expect his counsel to be accepted by such a stubborn ruler (the taunting role will later be taken up by the Fool). Kent's counsel seems to involve a certain amount of pride in his role: he wants to be Lear's 'physician' (line 163).[31] Plato (in *Lysis*) paralleled the role of the friend with that of the physician – as one who is *useful* – and here we see Kent insisting on his own usefulness. He also wants to be 'the true blank of thine eye' (line 159 – i.e. the centre of the target at which his eye/mind aims), suggesting a demand for exclusive attention. Although a feudal subordinate, Kent is making grand claims on his King in this scene, and his whole part in the play can be seen as an attempt to press his claim on Lear's attentions and affections by his usefulness. In doing so, he asserts his place in the story, and his claim on the audience's attention. Kent's disguising himself as a servant indicates particularly strongly that dramatic self-assertion can be a more powerful motive than social self-advancement. His explicit motive – loyalty to the King – is deeply complicated by this subtler motivation.

A major feature of *King Lear*'s oddity is that the play's structure consistently tries to prejudice the audience against the titular hero. In the early acts the only thing that disposes us towards him is the loyalty of Kent after his banishment; we infer that he must be somehow worthy of this devotion. Yet this devotion is rather double-edged. Despite being only one of many servants to Lear, his continual desire to be Lear's truest focus drives all his actions. The egocentric force of the useful friend or affectionate servant has much more motivational power than simple friendship. The constant frustration of his desire – Lear focusses more on the Knights, the Fool, Poor Tom and Cordelia than he does on Kent – is an important secondary aspect of the play. We have seen Kent's self-assertion in the first scene, and most of his later actions seem rather oriented to assert his own position than to further the genuine interests of his master. His soliloquy when he first enters in disguise has only a subtle hint of this, as it emphasizes his pride in his ability to serve:

> Now, banish'd Kent,
> If thou canst serve where thou dost stand condemn'd,
> So may it come, thy master, whom thou lov'st,
> Shall find thee full of labours. (I. iv. 4–7)

Love here is balanced with a stubborn desire to prove himself. He chooses the role of saucy servant because it suits his own character, not because it suits Lear's needs. Although he does not initiate the misconduct of Lear's retinue at his daughters' houses, he does nothing to prevent it, and indeed contributes the most notable example of it. His self-assertion now takes the form of asserting the King's rights, even though this is against the King's direct interests. Rather than being a wise counsellor and stopping the King from destroying his position, he does what the King wants him to do, and thus helps precipitate his disaster. Cornwall's diagnosis of 'Caius's' character is disturbingly accurate:

> This is some fellow
> Who, having been prais'd for bluntness, doth affect
> A saucy roughness and constrains the garb
> Quite from his nature. (II. ii. 95–8)

Samuel Johnson thinks that this means 'Forces his "outside" or his "appearance" to something totally different from his natural disposition.'[32] R. A. Foakes thinks that it means 'coerces the manner (of speaking the truth bluntly) quite against its nature, and thus turns it into a mode of deception'.[33] Johnson's reading seems more natural, Foakes's better for the context. An alternative, though, is: he turns the nature of a servant's livery against itself and thus does his master more harm than good. A. C. Bradley aptly comments on this that 'he illustrates the truth that to run one's head unselfishly against a wall is not the best way to help one's friends'.[34] Seduced into misbehaviour by Lear's example and approval, Kent turns his role into a self-thwarting one. As an extension of his master's will, he provides an active parody of the King's wilfulness. The paradox of a proud servant who believes that 'anger hath a privilege' (II. ii. 70) is bound to lead to humiliation. His being placed in the stocks is an insult to Lear, whose livery he wears. His conduct allows the King to be insulted. A servant is more an aspect of a man's honour than a friend could ever be. Kent's self-assertion as a servant of the King merely shows Lear how little value is now placed on his empty royalty.

When he finds Kent in the stocks Lear is only concerned for the insult to himself: he shows no sympathy for 'Caius' himself. Only on the heath does he begin to sympathize with the sufferings of Kent and the Fool, and that is only because he is sharing in them. Kent's major role at the centre of the play is to be the voice of sanity on the heath, though he achieves little or nothing here and seems out of his depth. By this stage he has abandoned his Caius voice, having (in III. i) communicated the plans for a martial/political solution to the crisis. He is concerned to get Lear to safety during the storm, repeatedly urging him indoors to the hovel. Kent's voice is joined by that of Gloucester, who calls him 'friend' (III. iv. 165, 168), but although they succeed in saving Lear, and in getting him off to Dover, their prosaic help is destined to be unappreciated. Doing good service in *King Lear* seems curiously inappropriate and irrelevant. This is a play, after all, in which the best act a servant does is to kill his master Cornwall. The play's chaotic world of service may be explained by Regan when she says:

> How in one house
> Should many people under two commands
> Hold amity? 'Tis hard, almost impossible. (II. iv. 240–2)

Everyone's loyalties are conflicting in this play, not just those of a central character with classic twin imperatives. Amity is dependent, it is implied, on unified authority.

The play's discourse of friendship *per se* is as confused as its discourse of service, and for related reasons. After seeing the King on the heath,

Gloucester addresses anyone who can help him or the King as 'friend' (to Kent – III. vi. 86, 88, 91; to the old man – IV. i. 15; to Edgar – IV. vi. 28). Edgar refers to the letters he obtains from Oswald as his 'friends' (IV. vi. 257). And at the play's conclusion Albany calls Kent and Edgar 'noble friends' (V. iii. 297) and 'friends of my soul' (line 320). There is a collective attempt to recover the uniting effects of friendship from the play's moral chaos, but it rings falsely and is hopeless. Where the loyalties of service have collapsed, more affectionate loyalties cannot be recovered. At the end of the play, Kent makes an attempt to get recognition for his friendly service to the King by revealing his identity.[35] As this takes place in the midst of Cordelia's dying scene, it only seems incongruous, even if it is a well-meaning attempt to distract Lear from his intolerable grief. He may have said earlier (to Cordelia) that 'To be acknowledg'd, madam, is o'erpaid' (IV. vii. 4), but he clearly does want acknowledgement in the end. Edgar introduces him to Lear as 'noble Kent, your friend' (V. iii. 269), but Lear (understandably in the circumstances), fails to recognize him at first, even including him amongst the 'murderers, traitors, all!' (line 270) and when he reveals that he played the role of Caius, Lear can only say 'you're welcome hither' (line 290). Kent is rather melodramatic in revealing himself, but this has no effect on Lear. Nor does his attempt to cheer his master up by telling him that Goneril and Regan are dead. The death of Cordelia has cancelled all possibility of other emotion, be it grateful recognition or vengeful pleasure. Kent's theatricality here is thus distasteful, exemplified by his self-assertively humble line, 'Your servant Kent. Where is your servant Caius?' (line 284). Trying to steal the scene from the dead Cordelia echoes the first scene, where he tried to trump Cordelia's defiance. Kent even tries to upstage Lear's death by his claim that he must follow his master to the grave. He refuses the reins of authority from Albany, saying

> I have a journey, sir, shortly to go:
> My master calls me, I must not say no. (lines 322–3)

He is the ultimate *follower*, his selfhood defined by service – a relationship more powerfully symbiotic than any idealized form of friendship could be. Faced with such cosmic drama, Kent can only assert his own place in the story. He does not come to a powerful self-recognition as some Shakespearean characters do. Like *Hamlet*'s Horatio, he can only realize himself by the desire to follow the play's hero to death.

Self-assertion within the servile relationship tests its limits, and therefore the limits of any kind of loyalty. Men like Kent can identify with their masters, without necessarily advancing their interests. Both comedy and tragedy are accentuated by servants being pulled into their masters' vortices. Only those with an ironic and non-committal mode of selfhood – such as Edgar – can escape Lear's tragedy. As we shall see in the next chapter, personal loyalties play a lesser role in the world of politics, even if the rhetoric of personal friendship is still used.

CHAPTER 6

Political friendship

Whilst service necessarily involves social differences, there must always be a particularly acute, even categorical difference in a king's friendships, thus making ideal friendship impossible, but even attempts to act as the *guarantor* of friendship are shown to be equally futile in the history plays and in *Macbeth*. On the other hand, some plays, particularly the two parts of *Henry IV* and *Hamlet*, find different ways for the monarch to have symbiotic connections with friends, and thereby to realize his individuality and that of others. The word *friend* has what amounts to a specialized meaning in a political context – stripped of its affective component, it simply refers to allies and supporters. We must be wary, though, of taking this meaning as normative; rather, it is the affective meaning that is invoked, however distantly, whenever the word is used for political purposes in drama; the idea of an amity that binds the nation together is also never far away. The audience's reception of the word is split – part of us is sophisticated (or cynical) enough to recognize that political friendship is purely transactional, but there is a residual part of us which retains a naive or nostalgic sense that the core emotive meaning is or ought to be present. The monarch, Richard II for example, expects to be loved for himself, and expects that love to be the principle that holds the whole country together. He connects this with his own legitimacy, but it is precisely because of an excessive belief in this ideal that he loses his throne. A version of this idea is later reflected in Falstaff, who is thwarted in his desire to become a royal favourite, but whose character demonstrates the real nature of the bond between subject and monarch, which has a limited, but nonetheless powerful affective component.[1]

Kingship involves a crucial paradox regarding friendship: on the one hand the king needs supporters, ideally bound to him by bonds of genuine affection, as may really have happened with medieval kings;[2] on the other hand, any particular friendship can be construed as excessive favour, and can therefore create jealous enemies who threaten the king's position. Laurie Shannon has argued that the *Henry IV* plays reflect a development of a modern mode of government in which affective loyalties are attenuated, in which 'The subordinated sovereign is denied the power of any but the most generalized affectivities.'³ Yet it is hard to find any real sense of friendly loyalty in the earlier history plays. Shakespeare's first tetralogy of history plays exhibit a constant nostalgia for a lost world of friendship, implying a connection between real affective bonds and royal legitimacy. But when Shakespeare moves back to the roots of the Roses conflict, first in *1 Henry VI* (now generally acknowledged to have been written after parts 2 and 3), and then in the second tetralogy, such a world of friendship is shown to be a mirage.

There is a continual sense in the first tetralogy that true friendship is dead. Political friendship is represented without its affective connotations, and the word *friend* starkly denotes anyone who will provide support, whether on the basis of kinship ties, past obligations, or mutual hostility to another. Shakespeare's earliest history plays play an almost insistent game with the concept of friendship. Both kin relationship and friendship are seen as providing only provisional alliances. As royal legitimacy is in abeyance, so is any essentialist concept of the affective power of friendship or blood ties. There is a nostalgic yearning for a feudal and chivalric world of legitimate kings which saw no dissonance between friendship, patriotism and familial loyalty. *1 Henry VI* signals the death of chivalric comradeship in the death of Salisbury, who has just called Talbot, 'my life, my joy' (1. iv. 23). Talbot, whose presentation calls up nostalgia for old heroic modes of being, takes up an Achillean role as noble avenger of his friend and fights his doomed patriotic war with the passion of friendship behind him. But in the emergent world of civil conflict in these plays he is seen as a last remaining anachronism. In the plays which present the conflict over the throne, King Henry himself, who ought to be the guarantor of national amity, can only express a dream of friendship in the shadow of death as he gazes at his rival's head staked to the city walls of York:

> Ah, cousin York, would thy best friends did know
> How it doth grieve me that thy head is here!
> (*3 Henry VI*, 11. ii. 54–5)

There is what seems to him a grievously paradoxical detachment here between friendship and blood relationship. His grief here is not just for an individual, but for a whole lost world of friendship and kin ties. Where there is no legitimacy and no strong ruler there can be no constancy, no friendship. Only a death-lament can express the residual feelings of friendship.

'Kingmaker' Warwick holds the balance of power in *3 Henry VI*, his treacherous friendship being exemplary of the universal fickleness in the play, which spreads throughout society. His changes of side are bewildering, and are imitated by others, including even the fickle gamekeepers who capture the King (III. i), suggesting that it is his spirit that guides the nation. No sooner has Warwick put Edward on the throne than he turns back to supporting the Lancastrian cause, Shakespeare's compression of historical time here highlighting the treachery. Queen Margaret accepts this treacherous man with easy words of friendship. Here friendship is less about remembering past services than it is about forgetting past sins:

> Warwick, these words have turn'd my hate to love,
> And I forgive and quite forget old faults,
> And joy that thou becom'st King Henry's friend. (III. iii. 199–201)

He calls himself Henry's 'unfeigned friend' (line 202) with a disingenuousness which goes beyond irony. Clarence's shift to the Lancastrian side further erodes any sense of loyalty, and the atmosphere of distrust is built up around a hollowing of the concept of friendship. Edward says that he would rather have Hastings and Montague as 'foes than hollow friends' (IV. i. 139), but all friendship now seems to be hollow. Warwick has to ask Clarence and Somerset 'are we all friends?' (IV. ii. 4), but by now the question is otiose. He tries to inspire his troops with a speech that prefigures Henry V's, but which reveals that their only allegiance is to him: 'For Warwick and his friends, God and Saint George!' (line 29). By this stage, we have no idea who Warwick's true friends are (and still less where God and St George stand). The troops are fighting for Warwick alone. In this atmosphere it becomes every man (or at least every nobleman) for himself. No one is left with the binding charisma of leadership, which relies on the proper manipulation of friendship.

The shifting network of loyalties in this play gives no individual sufficient or permanent enough prominence to hold the play or the nation together. We are left with isolated and entirely self-oriented individuals. This finds its fullest development in Richard of Gloucester, who says he

> can add colours to the chameleon,
> Change shapes with Proteus for advantages,
> And set the murderous Machiavel to school. (III. ii. 191–3)

Constancy is the keystone of ideal friendship, as it is of political stability, and Richard is its nemesis, signalling the end of any meaning to the idea of friendship or kin ties most radically (and wittily) when he orders Tyrrel to murder the princes in the Tower:

> K. RICH. Dar'st thou resolve to kill a friend of mine?
> TYR. Please you;
> But I had rather kill two enemies.
> K. RICH. Why, there thou hast it; two deep enemies,
> Foes to my rest, and my sweet sleep's disturbers.
> (*Richard III*, IV. ii. 69–73)

Richard's individual and subjective interests have come to define friendship and enmity. The word *friend* can only be used ironically. Richard is wholly alone. This gives him temporary success, but ultimately all his betrayals come back to haunt him, literally, before the battle of Bosworth. Before that battle, he expresses the hope that his 'friends prove all true' (V. iii. 213), but he has abused the concept of friendship so much that he has no right to expect that they will. All those ghosts who appeared before him in the night were nominally friends of one sort or another and it is their prophecies of his death that will prove true. All his living friends, either familial or political, abandon him. He has neither Henry VI's doomed nostalgia for friendship, nor any truly Machiavellian ability to manipulate friendship.

Richard III's one friend is Buckingham, who considers himself a kingmaker, but never quite gets to be a royal favourite. As soon as Richard becomes king, he begins to suspect that Buckingham's 'kindness' to him is cooling (IV. ii. 22), and he decides that his 'high-reaching' friend must be disposed of (line 31). This reflects the basic similarity between the men, but Richard is the original and Buckingham a mere copy. When Richard calls him his 'other self' (II. ii. 151), Buckingham may assume that they have the soul-connection of classical friendship, but Richard means only that Buckingham is his instrument. Bacon argued that the friend was another self in that he can be a 'deputy', doing things for one that one cannot do for oneself.[4] Richard directs Buckingham as if he were a 'tragedian' (III. v. 5), and we generally see him as Richard's smooth-talking mouthpiece, with little personality of his own. One particular duty that Bacon gave to the deputizing friend was praise, and it is this which Richard uses as Buckingham is deuteragonist in Richard's play of power before the Lord Mayor (III. vii). Such an easily manipulated actor can be easily cast aside when he hesitates to act in the murder of the princes. Buckingham draws his own morals on his fall (v. i. 13–22), understanding that it is caused by his betrayal of King Edward's family and his trust of Richard's flattery. Humanists would not see friendship in a bad cause as true friendship, but the virtuous counsellor has no better of it in the early histories. Humphrey, Duke of Gloucester, Henry VI's 'crutch' (2 *Henry VI*, III. i. 189) is levered away from the protectorship by spurious charges against his wife. His desperate attempts to help the King underpin friendship in the kingdom (1 *Henry VI*, III. i. 137, 145) have come to nothing. Despite his 'friendly counsel' (line 184), the world of the early histories is empty of friendship.

One purpose of the second tetralogy is going back to the roots of this problem, and it is false friendship that drives out true (a version of Gresham's Law). The roots of the destruction of royal legitimacy in *Richard II* are based on Bolingbroke's success in assembling useful friends. These friends are not motivated by affection for him but by enmity to Richard or the promise of gain should Richard be deposed. The second tetralogy's discourse of friendship is more about remembering friends than forgetting enmities, but to remember friendship is also to remember its basis in enmity, and provokes further cycles of rebellion. On meeting Harry, Percy Bolingbroke explains his position with a revealing mixture of affective and commercial language:

> I count myself in nothing else so happy
> As in a soul rememb'ring my good friends,
> And as my fortune ripens with my love,
> It shall be still thy true heart's recompense. (II. iii. 46–9)

Bolingbroke seems here to hope that when his fortune ripens and he becomes king he will gain the love (active and passive) that will underpin his position, but the idea is deeply associated with political transactionalism rather than a real faith in the affective power of kingship. Bolingbroke exercises a skilful courtesy that Richard, who believes in friendship as a form of love, despises. Richard rebukes Bolingbroke for his superficiality, saying that he is 'unpleased' by his cousin's 'courtesy' (III. iii. 193) in kneeling to him; he would rather have 'love' (line 192), but it is hard to see how Bolingbroke could demonstrate this.

Given the use of the word 'friend' to mean kin, there is some complication in the development of enmity between Bolingbroke and his kinsman the King. In the first scene, he renounces his status as the King's kinsman in order to accept Mowbray's challenge:

> Pale trembling coward, there I throw my gage,
> Disclaiming here the kindred of the King,
> And lay aside my high blood's royalty,
> Which fear, not reverence, makes thee to except. (I. i. 69–72)

This gesture has symbolic resonance throughout the play and in a sense reduces the impiety of his rebellion (there is no longer a Macbeth-like 'double trust' of kin and allegiance). Richard, after Bolingbroke's banishment, recognizes that kinship and friendship have now been separated. He tells Aumerle:

> He is our cousin, cousin, but 'tis doubt,
> When time shall call him home from banishment,
> Whether our kinsman come to see his friends. (I. iv. 20–2)[5]

If Bolingbroke is not a friend, as Richard believes, he can only be an enemy. Kinship is of no relevance and the strain in the word *friend* is evident. Its range of meanings – affection, kinship, support – which were once, it is supposed, bound together, can now no longer be taken as implying each other. *Richard II* suggests that such a world never existed outside the King's own mind. Richard is unable to 'make' Bolingbroke and Mowbray friends at the start of the play; he aborts the combat that might settle the issue between them. His favourites have advised him to do this, and they thus subvert one ritual that might underpin his royal charisma and authority.

Because, in the Ciceronian view of friendship, friends have to be equal, kings can never have true friends. Shakespeare takes it for granted that Richard's favourites are false friends, but he gives them little attention. Any attempt to choose a close friend leaves a king open to charges of favouritism. This was an important political theme of Shakespeare's time: favourites could be very unpopular – Ralegh for example – and even a serious minister such as Burghley could be accused of being a favourite.[6] Shakespeare's presentation of the theme is much more muted than that of his contemporaries, but it remains crucial to ideas of friendship in the political sphere. Although we could argue that Shakespeare is exhibiting political caution in downplaying the roles of Bushy, Bagot and Greene, he may also be creating a deliberate contrast between his play and its main dramatic sources, Marlowe's *Edward II* and the anonymous *Woodstock*. We may be supposed to think of Gaveston and see how emotionally empty Richard's favouritism is. *Richard II*, then, demonstrates that friendship had no real role even in the destruction of the legitimate monarch, and is merely a pretext for those who want to depose him.

Marlowe's Edward II really believes in his friendship with Gaveston. He attempts to get round the problem of kingly friendship, by making Gaveston a king and therefore his equal, giving him the title 'Chief Secretary to the state and me, / Earl of Cornwall, King and Lord of Man' (1. i. 154–5).[7] The different roles emphasize Gaveston's elevation whilst also binding him to Edward. Edward centres his kingly state on his favourite: when Gaveston says he is not worthy of his titles, Edward replies that Gaveston's worth 'is far above my gifts; / Therefore to equal it, receive my heart', going so far as to say that 'but to honour thee / Is Edward pleased with kingly regiment' (lines 160–1; 163–4). Shakespeare's Richard II expresses no such devotion to his favourites.

Edward constantly tries to realize the Humanist ideal of one soul in bodies twain, by rhetorically transferring his own feelings and attitudes onto Gaveston. In the first scene, he refuses Gaveston's homage with shock at what his new status has brought him and insists that their friendship remains mutual:

> Why shouldst thou kneel? Knowest thou not who I am?
> Thy friend, thy self, another Gaveston!
> Not Hylas was more mourned of Hercules
> Than thou hast been of me since thy exile. (lines 142–5)

Shakespeare's Richard's refusal of Bolingbroke's courteous kneeling clearly derives from this scene, but Edward is concerned with individual love rather than familial loyalty. The image of the King as grieving Hercules is tragically proleptic, and yet again shows that friendship is more likely to be expressed in grief at its loss than in pleasure at its fulfilment. More than his extravagant gifts, more than his revels with Gaveston (which we never actually see), the main image of Edward as a friend is his grief, losing Gaveston first by his banishment, then by his death; and finally torn away from Gaveston's replacement, Spencer.

Despite his apparent fickleness in taking Spencer as a favourite almost as soon as Gaveston is dead, Edward's grief for his friends, and his assertion of mutuality in an impossible situation, remain heartfelt. When his abandonment by all the nobles is confirmed by his brother's desertion, Edward can only lament for 'Poor Gaveston, that hast no friend but me' (ii. ii. 219). Yet it is clear that it is Edward who has no friend – the projection of his own loneliness onto Gaveston is a last desperate attempt to preserve the dream of complete mutuality. Gaveston's death, it must be said, does not destroy Edward, because he has Spencer and Baldock to shore him up, but the loss of these is the end for him – 'Life, farewell, with my friends' (iv. vii. 99). This may be histrionic, and a sign of a lack of personal resilience, but this is a man who has found in friendship the only meaning in his life. As he reflects on death, he can only put meaning into it by insisting that it is for friendship's sake:

> O Gaveston, it is for thee that I am wronged;
> For me, both thou and both the Spencers died,
> And for your sakes a thousand wrongs I'll take,
> The Spencers' ghosts, where ever they remain,
> Wish well to mine; then tush, for them I'll die. (v. iii. 41–5)

Only in death can there be mutuality. *Richard II* gives Bushy, Bagot and Greene none of this force of individual friendship; Richard can only give dramatic prominence to himself.

Woodstock (?1592)[8] provides Richard with five favourites – Bushy, Bagot, Greene, Scroope and Tresilian (the last of whom is discarded by Shakespeare, not least because he was historically a power much earlier in the reign than the others). The emphasis is semi-comically on their extravagant introduction of absurd fashions to the court, providing a visual contrast with the sartorial austerity of Thomas of Woodstock. Richard wants their youth to 'beautify our princely throne' (ii. i. 5); his fault in this play is 'headstrong youth' (i. i. 186) as well as susceptibility to his 'flattering minions' (line 48). The favourites are obvious villains, starting the play with the attempted murder of Richard's uncles, and getting key posts before Richard ultimately farms the realm out to them with Marlovian extravagance, telling them

> like an emperor shall king Richard reign
> And you so many kings attend on him. (iii. i. 2–3)

Like Edward, he wants to assert his own generosity, but unlike Edward he does not want to make them equals – indeed, he wants to raise himself from king to emperor. It is clear that the playwright intends his audience to disapprove wholeheartedly of these upstart fops who impose excessive and illegal taxation on the kingdom. Richard is seen as misled rather than villainous – in the end he tries to countermand the order for Woodstock's murder. He is also aware of history's likely adverse verdict (IV. i. 138–49). The favourites' unhistorical routing by the Royal Dukes' rebellion brings a satisfying end to the injustices. Richard's favouritism is a matter of youthful vanity rather than real affection, and this is emphasized by the fact that there are so many favourites, and real friendship can only work (according to Humanist theory) on a one-to-one basis.

Whilst *Richard II* is not a straight 'sequel' to *Woodstock*, the play is hard to understand without at least a passing awareness of its predecessor.[9] Shakespeare downplays the role of the favourites in order to present the full moral and political ambiguity of the deposed king, without displacing too many of his sins onto the favourites. He is nowhere near as keen as Marlowe to present the affective side of royal friendship: the impossible mutuality for which Edward II yearns isn't even entertained as a possibility in *Richard II*. Richard is far too inwardly preoccupied with increasing the dramatic prominence of his own kingly image for that. Charles R. Forker observes that 'Edward's infatuation with Gaveston and afterwards with the younger Spencer is shown to be the direct cause of his doom, while Bushy, Bagot and Green are treated as mere adjuncts of Richard's collapse and seem to share but little of their master's intimate or interior life.'[10] Though Gaveston doesn't share Edward's interior life, Edward thinks (or at least hopes) that he does. Bushy, Bagot and Greene are colourless individuals and Richard expresses no particularized affection for them. Bolingbroke charges Bushy and Greene with misleading their king, with more than a slight suggestion that they are guilty of sodomitical relations with him:

> You have misled a prince, a royal king,
> A happy gentleman in blood and lineaments,
> By you unhappied and disfigured clean;
> You have in manner with your sinful hours
> Made a divorce betwixt his queen and him,
> Broke the possession of a royal bed ... (III. i. 8–13)

The accusations are puzzling as they do not fit with what we see of Richard's relations with Queen Isabel, and the excessive charges reflect Bolingbroke's outrage at the idea that a king may arbitrarily choose his own friends. We are surely meant to think here of Gaveston and make the contrast. The core truth of the charges, insofar as the favourites have harmed the King, is that they have prevented him from begetting an heir and thereby securing his position, but it is not friendship that has destroyed this king. These 'caterpillars' (II. iii. 166) do not have the power of fascination possessed by Gaveston. Part of Richard's tragedy is that he believes abstractly in friendship, but has no friends. As Forker points out, 'Bushy, Bagot and Green, the "caterpillars" of Richard's ill-tended garden, are meant to function chiefly as self-aggrandizing parasites and the givers of bad counsel to a youthfully impressionable and emotionally unstable king, although this action is merely implied rather than shown.'[11] This is all *shown* very well in *Woodstock*, and the puzzle is why this dramatically effective material is so muted in Shakespeare's play. Forker also notes that whilst Bushy and Green are executed, Bagot survives and is implicitly disloyal to Richard in accusing Aumerle of Gloucester's (Woodstock's) murder. 'This base man' (IV. i. 20), as Aumerle calls him, is forbidden by Bolingbroke from accepting Aumerle's consequent challenge. The favourite is not allowed a dramatic final scene even in betrayal, being pushed to the background whilst others argue over the accusation. Richard is dramatically diminished as well as politically compromised by having such worthless friends. Richard plays 'in one person many people' (v. v. 31); a king of such multiplicity (which is different from the protean Machiavellianism of Richard III) does not need friends in the end, however much he may have felt the need for an audience. His belief in friendship is more a belief in his own largeness than it is in the real values of social relations.

In deliberate and obvious contrast to Richard II, Prince Hal/Henry V recognizes that his royal status depends on social agreement and is not essential to him. Consequently, he knows that all social relationships have to be negotiated and cannot be taken for granted. When Hal says that he will uphold his friends' idleness 'awhile' (*1 Henry IV*, I. ii. 195–6), he is declaring himself against the long-term nature of true friendship – he is no Edward II to equate life and friendship. Hal knows that when he comes to be King he must be alone: he is Shakespeare's most solitary hero, despite appearing in company so often. The group at Eastcheap provides a way for Hal to avoid having to 'remember' aristocratic friends as his father did. Hotspur, his nearest equal, may be as witty as Hal in his exchanges with Glendower, but his insults to the Welshman cause him political disadvantage and earn the distrust of his uncle Worcester. There is nothing to be lost in insulting Falstaff. The Eastcheap fellowship allows him to return to court with mystique and authority even over his brothers, as we saw in chapter 3 above. Falstaff is easily banished, but he is not replaced by any new intimates. Hal will rule alone, and his Eastcheap milieu has merely enabled him to avoid entanglements and obligations at court.

Although Falstaff thinks he is in line to be a favourite (even to become Lord Chief Justice),[12] Hal never contemplates this. His contempt for his fat friend is constant, nowhere more so than at Shrewsbury. Before the battle he tells Falstaff 'thou owest God a death' (v. i. 126). At this point he refuses even the most basic chivalric aid to his supposed friend:

FAL. Hal, if thou seest me down in the battle and bestride me, so; 'tis a point of friendship.
HAL. Nothing but a Colossus can do thee that friendship. Say thy prayers, and farewell. (v. i. 121–4)

Yet when he thinks that Falstaff is dead, his reaction is decidedly ambivalent:

What, old acquaintance! could not all this flesh
Keep in a little life? Poor Jack, farewell!
I could have better spar'd a better man.
O, I should have a heavy miss of thee
If I were much in love with vanity!
Death hath not struck so fat a deer today,
Though many dearer, in this bloody fray. (v. iv. 102–8)

This seems initially heartless, but it suggests the suppression of emotion. Hal cannot bring himself to call Falstaff 'friend', regarding him only as an 'acquaintance'. The obsession with Falstaff's excess flesh makes him seem a grand symbol of mortality, and the vanity of human life. There are considerable emotional ambiguities here, especially in the gnomic line 'I could have better spar'd a better man' – does this mean 'I would prefer that a better man were allowed to live' or (more likely, I think) 'I could more easily have done without a better man'? If the latter, this is a rare instance of Hal being surprised at his emotions. Others may be dearer and better than Falstaff, but Hal finds that he is nonetheless difficult to do without. The *if* here is an important arbiter – whilst it implies that Hal does not love Falstaff and his vanity, it also shows that he sees the possibility, and is genuinely tempted, despite himself, into true feelings of friendship for this man; there is a strange, almost symbiotic affinity between the men. The audience, meanwhile, may share in Hal's grief, for they may believe Falstaff to be really dead. We have seen that friendship finds its fullest expression in death, and Falstaff, who has no reason to continue playing dead once Hotspur has been killed, may be deliberately doing so in order to overhear this apotheosis of his friendship. This eulogy, feeble as it is, seems to resurrect Falstaff, such power does friendship have for him: for him, life and friendship *are* equated. Hal's pre-battle sentiments are belied because of the power of friendship, even if it is only one-way.

Falstaff has a fantasy of mutuality every bit as intense as Edward II's. This represents a brilliant inversion of Marlowe, for Falstaff's task in making himself equal to the Prince is even more difficult than Edward's in making Gaveston his equal. When Hal and Poins twit Falstaff with his cowardice at Gad's Hill and his dishonesty about the exploit, Hal is clearly relatively in the right, and yet Falstaff comes out of the scene better. His lies are absurd – Hal, in calling them 'open, palpable' (ii. iv. 226), almost acknowledges that they (like their father Falstaff) are harmless. Falstaff excuses his cowardice by claiming that he instinctively knew not to attack his prince:

By the Lord, I knew ye as well as he that made ye. Why, hear you, my masters, was it for me to kill the heir apparent? Should I turn upon the true prince? Why, thou knowest I am as valiant as Hercules; but beware instinct – the lion will not touch the true prince. Instinct is a great matter. I was now a coward on instinct. I shall think the better of myself, and thee, during my life; I for a valiant lion and thou for a true prince. (lines 267–75)

This stunning bit of sophistry has one clear suggestion: the incidents of the night have not only proved the special relationship between Hal and Falstaff, but have also proved that Hal's doubtful claim to true royalty is divinely endorsed, and that Falstaff is the touchstone or guarantor of royalty. David Scott Kastan argues that 'the episode becomes, in the shameless lie, proof not only of Falstaff's instinctive virtue but even of the Prince's legitimacy'.[13] This is a grand claim indeed, suggesting a friendship that underwrites royal status, rather than undermine it as did the friendships of Edward II and Richard II.

Falstaff's claim to be the true Royal Lion, the mascot of the English Crown, gives him other entitlements. In part 2 he responds with further sophistry to charges that he has abused Hal: 'I disprais'd him [Hal] before the wicked that the wicked [*turns to the Prince*] might not fall in love with thee: in which doing, I have done the part of a careful friend and a true subject, and thy father is to give me thanks for it' (*2 Henry IV*, II. iv. 319–23). There is a claim of exclusive friendship here that extends almost to exclusive subjecthood: Falstaff is the Prince's only true subject and friend. Again he is underwriting Hal's royalty, but here he is undermining it as well, suggesting that Hal's royalty can only be fully expressed with Falstaff. Falstaff's claim that his friendship brings true royalty to Hal reaches its heights towards the end of part 2. He laments that Hal's brother Lancaster does not love him (Falstaff) and may perhaps be a little jealous of the blood relationship, but then he considers that he has a truer relationship to Hal through sherris-sack, which 'illumineth the face, which, as a beacon, gives warning to all the rest of this little kingdom, man' (IV. iii. 107–9), and which brings true valour to a man. By introducing Hal to this drink, Falstaff has made him truly royal, in a way that his blood could not:

Hereof comes it that Prince Harry is valiant, for the cold blood he did naturally inherit of his father he hath like lean, sterile, and bare land, manur'd, husbanded and till'd, with excellent endeavour of drinking good and good store of fertile sherris, that he is become very hot and valiant. (lines 117–22)

The friend Falstaff has become superior to father and brother, providing the true and non-genetic, non-blood-based origin of kingship. Falstaff is a reminder to the common man of the appetitive selfishness that really underlies his commitment to king and country, whilst not denying that that commitment is real, nor that his commitment is a crucial element of the monarch's hold on power. Both subject and king gain in this symbiotic fiction; the special connection asserts the dramatic and social place of each.

The general claim is that Falstaff has corrupted Hal (one might compare this to the charges against Socrates), but he insists that Hal has corrupted or even 'bewitch'd' him (*1 Henry IV*, II. ii. 17), and later that Hal has 'misled' him (*2 Henry IV*, I. ii. 145). But he doesn't really see himself as corrupted or in moral danger – this is simply joyful attribution of his faults to Hal, suggesting their mutuality in the same way that Shakespeare passes the buck of sin around in the *Sonnets*. Falstaff insults Hal, and comes to see himself as the Prince's superior. In one startling image, he says that 'I am the fellow with the great belly, and he [Hal] my dog' (*2 Henry IV*, I. ii. 145–6). This claim of superiority is even harder to sustain than claims of mutuality, and is a form of *hubris* in friendship that will lead to Falstaff's fall. A few scenes later Hal will reverse the hierarchy of this image as he reversed the hierarchy when he and Falstaff played at king and prince (or father and son), saying 'I do allow this wen to be as familiar with me as my dog' (II. ii. 106–8). Mutuality has now become a power struggle: the men's images are now in conflict rather than witty dialogue. Falstaff has become a parasite, a wen or wart, and must be removed. The Lord Chief Justice sees how Falstaff has over-reached, saying that he claims the 'power to do wrong' (II. i. 129). This power parallels the 'power to hurt' (sonnet 94) of superior people in relationships. In the end it is Hal who reasserts this power in his rejection of Falstaff. In saying 'I know thee not' (v. v. 47), Hal gives us the ultimate inversion of the friendly recognition, denying friendship as a way of asserting a new self, and allowing himself to be recognized as truly king.

Aristotle posited that one of the main purposes of virtuous friendship was to improve the friend's *eudaimonia* – his moral well-being – and this may involve a sacrifice of virtue on the other friend's part.[14] Allan Bloom argues that the relationship between Hal and Falstaff is 'a parody of Aristotelian friendship'.[15] In giving Falstaff the honours at Shrewsbury, Hal has done this in a parodic manner, sacrificing his honour for his friend's: and at the end of part 2 the new King Henry V reclaims his honour by banishing his friend. It matters little that Falstaff is an involuntary sacrifice: David Womersley argues that the structure of the plays is designed to shift some of the martyred Oldcastle's piety onto the King, that it was 'the playwright's intention to unify political and spiritual authority in the person of Henry. The sanctifying of the king demanded the secularization of the subject.'[16] That it is the playwright rather than Falstaff himself who has effected this gift to the King means that we obviously cannot attribute any generosity to Falstaff in this, but in making a sacrifice of Falstaff Shakespeare has made him a valuable friend, one who creates virtue, without any of the equality, generosity or virtue a Ciceronian might expect from true friendship. Falstaff himself, 'the cause that wit is in other men' (*2 Henry IV*, I. ii. 10), would appreciate the irony. His claims to a special relationship with the King are in some sort vindicated.

We might also see their relationship in Platonic terms, with Falstaff a parodic educator of the younger man. Falstaff's parallel to Socrates is primarily to be found in the fact that he is a cause of other men's wit, but this *wit* is not to be equated with philosophy – it is an ironic, deflating mode of thought, often instrumental and sophistical rather than directed towards truth. This is often a property of Plato's Socrates, a property that later traditions of philosophy have attempted to clear away. It is associated with the underlying pederasty of Socrates' educational method, yet this pederasty is not present in Falstaff, whose desires are expressed in other terms – the need for food and drink, sexual desire for women, even the desire to be Chief Justice. Without sexual desire for Hal, Falstaff's desire to be friends with the Prince becomes polymorphous and perhaps more subversive than sexual desire would be. In the *Symposium*, Socrates' wisdom has managed to convert his desire for Alcibiades into Alcibiades' desiring Socrates, despite his physical ugliness. No such reversal takes place between Hal and Falstaff, because Falstaff's wit is less powerful than Socrates' wisdom. The friendship is a parody of the already parodic relationship between Socrates and Alcibiades: in this case, all the desire is on the part of the older man – even Alcibiades' drunkenness is transferred to him. Hal retains only Alcibiades' martial abilities. All the supposedly good things – temperance, wisdom, martial skill – are given to Hal; all the bad things – drunkenness, desire, ugliness – to Falstaff. Hal even gets the better of the wit contests. As Dr Johnson points out 'the fat knight has never uttered a sentiment of generosity'.[17] So even the desire to do others good must be denied to Falstaff, making this the most unequal friendship imaginable. Hal and Falstaff are engaged in a version of Aristotelian moral competition – in which there should be mutual augmentation of virtue or moral well-being. In this grotesque and Machiavellian inversion of the concept, Hal increases his own *eudaimonia* and destroys Falstaff's. In the end, it is this imbalance that rescues Falstaff in our esteem: he is the better friend, because his friend's *eudaimonia* is enhanced more by the friendship than his own. Hal wins the obvious moral competition, but Falstaff wins the underlying competition of friendship, because he has been the one to give Hal something. In some peculiar sense, Falstaff has made Hal king. Albeit involuntarily, he has become a sacrificial figure, validating Hal's role. His friendship, though pleasure-oriented and instrumental, more witty than wise, was real and individual, embodying fellowship but with the addition of particularity. It therefore confers legitimacy on Henry V more powerfully than any merely political friendship could. Despite his social humiliation, he gains dramatic prominence – for himself and for his prince.

King Henry has learned to banish friendship, whilst keeping up the pretence of virtuous connections with others. Throughout *Henry V* the King insists on his own difference from his subjects, whilst claiming their friendship. In his soliloquy on ceremony, he can only think of all others apart from himself as 'slaves' (IV. i. 281). Nonetheless when he stirs up his army there is a continual rhetorical sleight of hand which insists upon equality:

> We would not die in that man's company
> That fears his fellowship to die with us. (IV. iii. 38–9)

Despite its gracious terms, this remains a command, and the men are being asked to die for him, more likely than with him. The use here of the royal *we* insists on the mystical difference of kingship. It also jars with the following lines which use the normal *we* to assert the companionship of the army:

> We few, we happy few, we band of brothers;
> For he today that sheds his blood with me
> Shall be my brother; be he ne'er so vile,
> This day shall gentle his condition. (IV. iii. 60–3)

This is so much hollow rhetoric: peasants at the battle were not made gentlemen.[18] On a more personal level we see Harry using different tactics to drive away intimacy. First he toys with the traitors at Southampton, before rounding on them, attacking Scroop in particular on the basis of their former intimacy, as he was once his 'bedfellow' (as Exeter tells us – II. ii. 8) and knew 'the very bottom of my soul' (II. ii. 97); in making the treachery personal Henry is claiming that he values friendship, but his motives are clearly always political. Unlike his father, Henry V has not compromised himself with aristocratic friends. When Henry IV tells Hal that he should not make himself 'common-hackney'd in the eyes of men' (*1 Henry IV*, III. ii. 40) as Richard II did, he might also be advising his son not to act as he himself did – after all, it is Bolingbroke, not Richard who appears a populist in *Richard II*. In giving his son deathbed counsel, Henry IV is clear that supposed friends are really just toothless enemies. He tells him 'all my friends, which thou must make thy friends, / Have but their stings and teeth new ta'en out' (*2 Henry IV*, IV. v. 204–5). Friends cannot be simply inherited. It is this recognition that separates the non-legitimate Lancastrian kings of the second tetralogy from the legitimate Richard II. Henrys IV and V know that they must actively negotiate friendship to shore up their political power, whereas Richard II believes that friendship is owed to him on account of the divine sanction of his royalty and of his special feudal connection to the land and its people. All these negotiations tend to diminish any sense of real selfhood in the royal personages; possession of immortal kingship makes them less alive than the bad friend Falstaff.

The tragedies *Macbeth* and *Hamlet* make some attempts to negotiate the tensions between friendship and power that we have seen in the history plays. *Macbeth* partially revises the ideas of the histories in connecting legitimacy with successful friendship and usurpation with solitude, but the former connection is decidedly fragile. The play ultimately suggests a bleak outlook for reliable social bonds, which will be replaced by untrusting, highly conditional alliances. *Hamlet*, however, finds at least a limited role for friendship in the political sphere, developing possibilities adumbrated but rejected in the figure of Falstaff.

Macbeth is, amongst other things, a play about the destruction of friendship in the political sphere. Duncan, the source of friendship, is killed, and replaced by the rampant individualism of Macbeth.[19] Nonetheless, Macbeth is paradoxically a man who yearns for friendship. His nature is famously 'too full o' th' milk of human kindness' (1. v. 17). The generalized nature of this phrase suggests that he sees himself as kin to the rest of humanity. His relationship to Duncan is also overdetermined. In his great soliloquy meditating the murder, Macbeth reflects on his relationship to Duncan:

> He's here in double trust:
> First, as I am his kinsman and his subject,
> Strong both against the deed; then, as his host,
> Who should against his murderer shut the door,
> Not bear the knife myself. (1. vii. 12–16)

The ramification of double into triple trust (kinsman, subject, host) shows the overdetermination of the relationship. The problem is, how can feeling match up to such an excessive relationship?

Ironically, the language of excess is started by Duncan, whose assessment of Macbeth's deserts may contain an element of fear that Macbeth has forced too much indebtedness on the King:

> O worthiest cousin!
> The sin of my ingratitude even now
> Was heavy on me. Thou art so before,
> That swiftest wing of recompense is slow
> To overtake thee. Would thou hadst less deserv'd,
> That the proportion both of thanks and payment
> Might have been mine! Only I have left to say,
> More is thy due than more than all can pay. (1. iv. 14–21)

This is going beyond the normal ratio of friendship. The phrase, 'would thou hadst less deserv'd' may be formal, but it also reveals Duncan's worry that their relationship as ruler and subject has become imbalanced. Macbeth is to take 'more than all' in killing Duncan. The idea of reciprocation cannot work in a relationship between a king and his subject, any more than the idea of equality. Even a seemingly perfect king such as Duncan cannot guarantee amity.

Shakespeare's approach to the role of Macbeth's friend Banquo is curious. His motive for removing from the sources Banquo's complicity in the murder of Duncan was clearly a desire not to malign an ancestor of James I, but the effect this has on the play goes beyond contemporary political expediency. Crucially, by denying Macbeth a male accomplice, Shakespeare makes the origin of the regicide domestic rather than martial. Banquo is not completely whitewashed, however: Shakespeare retains an element of complicity between him and Macbeth by having them both meet the witches, something he could have removed along with Banquo's involvement in the murder itself. This retains some of the friendship that Holinshed's Mackbeth has for Banquho, but in a modified and under-motivated form. Our first impression of Macbeth and Banquo is that they are friends, but this relationship is not established by any direct means (Holinshed emphasizes that Banquho is the 'chiefest' of Mackbeth's 'trustie friends').[20] Instead, we gain the impression from the simple matter of their companionship on first entrance, and the open banter that passes between them. The practical reason for having Banquo with Macbeth is to demonstrate that the Weird Sisters are real (rather as the guards and Horatio validate the reality of *Hamlet*'s ghost). The consequence is that Macbeth is immediately put in a context of friendship. Their tone after the Weird Sisters have made their prophecies is half banter, half an attempt to sound one another out:

> MACBETH. Your children shall be kings.
> BANQUO.   You shall be King.
> MACBETH. And Thane of Cawdor too; went it not so? (I. iii. 86–7)

The shared lines here suggest two men about to enter into conspiracy, an impression that is reinforced at the end of the scene when Macbeth indicates they will speak further. Macbeth, having been made Thane of Cawdor, speaks privately to Banquo, as sharer of his secret:

> Think you upon what hath chanc'd; and at more time,
> The interim having weigh'd it, let us speak
> Our free hearts each to other.
> BANQUO.   Very gladly. (lines 153–5)

The fact that they talk to each other apart from their other 'friends' (line 156) here suggests a special pact, but the play makes nothing more of this, largely because Lady Macbeth intervenes to spur her husband, pulling him away from the 'friendly' conspiracy that might support him. Any sense of mutual interest between the men is removed.

After Macbeth has come under his wife's influence, he refuses to speak freely to Banquo. When Banquo broaches the subject of the witches' prophecy, Macbeth denies thinking of them. He puts his friend off until later:

> when we can entreat an hour to serve,
> We would spend it in some words upon that business,
> If you would grant the time.
> BANQUO.   At your kind'st leisure.
> MACBETH. If you shall cleave to my consent, when 'tis,
> It shall make honour for you.
> BANQUO.   So I lose none
> In seeking to augment it, but still keep
> My bosom franchis'd, and allegiance clear,
> I shall be counsell'd. (II. i 22–9)

This clotted language is hardly speaking freely, but it looks very like conspiracy. It is notable that Macbeth is treating Banquo high-handedly here: lines 22–3 look very much as if Macbeth is proleptically using the royal *we*. Rather than a free heart, Banquo wants an enfranchised one. Macbeth is clearly sounding Banquo out as a *future* supporter, but conspiratorial friendship is for the moment out of the question.

One of Macbeth's motives for killing Banquo is that his friend is more truly kingly than himself. Banquo's 'royalty of nature' (III. i. 49) is to be feared, and we have seen this in action immediately on the announcement of Duncan's murder, when Banquo takes charge of the situation, though he is in Macbeth's house. Macbeth also believes that

> under him
> My Genius is rebuk'd, as it is said
> Mark Antony's was by Caesar. (III. i. 54–6)

This implies some special connection between them, a kind of negative affinity that shapes Macbeth's character. Banquo's ghostly appearance at Macbeth's banquet further underlines a connection between them that goes beyond death. Macbeth, toasting his friend, ironically refers to 'our dear friend Banquo, whom we miss; / Would he were here' (III. iv. 89–90). Macbeth is desperate for friends to support his royal status, and Banquo is the particular friend we have seen him with. His murder of this friend signals his destruction of political amity, and the personal and political elements of Macbeth's loss of friendship are deeply bound up, with neither being of predominant importance. As Angus comments, he goes about shoring up his rule in exactly the wrong way – 'Those he commands move only in command, / Nothing in love' (v. ii. 19–20). Malcolm also comments that all who serve Macbeth are 'constrained things' (v. iv. 13). Macbeth himself sees the poignancy of this as he is left alone in the world:

> I have liv'd long enough: my way of life
> Is fall'n into the sere, the yellow leaf,
> And that which should accompany old age,
> As honour, love, obedience, troops of friends,
> I must not look to have. (v. iii. 22–6)

It is noticeable that this realization of being cut off from humanity is expressed in military terms: he wants *troops* of friends. Yet he murders friendship in the play. He is the opposite of those blessed by the Old Man, who 'would make good of bad, and friends of foes' (II. iv. 41). It is significant that the play ends with Malcolm wishing for the return of 'the friends we miss' (v. ix. 1) and setting himself the task of 'calling home our exil'd friends abroad' (line 32). Macbeth's overdetermined individualism has turned the whole world into his enemy. Yet we feel his loss: he ends the play as a 'poor player' (v. v. 24), wholly alone after his wife's death. As Bacon suggests, without friends, he cannot play his part properly and may as well 'quit the stage'.[21]

By stark contrast, Horatio in *Hamlet* is the character in whom we most clearly see a balance of political usefulness, personal affection and the use of friendship to rise in social status. As a relatively humble friend to the heir presumptive, Horatio has some superficial similarity to Falstaff, but his career is a much greater success. Whereas Falstaff is sacrificed to Prince Hal's royal career, it is the lower-status friend who survives in *Hamlet*, as bearer of his friend's legacy. Whilst Hamlet's choice of Horatio as friend is rather abrupt, it is the more emphatic for it. The point is that the Prince has deliberately and explicitly chosen someone appropriate for his predicament, and we are shown the terms of this choice. In drama we rarely see the 'longe deliberation and profe' that Sir Thomas Elyot recommended as essential to true friendship.[22] Horatio is chosen in definite contrast to other potential friends – Marcellus, and Rosencrantz and Guildenstern. Unlike Marcellus, he is a scholar rather than a soldier, suggesting that Hamlet leans towards words rather than action; unlike Rosencrantz and Guildenstern he has no competing allegiance to Claudius and thus can be a pure, unflattering friend to Hamlet. Horatio's position is purposefully ambiguous. The special position that he attains depends entirely on his relationship with Hamlet: at no stage does he talk to the King, suggesting that he has no real status at court. When Hamlet has to explain the King's customs to him, Horatio barely seems to be a native of Denmark. Marcellus seems more at home in the court, knowing in the first scene where they might find Hamlet, but he disappears from the play, removing any sense that Hamlet may have a number of armed 'friends'. No political group supports him nor can he get a mob together as Laertes does (though Claudius does mention his popularity with 'the distracted multitude' (IV. iii. 4)). If Hamlet is to have support, it is to be personal and friendly rather than political.

The second act contains no role for Horatio. Instead, Hamlet encounters the two false and treacherous friends Rosencrantz and Guildenstern. The ease with which Hamlet sees through this pair suggests that he has a fundamentally distrustful nature. In this, he has a touch of Prince Hal. Gertrude says that Rosencrantz and Guildenstern were 'brought up with him' and that 'two men there is not living / To whom he more adheres' (II. ii. 20–1). Hamlet's attitude to Rosencrantz and Guildenstern contrasts strongly with the courtesy he extended to Horatio and Marcellus:

ROSENCRANTZ AND GUILDENSTERN. We'll wait upon you.
HAMLET. No such matter. I will not sort you with the rest of my
    servants; for to speak to you like an honest man, I am most
    dreadfully attended. But in the beaten way of friendship, what make
    you at Elsinore? (II. ii. 266–70)

Far from courtesy, this is downright rudeness: whereas he told Horatio that he was a 'good friend' and not a servant (I. ii. 162–3), he refuses even their service. He also speaks with unconcealed boredom of the 'beaten way of friendship', as if only habit keeps him from using the term *friend* for these two. His enthusiasm for the players, whose leader he calls 'old friend', and whom he collectively addresses as 'good friends' (II. ii. 422), contrasts radically with this. There are some peculiar (if commonplace) lines on friendship in the Player King's speech which may be directed at Rosencrantz and Guildenstern:

> 'tis a question left us yet to prove,
> Whether love lead fortune, or else fortune love.
> The great man down, you mark his favourite flies,
> The poor advanc'd makes friends of enemies.
> And hitherto doth love on fortune tend,
> For who not needs shall never lack a friend,
> And who in want a hollow friend doth try,
> Directly seasons him his enemy. (III. ii. 202–9)

These lines anticipate and justify Hamlet having his old friends killed, a ruthlessness worthy of Henry V.

Before the play, Hamlet tells Horatio, insisting that he has no need to flatter him, 'thou art e'en as just a man / As e'er my conversation cop'd withal' (III. ii. 54–5). Hamlet seems to be appointing this man who 'is not passion's slave' (line 72) as his Chief Justice, the role Falstaff fondly hoped for, in order to have clear judgement of the effect of the play. He himself has tried his friend through (unrepresented) conversation and now will use him, but he also expresses deep affection for his friend on a personal level, promising to keep him 'In my heart's core, ay, in my heart of heart' (line 73). In act IV, Horatio becomes, as Bacon suggested a friend might usefully be, a deputy for Hamlet. He does not go to England with the banished Prince, who is accompanied instead by Rosencrantz and Guildenstern: by this time the pair are clearly 'friends' to Claudius (IV. i. 33) and Hamlet has called them 'my two schoolfellows, / Whom I will trust as I will adders fang'd' (III. iv. 202–3). Horatio is left at Elsinore, where he has a rather pointless discussion with Gertrude about Ophelia (IV. v). At this point in the play he seems more like a courtier than at any other time. His presence at Elsinore is dramatically important only in one respect, in that he acts as Hamlet's representative (or second self) whilst he is away, urging Gertrude to see Ophelia, and reading Hamlet's letter on his escape from the ship to England. He points up our sense of Hamlet's absence, and through the rather awkward device of the letter (IV. vi) establishes his position as Hamlet's sole confidant. (In the 'Bad' Quarto of the play, Horatio discusses Hamlet's plans with Gertrude, a crucial scene that puts the Queen firmly on her son's side.)[23] As Claudius is ranging up his alliance with Laertes against Hamlet, Horatio's presence makes us feel that Hamlet is not totally alone (as he was in act II in Horatio's unexplained absence).

In act v, Horatio's role is very much a backing-up one. He has taken on much more of the role played by Pylades in Aeschylus's *Choephori*, the quietly accompanying friend who validates the hero's actions. Horatio is now a sounding board for speeches that would otherwise be soliloquies. Yet it is important that he is present, for the new, more patient and mature Hamlet must not indulge himself in self-examining soliloquy. The fact that Horatio shares in Hamlet's mockery of Osric (v. ii) stresses their camaraderie, and provides a light and convincing moment of friendly sharing. The key moment of the early part of this scene, though, comes when Hamlet decides to accept Laertes' challenge. Horatio's reply is simple, direct, honest and pertinent: 'You will lose, my lord' (line 209). Hamlet ignores the advice, saying that he has been practising his swordsmanship; he accepts the fact that he will lose as a matter of indifference. He has accepted his fate as the hero of a revenge tragedy, which means that he will inevitably be destroyed himself. Hamlet has a vastly richer consciousness than Horatio, but Horatio's famous 'philosophy', limited though it may be, has a necessary directness that anchors Hamlet in reality.

Much of Horatio's support for Hamlet may be rather commonplace but in the final scene he contributes to one of the play's greatest moments. Hamlet's near-attempt at suicide pushes the boundaries of high comedy and risks the whole tragic effect of the play's conclusion:

> . . . Horatio, I am dead,
> Thou livest. Report me and my cause aright
> To the unsatisfied.
> Horatio.   Never believe it;
> I am more an antique Roman than a Dane.
> Here's yet some liquor left.
> HAMLET.   As th' art a man
> Give me the cup. Let go! By heaven, I'll ha't!
> O God, Horatio, what a wounded name,
> Things standing thus unknown, shall I leave behind me!
> If thou didst ever hold me in thy heart,
> Absent thee from felicity awhile,
> And in this harsh world draw thy breath in pain
> To tell my story. (v. ii. 338–49)

This might seem egoistic on Hamlet's part, but he shares his egoism with his friend, knowing that only arguments in his own favour will sway the loyal Horatio (whose name now takes on tones of *oratio* – the speaker of Hamlet's fame). Bacon saw praise, and the continuation of one's works after death, as the sense in which the friend can be a second (or auxiliary) self, arguing that 'If a man have a true friend, he may rest almost secure that the care of [his works] will continue after him. So that a man has, as it were, two lives in his desires.'[24] Hamlet is handing over to Horatio as his 'deputy'. He echoes the ghost's 'if thou didst ever thy dear father love' (I. v. 23), but here it is speech rather than action that is required to redress injuries. The speeches of friendship are the mark of civilization's escape from patterns of revenge. This conclusion is more satisfying than the transformation of the Furies into the Eumenides that marks the *Oresteia*'s conclusion. For Aeschylus, patterns of vengeance are resolved into the Law: for Shakespeare they come out into friendly speech, in Horatio's great lines 'Good night, sweet prince, / And flights of angels sing thee to thy rest' (v. ii. 359–60). Hamlet's 'Let go' releases Horatio and his linguistic capacities from the curse. Dennis Kay argued that we must imagine a wholly satisfying recognition scene outside the play in Horatio's telling of the story;[25] Horatio is the one who gives Hamlet his due dramatic honour, even if his initial summary of Hamlet's story misses out much that we have understood from the soliloquies, as James Shapiro observes.[26] He is our point of contact with Hamlet, preventing him from being an echo-chamber of a character like Richard II. He is also, crucially, the bearer of Hamlet's 'dying voice' (line 356) to Fortinbras. This makes him a kingmaker, a role that Robert Cecil and the Earl of Essex had vied to perform for James I. Horatio advises the presumptive new king how best to secure his position by presenting the bodies 'High on a stage' (line 378):

> ... let this same be presently perform'd
> Even while men's minds are wild, lest more mischance
> On plots and errors happen. (lines 393–5)

This puts him in a strong position to be counsellor to the new king, a wiser Polonius. His philosophical merits may balance the martial nature of Fortinbras. Through true, disinterested friendship to Hamlet, a poor scholar has risen to the centre of power. He asserts himself both socially and dramatically, without any diminution of his friend. Unlike most of the friends discussed in this book, Horatio does not add much to our understanding of his friend's character, but there is a special connection between them; Horatio gains social and dramatic prominence from the friendship, and Hamlet gets some sort of closure to his drama, even if this is only the hope of heaven and the placing of his body in a position of mute prominence. Horatio is the apotheosis of particular friendship, emerging from a situation which has seemed in other plays to offer minimal scope for friendship to express itself. He is a rare example of the virtue that can truly aid a prince, and it is precisely due to his rarity that he is valued. All others – Marcellus, Rosencrantz and Guildenstern – must be winnowed away for this friendship to win out.

The hollowing of friendship in a political context produces two models of selfhood in kings – Richard II and Hal/Henry V are both ultimately friendless, but Richard comes to destruction through an abstract belief in friendship, Hal to power through a rather chilling but successful manipulation of friendship; yet in Hal's plays it is Falstaff who gets to be magnanimous, however strangely, like Richard II. The hollow nature of kingly power is expressed in their inability to make friendly connections to others. *Macbeth* shows a more extreme mode of royal individuation, with a deeper sense of personal loss, whereas *Hamlet*, through the figure of Horatio, presents a much more positive way in which particularized friendship, however unequal, can be advantageous to both prince and friend. Whilst the intensities of high politics in these plays constitute one important, even central, aspect of the social world, the particular pressure they place on friendship – which is always conceived in relation to issues of political allegiance – is only one way Shakepeare has of representing friendship's relation to the wider world. Other social bonds, in the representation of the more ordinary bonds between men, will be the subject of the next chapter.

CHAPTER 7

Fellowship

The friendship of exclusive pairs may be the ideal, but it is not the norm. The social world is more frequently made up of more complex interactions amongst groups, and Shakespeare's plays reflect this, more frequently giving us scenes of groups of men (three or more) rather than two-handers. We read the dramatic and social status of individuals on the basis of their centrality (or otherwise) to their group, and get a sense of their sociability from the size of the group around them; the group can attenuate the self-assertion of the individual, but can also give the individual a clearer shape; shifting power relations in the group are crucial to this, allowing individuals to develop new kinds of prominence. Often the only claim to friendship that these groups have is that they share some goal or interest in common; sometimes they are simply thrown together by chance. I shall reflect the vagueness of these groupings by calling them fellowships. Montaigne says that 'There seems to be nothing for which nature has better prepared us than for fellowship', though it is much lower than perfect friendship – which can emerge from it.[1] The emergence of special individual connections within fellowship is always rather embattled. C. S. Lewis says that 'companionship' is not the same as friendship, though it is its matrix.[2] Fellowship, then, is one of the inevitable features of life, but its relationship to friendship is complicated. Lewis also observes that the 'pack or herd – the community – may even dislike and distrust' friendship,[3] arguing that companionship is natural, but friendship something beyond our natural needs. Yet he finds it hard to make a clear dividing line between companionship and what he sees as true friendship. In Shakespeare's plays true friendship struggles to emerge from friendly groupings. This is not to say that Shakespeare insists on the group ahead of the individual, but that he recognizes the limitations of individual friendship; it is never able to isolate itself, however much this may be the wish of the *Sonnets*.

Whilst *Timon of Athens* clearly has friendship as its main subject, the chief problem in understanding the play in these terms is that there are no particular friendships in it.[4] It is easy to see it as a formulaic fable about failed reciprocity and the folly of human optimism – more an economic fable than one about friendship as such. Yet Timon is a character of some grandeur: he has taken the logic of friendship theory to extremes, without the human feelings that must underpin friendship and that are so hard to theorize. G. Wilson Knight regarded Timon as a superman or even a Christ-figure, but this is surely going too far; he argues that 'Timon, in love or hate, bears truly a heart of gold. He is a thing apart, a choice soul crucified',[5] but it is his *apartness* not his special qualities that is truly significant; he is not tragic because of his superiority to his human environment, but because he lacks a genuine capacity for friendship. He places himself at the centre of every scene like a king; he is like a private, bourgeois version of Richard II, wanting an abstract friendship in which he is always to be the centre. In this he is as deluded and doomed as the English King.

The plot of *Timon* is less baroque than any other Shakespeare play, and a considerable contribution to its simplicity is the lack of women in it – nowhere else does Shakespeare present so masculine a world, and this promotes the stark limitation of feelings in the play. Other than the Amazons in act I's dance, the only women in the play are the whores brought on by Alcibiades in act IV. Karl Klein comments: 'The revolting picture they offer ties in with Timon's desire to erase women from his life.'[6] At one level, then, the play is about the folly of putting all your eggs into the basket of friendship – a theme that comes up with some frequency in Shakespeare: there is an implied critique of an excessive devotion to what Shannon, following Michel Foucault, calls 'homonormativity'.[7] An over-reliance on friendship puts life out of balance, and tends to produce melancholic or tragic results. Yet there is no excessive valuation of one other man in Timon's case – unlike that of Antonio in *The Merchant of Venice*. Instead, his friendship is seen as barren, even masturbatory. As Clifford Davidson observes, 'Despite the obvious double meaning which would seem to connect Timon's "spending" of gold with "spending" in the sexual sense, Shakespeare seems content with the iconography of a man ecstatically scattering his worldly wealth.'[8] The play's suggestion is that if you only have friendship, you have nothing – though that is not to say that friendship is nothing, but that other feelings are needed to bind a man into society. We might perhaps add that without women to bind society together, the pure friendship of men seems empty.

Una Ellis-Fermor argues that *Timon* is a failure in conception as well as execution because the hero has no relationships in the present and none are indicated that have shaped him in the past.[9] E. A. J. Honigmann contends that Timon's isolation is less the problem than the fact that none of the other characters have much relationship to each other.[10] The play clearly exhibits a desire to separate and simplify human relationships, which means that none of these relationships can have real force or meaning. This may of course be the point of the play – that relationships, particularly friendship, lose their value if you demand that they be clear and simple.

As Klein notes, the first half of the play is 'ceremonial',[11] giving no time for reflection on the part of any character. This attenuates our sympathy. Timon is absurdly generous, and then, when needs press, he finds that none of his fair-weather friends will help him. In the second half Timon gives way to rage at all humanity – despite finding gold in the hills – before dying. In the meanwhile Alcibiades, feeling that the Senate of Athens have dishonoured him, raises an army and attacks the city, which capitulates to him. No other Shakespeare play can be described so simply (at least without us feeling that we've left something crucial out). Normally, Shakespeare uses fellowship to provide a sense of a wider social world beyond his central plot, but here, having made friendship the centre, there can be no such sense and therefore no complications or ramification of plot. This limitation parallels the emotional limitation Timon himself suffers as a result of his attempt to make fellowship the centre of his life (whilst thinking of it as true friendship). He is certain of its absolute value, and preens himself not a little on being an exemplary friend. When he gives a generous marriage portion to his servant Lucilius it is obvious that this is an unusual act, but Timon modestly argues that it is normal, saying ''Tis a bond in men' (1. i. 147). On the one hand, Timon would like such generosity to be the human norm, just as theorists of friendship would like it to be common; on the other hand, he wants it to be recognized that he is the only person around who is true to this bond, just as friendship narrators like Elyot want their stories to be recognized as exceptional. This does not mean that Timon is insincere, just that his motives are more complicated than he would like to think. He is convinced of the purity of his motives, and is very keen to differentiate his friendship from mere outward courtesy. He tells Ventidius (whom he has had released from debtors' gaol):

> Ceremony was but devis'd at first
> To set a gloss on faint deeds, hollow welcomes,

> Recanting goodness, sorry ere 'tis shown;
> But where there is true friendship, there needs none. (I. ii. 15–18)

Such attempts to disclaim the outward show of friendship in the name of asserting 'true' friendship are themselves a politeness formula, but there is something more here: Timon does not want to be repaid. He almost peevishly refuses any attempts to reciprocate his friendship; as Nuttall puts it 'some dark, driving necessity of his inner nature will not allow him to take his turn as beneficiary in the financial dance of amity'.[12] He is anxious that his own friendship be the greatest, that he can do more for others than any others can do for him. This is reminiscent of a Calvinist God, who will not allow any merit on the part of his creations. Timon is at times putting on the role of a god who dispenses all, and whilst he may pretend an aversion to ceremony, he does not object to his friends *'adoring'* him (I. ii. 145 SD). Such grand claims on social life effectively blind Timon to the absence of true affection behind the signs of friendship, something that Apemantus sees and is almost joyfully bewildered by:

> That there should be small love amongst these sweet knaves,
> And all this courtesy! (I. i. 249–50)

On the other hand, Timon is quite pleased when he gets the chance to test his friends, again, perhaps, in the manner of a god. There is something almost calculating about his spendthrift nature, as if he is eager for the chance to test his friends. There are hints (e.g. when he says that he will 'strain' to help Lucilius marry (I. i. 144)) that he at some level knows that he is bankrupting himself, and he is less than devastated when his steward Flavius finally brings it home to him that he is in dire straits:

> in some sort these wants of mine are crown'd,
> That I account them blessings; for by these
> Shall I try friends. You shall perceive how you
> Mistake my fortunes; I am wealthy in my friends. (II. ii. 181–4)

This may just be putting a brave face on things, but he turns the situation around into an assertive pleasure which suggests an underlying and unconscious motivation for his earlier giving. Earlier he had said, in his most extravagant speech about friendship:

O you gods, think I, what we need have any friends, if we should ne'er have need of 'em? They were the most needless creatures living, should we ne'er have use for 'em; and would most resemble sweet instruments hung up in cases, that keeps their sounds to themselves. Why, I have often wish'd myself poorer, that I might come nearer to you. We are born to do benefits; and what better or properer can we call our own than the riches of our friends? (I. ii. 95–103)

Contrary to the view expressed in Plato's *Lysis* that a good man cannot *need* friends, Timon believes that friendship must be needed; the use of the words *need* and *use* suggest a friendship of utility is being invoked – and there is a clear claim on the friends' possessions. As the friends depart at the end of the scene Timon says 'I'll call to you' (line 217) – the primary meaning is that he'll come round to bring gifts, but there is also the ironic suggestion that Timon intends to call in debts. He wants to have his cake and eat it. Nuttall argues that it is 'too easy' to argue that Timon tries to buy friendship,[13] and he does take friendship for granted, regarding it as too valuable to be bought; but as he expresses friendship through giving, confusing the economic and the affective, he naturally expects others to do the same.

His later misanthropy is therefore based on a category error, and on the expectation that others will see the world exactly as he does. Timon believes that without true friendship – that evanescent and ultimately undemonstrable thing – society is worthless. He rages, *solus*,

> Breath, infect breath,
> That their society (as their friendship) may
> Be merely poison! (IV. i. 30–2)

But Timon himself has emptied out the concept of friendship, proved it hollow by his too purist attitude. The empty banquet in act III scene vi represents the emptiness of friendship of pleasure or utility as far as Timon is concerned, but once those are taken away it is clear that there is nothing left of friendship, which can only reasonably or dramatically exist on the basis of its outward signs. This is Shakespeare's most frequent technique when someone presses too hard at the concept of *true* friendship – to show its emptiness, and the bafflement of those who naively believed that there was something detachable from utility or pleasure at the core of friendship. This is not to say that there is no such thing as true affection, only that it must be attached to its signs. In the final act, the word *friend* is emptied again, as Timon advises his 'friends' to hang themselves (V. i. 207). The only friendly counsel he can give the poet and the painter at the end is to separate from each other, and even from themselves:

> [*To one*] If where thou art, two villains shall not be,
> Come not near him. [*To the other*] If thou wouldst not reside
> But where one villain is, then him abandon. (v. i. 109–11).

This riddling of a basically simple idea is a radical reversal of the doctrine of 'One Soul in Bodies Twain'. If men cannot be true friends, the argument goes, then they should not be together at all – but given that true friendship is rare (that's why it's valuable), the implication is radical isolationism.

Timon's attitude is central to the play, but it is not the only one, and obviously cannot be endorsed. The supposed friends are equally obviously to be condemned, but are not really bad enough to provoke such misanthropy. There's something rather delightful about their refusals of Timon in act 3 (an elegant act, whose unusual structural formality was probably the work of Thomas Middleton rather than Shakespeare).[14] Lucullus's response to the servant's request for aid is brilliant in its simplicity – 'Every man has his fault, and honesty is his' (III. i. 27–8), and he even claims to have urged Timon to rein in his spending. The accidental candour – 'I'm not honest, thankfully' – can't help but provoke our admiration. Lucius is similarly blithe, telling the strangers that he would help Timon, but then immediately refusing when asked. Sempronius's twists and turns, saying he thinks the others should be asked first, and then taking offence at being asked last when he's told that the others have already been tried, are particularly powerful in their absolute disdain for honesty and consistency. We don't approve of these men, but they are funny – their conscienceless denial of vaunted values makes them resemble some of Shakespeare's other great ambivalently comic creations, such as Falstaff and the Fools. It's not worth being angry with these men – because it wasn't worth being friends with them in the first place. Such indiscriminate friendship as Timon's cannot be regarded as true friendship, however good Timon's will. The friends seem to think Timon's friendship a game, and to some extent they are right – though Timon takes the game seriously. In the fake banquet scene (III. vi), the friends think Timon has been testing them, and even later this idea is mooted (v. i – by the poet and painter). It is taken as axiomatic that someone might want to test friendship, which suggests that it is natural to be anxious about it.

Alcibiades holds a much more particularized place in the play than Timon's other friends, though his structural position is peculiarly unresolved (it's the strongest mark of the play's incompletion). As a major historical figure, and one who is associated with friendship in Plato's *Symposium*, and as the particular friend of Timon in one of Shakespeare's sources, he should, we feel, have more importance than at first he does. In the first act, he is only a bit-part player, receiving no gifts from Timon, and asserting (I. ii. 76–80) that he'd rather be killing enemies than feasting with friends. Later in the play he is set up as a contrast to Timon, repaying the Senate's ingratitude to him by attacking the city rather than going off to sulk. In a sense, this is the manly response, *à la* Coriolanus – his mode of self-assertion is much more effective than Timon's; but Alcibiades' self-assertion is only that – it has no deeper human value behind it. Nominally, Alcibiades is banished for his too-defiant claims on behalf of an unnamed friend who has killed a man in a duel, but though he seems to be acting on behalf of friendship, he is really flexing his muscles and asserting the rights of the military man. Though more effective than Timon (and desiring to do Timon 'friendship' (IV. iii. 71)), it is Timon who gives him money for his campaign when they meet in the wilderness, and his whole motive is enmity rather than friendship.

Apemantus provides a richer contrast to Timon, and the scene between the two (IV. iii) in the wilderness is the play's dramatic highlight, at least in terms of the interaction between characters. Apemantus is 'a churlish Philosopher' (i.e. a cynic – *Dramatis Personae*), and as such is supposed to be 'opposite to humanity' (I. i. 273), but his misanthropy is of a different character to Timon's, not least because it lacks specific motivation. Nuttall notes that 'Apemantus is, for a declaredly antisocial man, oddly given to turning up at gatherings.'[15] This paradox may have some explanation in what the Poet says of him, declaring that men of all conditions love Timon, even

> Apemantus, that few things loves better
> Than to abhor himself; even he drops down
> The knee before him, and returns in peace
> Most rich in Timon's nod. (I. i. 59–62)

Although this does not chime with what we see of Apemantus's conduct, it does hint that the cynic has some grudging affection for Timon; this is clearly mingled with an appalled fascination at Timon's foolish goodheartedness. The idea of Apemantus having some affection for Timon is balanced by the fact that he is the only person that Timon dislikes in the first acts – saying he's not 'fit' for company (I. ii. 32). This gives the big scene between the two much of its dramatic energy. Apemantus in this scene is partly delighted that Timon has come round to his way of thinking, though this is paradoxical in that cynical misanthropy is not exactly a sociable philosophy. He therefore has to assert the superiority of his own cynicism, which is pure rather than externally motivated:

> This is in thee a nature but infected,
> A poor unmanly melancholy sprung
> From change of future. (IV. iii. 202–4)

Despite this self-assertive claim, Apemantus seems eager to prod at Timon as long as possible: his railing is his way of showing his version of affection. Timon, for his part, persists in his disdain for Apemantus, and refuses to see any similarity between them, saying, 'Were I like thee, I'd throw away myself' (line 219). Ironically, Apemantus agrees, telling him 'Thou shouldst desire to die, being miserable' (line 248). This is cold comfort, but it is, I think, meant as comfort – 'If you were really miserable, you'd want to die, but you don't so you aren't.' In the end, of course, Timon takes the advice and (it seems) kills himself. There is real (if negative) affinity between these two, which has a blackly comic aspect to it – it is an ironized anti-friendship, summed up in Apemantus's comment 'I love thee better now than e'er I did' (line 233), begging the question of how much he ever loved him. Their lengthy parting shows that these are the sort of negative friends that like saying goodbye (or good riddance) better than greeting; the tone of the exchanges is almost flirtatious. The first attempted parting comes in these terms:

APEMANTUS. When I know not what else to do, I'll see thee again.
TIMON. When there is nothing living but thee, thou shalt be welcome. I had rather be a beggar's dog than Apemantus. (lines 353–7)

But they don't part until forty lines later (after Timon has lobbed a stone at Apemantus):

TIMON. Thy back, I prithee.
APEMANTUS.   Live, and love thy misery.
TIMON. Long live so, and die. I am quit. (lines 395–6)

Whilst it is clear that it is Apemantus who is enjoying this more, there is an element of mutuality here that is amusing, indeed almost touching. Apemantus has promised to tell others of Timon's gold so that Timon can have the pleasure of abusing others. This scene of negative friendship has more to it, dramatically, than any expression of ideal or 'true' friendship. Misanthropic cynicism has its pleasures (at least for Apemantus) and it is not devoid of affection. Even such characters cannot help shaping themselves with regard to each other.

In focussing on a group of solid and established burghers who have little interest in women, *Timon of Athens* differs from most dramatic presentations of groups of friends, which more commonly concentrate on young men looking for wealth and marriage. Such groups are central to (mostly urban) comedy. In Jonson's *Every Man in His Humour* the group has one central friendship, between Well-Bred and Young Kno-well, and the others are their gulls. The older generation regards the group of gallants as subversive: Old Knowell says that his son is 'grown the idolater' of Well-Bred (i. i. 149); Kitely suspects the young men of designs on his wife; and Down-Right thinks them 'fiends' rather than friends (iv. i. 5). There is little of the ideal here, despite Well-Bred calling Young Knowell his 'Genius' (iii. i. 23). These two young men are always presented as part of a group: they do not meet on stage until iii. i, and are never alone together (though they sometimes speak aside, and their conversation in the presence of the gull Stephen might as well be private – iv. iii). The main bases of their friendship are pleasure and utility: pleasure, in exposing the gulls Bobadill, Matthew and Stephen; utility, in that Well-Bred helps Young Knowell to a good marriage with Kitely's sister. Similarly, in *Epicene* there is no ideal friendship between the wits Clerimont, Dauphine and True-Wit, who are bound together by their gulling of Daw and La Foole. These two fools become friends, and True-Wit calls them a 'Damon and Pythias' (iv. v. 333–4) and a 'Pylades and Orestes' (iv. vi. 72), thus making a mockery of cherished classical icons of ideal friendship.[16] Witty men know the folly of the trust implicit in such friendship. Dauphine begins the play not trusting True-Wit, who nearly spoils his plot against his uncle; Dauphine's witty vengeance is had when True-Wit has attempted to make love to Epicene (the boy disguised as his uncle's wife).

In not letting his friends in on his plot, Dauphine has shown the limits of such friendship. Such witty plots had a logical appeal to the audience of the Renaissance (and indeed Restoration) theatres, which often con-sisted of groups of young men.[17] Few of Shakespeare's plays foreground such a milieu. The most notable example, in *Love's Labour's Lost*, has an isolated and aristocratic setting, in contrast to the city setting of Jonson's plays. The group of young men in *The Taming of the Shrew* corresponds more neatly to the Jonsonian model. *Love's Labour's Lost*'s less socially realistic setting enables Shakespeare to explore the nature of male fellowship in a form of anthropological experiment. The understanding of male social interaction developed in this play gives way to more backgrounded milieux in *Romeo and Juliet*, *The Merchant of Venice* and the Henry IV/V plays. These groupings have a tendency to persist longer than more individualistic bonds, because they can outlast any individual. An individual's serious emotions cannot fit into such contexts. Romeo's love means that his camaraderie with Benvolio and Mercutio must end; Antonio's serious friendship for Bassanio is incompatible with the Venetian milieu; Hal's regal duties demand the abandonment of the frivolous Eastcheap crowd. Yet there are serious emotions and special symbiotic connections which arise from the frivolous fellowships: both Antonio and Falstaff desire exclusive friendship, and the fellowship provides the necessary intimacy for that desire to emerge, whilst making it impossible to attain exclusivity.

The world of the masculine fellowship tries to keep itself free of tension and is therefore inherently undramatic; *Love's Labour's Lost* is perhaps Shakespeare's least dramatic play in that there is virtually no tension between the characters. Similarly, in *The Taming of the Shrew* Hortensio hopes that he and Gremio can be 'happy rivals' (1. i. 117 – see chapter 5, above). Lucentio comes to Padua expecting to find friends rather than love and his words 'Such friends as time in Padua shall beget' (1. i. 45) suggest how natural it is that men should form bonds, without any anxiety about it. Friendship simply emerges over time: no grand claims are made for soul-bonding. Any mild tension between the men comes from their competitive pursuit of Bianca, which seems more like a game than a serious emotional struggle. The presence of women can only partly unsettle the pleasant, easy world of masculine fellowship. Women may temporarily upset the group dynamic, but the feeling of fellowship persists. Fellowship, being a social organism, is relatively indifferent to the individuals who are parts of it. There are no claims of shared souls in such a grouping, and therefore competition in love does not constitute a betrayal.

Women provide what little tension there is in *Love's Labour's Lost*. The quiet world of Navarre is disrupted not by competition in love but by the simple presence of the women. The play explores gender difference in both love and friendship but no intense emotions are brought out. More everyday social bonds are therefore foregrounded and subjected to a dramatic critique. The men in *Love's Labour's Lost* have come together as an academy, dedicated to 'Th' endeavour' (i. i. 5) of ensuring that 'Navarre shall be the wonder of the world' (i. i. 12). This opening scene has an underlying tension, in that the King is in a sense demoting himself from his position of royal authority in order for the men to arrive at the supposed equality of scholars. Yet he cannot get out of the habit of using the royal *we*: his references to 'Our late edict' (line 11) and 'Our court' (line 13) both suggest the habit of command. When he refers to Navarre as the wonder of the world, he could just as easily be referring by synecdoche to himself as to the kingdom. The desire to be 'fellow-scholars' (line 17) is a dream that cannot truly subvert the men's difference in status. This is accentuated by the fact that the King's overconfidence in his opening pronouncement is comic in itself. He seems to assume that in taking the oath they have been successful already, referring to them as 'brave conquerors' (line 8), and the grandeur of his language – that they shall be 'heirs of all eternity' (line 7) – combined with the certainty of the repeated *shalls*, is surely a mockery of the grand designs young men are prone to dreaming of. Men seem to need absurdly formal oaths on entering into any fellowship (one could instance guild oaths and the masons as well as schoolboy and student initiation ceremonies) partly to insist on the importance of their aims, but also because they seem to be rather suspicious of one another. In this case the oath (passed before the play's opening) has not been enough: they must also sign their names.

> Your oaths are pass'd, and now subscribe your names,
> That his own hand may strike his honour down
> That violates the smallest branch herein. (i. i. 19–21)

In drama, as perhaps in life, the need for such oaths automatically implies that they will be broken. Oath-swearing between political allies in the history plays and Roman plays also precedes treachery. Only in *Hamlet*, when Marcello and Horatio are sworn to secrecy on the matter of the ghost, does an oath have a genuinely sacramental ring, and that is endorsed by the ghost itself. In *Love's Labour's Lost* Berowne quickly undercuts the oath by observing that he only takes it reluctantly, calling it an 'abortive birth' (line 104). Paradoxically, this shows that he is the only one who takes it seriously, understanding its full implications.

The fact is that the oath has no sacred or other external underpinnings. It may be a matter of *honour*, but that honour is only valid within the group itself, which is a self-perpetuating and enclosed system. It matters to no one else, and the women are certainly not impressed by it; honour is a relative concept and is gender-specific; this kind of honour between men does not impress women. The Princess very neatly dismisses the whole concept by making it clear that the oath is a matter of choice, not necessity: 'Why, will shall break it, will, and nothing else' (ii. i. 100). Unfortunately, the men lack will, because they lack real personality – with the partial exception of Berowne. Will also suggests sexual, phallic energy, but the men merely have wit, and a linguistic construction of love in jokes, plays and bad poetry. They put their faith in language – the oath in particular – and more physical desires are regarded as external forces, as witnessed by the King's phrasing in the first scene: they must combat 'the huge army of the world's desires' (i. i. 10).

Lacking anything more than a linguistic personality, the men must rely on oaths to each other instead of a genuine affective bond. With suspicious neatness each independently chooses a different woman as his beloved, an arbitrary convention the women later highlight by masking themselves and allowing the men to court the wrong women (v. ii.). Will and choice do not come into it on the whole, but when Berowne bemoans his fate in falling for Rosaline an important point is made. He says it is his misfortune 'among three to love the worst of all' (iii. i. 195). Only *three* women were available for his choice. The Princess is clearly out of bounds, but why was there a choice at all? Berowne, at the time of his speech, does not yet know that Longaville and Dumaine have fallen for Katherine and Maria, so why did he choose the worst? We can infer that far from resisting the women on their arrival, the four men saw four women and simply leapt forward with adolescent enthusiasm to take a partner. They not chosen at all, but have done what the courtly and dramatic situation demanded. Berowne's use of the word *love* here is meaningless – or rather, it means merely 'talk to'. Each man thinks he is in love because good manners insisted that each talk to one woman. That the King talked to the Princess was a matter of etiquette, and the same can be said of all the men's loves.

With such formality dominating both the fellowship and the men's loves, it is clear that affective bonds are not in question any more than personality is amongst the men. Berowne at least has a head start on developing a personality. Firstly, because his role in the group is to be recalcitrant and a jester and secondly, in ending up with the least attractive lady he has to find the most depth in trying to love her. In addition, his awareness in the first scene that the oath would be broken by 'Necessity' (I. i. 149) showed his greater intelligence:

> For every man with his affects is born,
> Not by might mast'red, but by special grace. (151–2)

This view is Calvinist, and it absolves Berowne from his oath-based responsibilities.[18] Such a semi-theological argument for irresponsibility shows that he is a mere fellow-traveller to the concept of honour and therefore closer to the women's position than the other men. It is Berowne who reminds the King that the women are due to arrive – after Longaville and Dumaine have signed but before he himself signs – and that therefore one term of the oath is due to be invalidated. His frivolity is underpinned by realism, in the sense that he understands human nature *and* the impossibility of a king isolating himself.[19] Nevertheless, the King's authority ensures that his unrealistic position triumphs in the first scene. Formality dominates: all the men address one another as *you*, implying their mutual respect as would-be scholars.

When the men's respective loves are revealed, that formality breaks down. In the revelation scene the men call each other *thou* (with the exception of addresses to the King) and Berowne's position comes to dominate. Affection can develop in this (relative) adversity because this is a scene of recognition, of common plights rather than of elected common purpose. Only in such a recognition of common humanity is the question of status erased between the friends. Fellowship, although it may be established with higher cultural ends in view, works better for the simpler purposes that are the common denominators of life. This situation is more readily handled by Berowne's wit than by the King's attempted grandeur.

> KING. In love, I hope – sweet fellowship in shame.
> BEROWNE. *[aside]* One drunkard loves another of the name.
> LONGAVILLE. Am I the first that have been perjur'd so?
> BEROWNE. *[aside]* I could put thee in comfort; not by two that I know.
> Thou makest the triumviry, the corner-cap of society,
> The shape of love's Tyburn that hangs up simplicity. (IV. iii. 47–52)

David Bevington argues that Berowne becomes the leader in the competition to boast of love that is the new basis of the fellowship.[20] In this, he gains dramatic prominence which subverts the social superiority of the

King. He sees the others bonding and mocks from his privileged position of first viewer, taunting them for their 'hypocrisy' (line 149), with irony that is only exposed when his love is revealed and he is forced to admit 'that you three fools lack'd me fool to make up the mess' (line 203). The ensuing conversation, comparing loves, remains conventional, but its bantering tone, and Berowne's domination of the scene, create a more open friendship between the men, one which is not based on hierarchy or contract but on mutual understanding, something that the formal opening scene could not achieve through a notion of scholarly equality. Even if their loves are formalities, their friendship has deepened. But it is still a fellowship rather than an exclusive or idealized friendship; although the young men of *Love's Labour's Lost* look at each other in turn when they serially discover each other's loves, we do not see a mutual gaze, rather we see them 'ranged', always oriented to some external object – first against the world's desires, then towards the women. The key overall effect is the assertion of Berowne's position of dramatic prominence and the corresponding diminution of the King's.

Romeo's group at the start of *Romeo and Juliet* has reached about the same stage as the men have at the end of *Love's Labour's Lost*. The new element is conflict with another group of young men. Rather than expending their energies in insulting the lower orders as the young men of Navarre do, Romeo and his friends come to blows with the Capulet young men. The conflict is immature – enabling it to be the basis of *West Side Story*'s presentation of adolescent gangs – but it has a broader basis than Bernstein's musical. The conflict originates with and is ratified by the supposedly adult heads of the families, and it extends down to the servants who open the play. It is a microcosm of states at war. The general atmosphere of enmity creates comradely friendships – which are to an extent dependent on outside conflict and not necessarily affective in themselves. Being based on kin, they are also not so freely chosen as other friendships. The opposition of the citizens (i. i. 73–4) to both Montagues and Capulets serves to isolate the families still further. This isolation, unlike the quiet withdrawal of the King of Navarre's group, sets friendly groupings within a context of enmity and forces friendship to define itself against enmity. The language of the time, which referred to family members, even parents, as 'friends' (e.g. Montague at i. i. 146), but which nevertheless made a distinction between this meaning and the modern one, enacts some of the confusion about friendship which this play presents. The peace-making at the end of the play is based on dead love giving way to new friendship (in the sense of peaceful social amity) founded on a common grief. Though nominally a tragedy, this conclusion is comedic in its socially integrative results and driving out of exclusivist passion.

At the opening of the play, romantic love is as absurd as the loves of the young men of Navarre. Romeo is as much a self-conscious melancholy lover as Berowne and his group, without even Berowne's irony. Shakespeare needs to supersede this form of histrionic passion in order to move on to *Romeo and Juliet*'s main subject of mutual love; both forms of love are played out within a milieu of friends. Romeo is shown as being similar to his friends in loving Rosalind artificially, but his love for Juliet differentiates him from them in a manner quite alien to the world of *Love's Labour's Lost*. Reporting Romeo's behaviour to the Montagues, Benvolio, whose name suggests basic friendly goodwill, stresses his similarity to his friend:

> Madam, an hour before the worshipp'd sun
> Peer'd forth the golden window of the east,
> A troubled mind drove me to walk abroad,
> Where, underneath the grove of sycamore
> That westward rooteth from this city side,
> So early walking did I see your son.
> Towards him I made, but he was ware of me,
> And stole into the covert of the wood.
> I, measuring his affections by my own,
> Which then most sought where most might not be found,
> Being one too many for my weary self,
> Pursued my humour not pursuing his,
> And gladly shunn'd who gladly fled from me. (1. i. 118–30)

Benvolio here declares his own supposedly private trouble and insists on his similarity to Romeo. His repeated references to himself show his self-conceit. His eager reporting to Romeo's parents shows him to be more similar to the sycophantic Rosencrantz and Guildenstern than to the confidential Horatio. When Romeo enters, Benvolio promises them that he will 'know his grievance, or be much denied' (line 157). And Romeo's mystery is not too deep to sound. Benvolio's sympathy with him is also conventional and artificial, if not entirely heartless. He has to state it rather than feelingly exhibit it:

ROMEO. Dost thou not laugh?
BENVOLIO.   No, coz, I rather weep.

ROMEO. Good heart, at what?
BENVOLIO.   At thy good heart's oppression.
                                                                (1. i. 183–4)

Their shared language (conventional as it is) means that with Benvolio
Romeo has at least the pleasure, amidst his supposed oppression, of
talking at length about the love that is obsessing him. This relatively frank
chatter depicts an everyday friendship between two averagely sensitive
young men with a good degree of verbal wit. Their similar background
and situation allow them to speak in identical registers. At this point, the
two men seem a good, if conventional, example of an exclusive friendship. Benvolio's suggestion that Romeo seek out 'other beauties' (line
228) shows his desire to calm passions (shown earlier when he attempted
to pacify the quarrelling servants), and reflects his distaste for intensity.
Benvolio's lack of genuine passion and the later appearance of Mercutio
as Romeo's other friend ensure that the pair are not an exclusive one. In
fact, Mercutio is the more important friend for the play's plot. He is
outside the family groupings and therefore seems more of a chosen friend
to Romeo. His death provokes Romeo to kill Tybalt – the hero's tragic
mistake. Being much more passionate by nature than Benvolio, he is a
much better mirror of the passionate side of Romeo that provides his
dramatic interest. Herbert McArthur argues that Mercutio's speech
'breaks through Romeo's artificial demeanor', and enables him to be a
true lover;[21] on the other hand, Joseph A. Porter argues that Mercutio
provides a 'warning away from love to the fellowship of men'.[22] As a
character whom Shakespeare added to his source, he shapes Romeo in
more complex ways than the simpler goodwill of Benvolio could.

   Romeo arrives at the Capulets' dance with a group of friends, though
only Benvolio and Mercutio are named speaking parts. They appear a
sociable gang. Mercutio urges Romeo to dance and banters with him
about his besottedness. Their fellowship, rather than true friendship, is
demonstrated by the fact that no one takes Romeo's love for Rosaline
seriously, and the failure to take the Rosaline passion seriously means that
they cannot take the Juliet one seriously later and cannot offer him help
or comfort as true friends should. Romeo's rebuke to Mercutio, inter-
rupting his Queen Mab speech, 'Thou talk'st of nothing' (1. iv. 96), is an
index of the lack of meaningful conversation amongst a fellowship of
young men. This friendship is as far from the solemn sympathy of
Hamlet's Horatio as one can imagine. Mercutio is attempting, like
Benvolio, to divert Romeo. This may be motivated partly by affection,

but it has rather more to do with a desire to keep uncomfortable passions out of the jolly social group. In his love for Juliet, Romeo must be alone, but not in the posturing solitude of his love for Rosaline. He must escape from his unsympathetic clique and find all his comfort in his beloved. Whether or not Romeo really jumps over a wall on stage, Benvolio's suggestion that he has done so (ii. i. 5) symbolically highlights his escape from his group after meeting Juliet. They pursue him with witty, vulgar shouting, but he is now beyond their companionship, whether bantering (in the case of Mercutio) or imitative (in the case of Benvolio). Romeo reflects on them, saying that 'He jests at scars that never felt a wound' (ii. ii. 1). This is rather ironic in relation to Mercutio, whose jesting will be stopped by Tybalt's sword. Romeo's revenge for him is a return to friendship, in a much more serious mode than their actual knowledge of each other could provoke. Only in death can Mercutio's friendship be serious. *Romeo and Juliet* begins as a comedy, to which the style of fellowship is appropriate. As the play becomes a tragedy, the fellowship disappears. Mercutio is killed, and Benvolio fades away. Serious feeling does not fit with such a milieu. Benvolio's disappearance is convenient for the play's plot, and is totally unexplained, though the 'Bad' Quarto (Q1) has the line 'And yong *Benuolio* is deceased too', at the equivalent of v. iii. 211. This is intriguing, as it may hint at an unexecuted authorial intention, or at an actor's sense that his role needed some completion. In tragic crises friends are an embarrassment to the playwright, and Shakespeare at this stage does not yet seem to know what to do with them. It is striking that the last words Benvolio utters before his disappearance are an attempt to mitigate Romeo's offence in killing Tybalt, ending with 'This is the truth, or let Benvolio die' (iii. i. 175). Having performed this last friendly office, he may not die, but we see no more of him.

In *Much Ado about Nothing*, we see another trio of friends getting involved with women. It is hard to discern the centre of this group. As a prince, Don Pedro is clearly to be deferred to, but his lack of a beloved marginalizes him in plot terms beside the apparent romantic hero Claudio. On the other hand, Benedick emerges a much more complex character than his friends. According to Don Pedro, 'from the crown of his head to the sole of this foot he is all mirth' (iii. ii. 8–10). He is very much a man's man, though not one given to intense private friendships. Benedick is all things to all men in a pleasing way: as the messenger says he is 'A lord to a lord, a man to a man, stuffed with all honourable virtues' (i. i. 56–7), rather as if virtues were cakes. Beatrice's initial descriptions of Benedick do not promise well for the man: he 'wears his face but as the fashion of his hat' (1. i. 75–6). There is no integrity in such a person, and we expect him to be either an absurd courtier like Osric or those in Donne's satires, or a better-spirited flatterer like Parolles. Most significantly, Beatrice says that 'He hath every month a new sworn brother' (lines 72–3). We therefore might expect a plot in which he betrays or cons his friend, especially when Beatrice says, 'God help the noble Claudio! If he have caught the Benedick, it will cost him a thousand pounds ere 'a be cur'd' (lines 88–90), but when conflict with Claudio comes it is on an honourable basis, and driven by Beatrice herself. As the scene and the play go on, we realize that the lady was protesting too much, but it takes a while for our first impression of any dramatic character to wear off. His claim that he is 'a profess'd tyrant to their sex' (lines 168–9) gives a hint of why Beatrice dislikes him, but continues the impression of him as a far from loveable rake, and probably a bad influence on the smooth and honourable young Claudio. In fact, of course, it is Claudio who treats a woman tyrannically in this play, and this brings him into conflict with Benedick.

Benedick begins the play as an embodiment of fellowship, but quickly becomes isolated from his male peer group. He is significantly absent when Don John raises suspicions about Hero, having quarrelled with Don Pedro and Claudio immediately before the bastard's entrance. Leaving with Leonato (and thus associating himself with the older generation), he calls his friends 'hobby-horses' (III. ii. 73), and is clearly putting away childish things. Don Pedro sees this as a 'break' with him (line 74), but a more significant division is to arise due to the childish self-righteousness of the Prince and Claudio. The latter having repudiated Hero at the altar, Beatrice urges Benedick to prove his love and 'kill Claudio' (IV. i. 289). Earlier, having received hoaxing notice of Beatrice's love, he said, answering Don Pedro's comments on his 'mirth', 'I am not as I have been' (III. ii. 15), claiming a new-found seriousness, which perhaps repudiates the friendships of his youth. As the play veers close to tragedy in the aborted wedding scene, Benedick steps forward with new alliances as an honourable avenger. Leonato says that if Claudio and Don Pedro prove wrong about Hero

> ... they shall find, awak'd in such a kind,
> Both strength of limb, and policy of mind,
> Ability in means and choice of friends,
> To quit me of them throughly. (IV. i. 197–200)

The first such friend he finds is Benedick, whose betrayal of his friends here shows that he values honour more than blind loyalty:

> ... though you know my inwardness and love
> Is very much unto the Prince and Claudio,
> Yet, by mine honour, I will deal in this
> As secretly and justly as your soul
> Should with your body. (lines 245–9)

Benedick turns out to be the play's truly chivalrous individual, able to make such a serious pledge, even against those friends who he thinks exhibit 'the very bent of honour' (lines 186). The seriousness with which he regards the killing of Claudio is demonstrated by his long hesitation at Beatrice's urging. She insists that he will be a 'friend' to her by killing him, the word here articulating the conflict of loyalties that she is deliberately setting before him as a test of love. She says that 'You dare easier be friends with me than fight with mine enemy' (lines 298–9); in the serious world one cannot be a friend to all. Beatrice herself had earlier jokingly argued against marriage by saying that 'Adam's sons are my brethren, and truly I hold it a sin to match in my kindred' (II. i. 63–5). This comic sense of universal fraternal friendship, an element of both Beatrice and Benedick, is broken as the play becomes tragic, and stark alliances have to be chosen.

From the very first, there have been tensions about women within the male fellowship: having set Don Pedro to woo Hero for him, Claudio worries that 'the Prince woos for himself' (II. i. 174); Don Pedro rather frivolously offers himself to Beatrice before deciding to get her together with Benedick. With three main young men, and only two main female characters, there is no chance of the symmetrical love arrangements of *Love's Labour's Lost*; consequently beneath the festive atmosphere there is an element of the love versus friendship plot in this play. Having chosen love over friendship, Benedick challenges Claudio in insulting and unfriendly terms ('boy' (v. i. 185) and 'my Lord Lack-beard' (line 192)). What began as part test, part genuine desire for revenge on Beatrice's part ends up wholly as a test. Benedick passes it, proving his greater loyalty to her (and, less than incidentally, to honour) than to Claudio. Both Don Pedro and Claudio are surprised that Benedick is 'in earnest' (v. i. 194) in his challenge. They are fundamentally more frivolous people than he, both seemingly indifferent to Hero's supposed death. In the final scene, after Hero's survival and innocence are revealed, Benedick is still somewhat unimpressed by Claudio's behaviour. Although he says 'Come, come, we are friends' (v. iv. 117) to Claudio, this is an emotionally empty declaration of peace. He has returned to his mirthful disposition, with the addition of joy in his forthcoming marriage, but he offers a mild rebuke to Claudio – 'I did think to have beaten thee, but in that thou art like to be my kinsman, live unbruis'd, and love my cousin' (lines 109–11). This is bantering over the cracks in their friendship, but surely reflects a certain reasonable contempt. Love, and the more structured kinship alliances it creates (not necessarily affective in themselves) have triumphed over amorphous good fellowship; at the same time, individual character has been shaped, giving prominence to Benedick, who now seems much wiser than his friends, and able to dispense justice in devising punishments for Don John. As in *Love's Labour's Lost* and *Romeo and Juliet* we see an individual emerging from the fellowship of men as a more serious, isolated character.

The Merchant of Venice places Antonio's serious friendship for Bassanio in the context of a friendly group which contrasts strongly with Shylock's almost solitary nature. Antonio's position within his milieu is similar to Romeo's in his. Antonio's melancholy may be less affected than Romeo's, but his companions are just as unable to help him, as useless to him as Rosencrantz and Guildenstern are to Hamlet. The explanations they offer for his mood (worry about his argosies, love) are met with resistance – 'Fie, fie!' he says (i. i. 46). He does not, however, see himself as an outsider. Even his melancholy is a part of an integrated society:

> I hold the world but as the world, Gratiano,
> A stage, where every man must play a part,
> And mine a sad one. (lines 77–9)

He knows his role in society. Later, he will regard himself as 'a tainted wether of the flock' (IV. i. 114): part of the social flock, he is the sacrifice that is necessary to sustain it. He may be self-sacrificing, but he is also self-dramatizing; although such friendship is sacrificed and subordinated to love and good fellowship, it allows the individual to claim a central place in the story even if he is not fully folded into its conclusion. Indeed, Antonio's relative isolation at the play's end is part of his claim to be the play's individual centre, and its titular hero; yet he is also 'dumb', a figure of silenced friendship (v. i. 279). Gratiano sees Antonio's melancholy as a pose, like Romeo's, except more politic:

> There are a sort of men whose visages
> Do cream and mantle like a standing pond,
> And do a wilful stillness entertain,
> With purpose to be dress'd in an opinion
> Of wisdom, gravity, profound conceit. (i. i. 88–92)

This hints at a certain self-promotion in Antonio's attitude, but it also helps to account for the unease he provokes in the other men. The group of men who hold the stage in the first scene are friendly but not too intimate; they are concerned to drive away negative thoughts. Bassanio's attitude to Antonio is not very different from that of the others (except that he is making a request for help) – it is only Antonio's attitude to Bassanio that is in excess of the low-key affection in the group's other relationships. But we have a sense of a living society, young men and older talking with some freedom about important matters.

Shylock is much more obviously outside the social context than Antonio. He does not show the enmity to other Jews displayed by Marlowe's Barabas.[23] The news Tubal brings of Shylock's absconded daughter is an act of real friendship (iii. i. 77–130), but their relationship is lacking in affection. Shylock is only enthusiastic about the news Tubal brings, not the presence of Tubal himself, which brings no comfort in itself. Tubal's presence only serves to prevent us from feeling too much pity for an isolated Shylock. His lack of social grace extends to hating Antonio's courtesy, likening him to a 'fawning publican' (i. iii. 41). His refusal to eat with the Christians makes clear his separation of business from social interaction. Antonio is also clear that Shylock's exaction of interest is antisocial:

> If thou wilt lend this money, lend it not
> As to thy friends, for when did friendship take
> A breed for barren metal of his friend? (lines 132–4)

Taking interest is a refusal to accept someone else's social credit.[24] Shylock pretends to regard his pound of flesh deal as 'a friendship' (line 168) and couches it in terms of bantering sociality, calling it a 'merry bond' (line 173). Shylock is never more sinister than when he thus subverts the language of social fellowship. On the other hand, the Christians use their new association with Shylock to deceive him. Lorenzo takes

Jessica and the money from Shylock's house after Shylock has gone out to dinner at Bassanio's house. Though there is no direct suggestion of collusion, we may suspect it. The gang of Christians who help Lorenzo abduct Jessica show the moral ambivalence of the social group. In one sense, they were acting as good friends, providing material help to Lorenzo in a difficult and important endeavour. From another perspective they appeared to be a persecuting pack, attacking a vulnerable man's possessions. Their assistance to Lorenzo is very different from the self-sacrificing help Antonio gives Bassanio.

The relationship between Antonio and Bassanio has attracted much comment, most of it inconclusive. There are two major problems: the nature of the relationship (is it homoerotic?); and our feelings about Antonio's position at the end of the play. Is he integrated into the comedic happy ending, or is he, more subtly but no less surely than Shylock, driven out from the social bonds? No wife is found for him, and this suggests that he has no happy ending within the conventions of comedy. He is the play's titular character and – as the one who most nearly loses his life – is the most serious figure in the play. Bassanio, in choosing the leaden casket, believes that the successful wooer of Portia must 'give and hazard all he hath' (II. vii. 16), but it is in fact Antonio who does so on Bassanio's behalf. His life is put at risk in order to provide Bassanio with the means to woo Portia. This is the self-sacrifice of the most intense friendship; it has an element of Christ-like *charitas*. In merely functional terms, Bassanio's acceptance of such help from his friend *ought* to imply that he recognizes (and therefore in some sense reciprocates) Antonio's love and the obligations it creates. But Bassanio is an insensitive creature, equally incapable of understanding or reciprocating Antonio's goodness. Antonio's love gives Bassanio the power to hurt him, but this is not an essential quality of the young man, originating rather in the nature of Antonio's feelings and the circumstances of their relationship. Bassanio has no more affection for Antonio than for the young men of his social group, including Gratiano and Lorenzo – and he is able himself to help the latter in his marriage project, rather as Antonio helped him. Social life is both complex and hierarchical: the kind of exclusive and symmetrical relationship that Antonio seems to want with Bassanio is simply not possible in such a context. Bassanio refuses to be drawn into the mutual recognitions of one-to-one, face-to-face friendship.

Antonio is a merchant first and foremost, and as such his concern should be with money rather than higher aims. Venice is a mercantile society, in which too much idealism about love or other matters cannot thrive. Antonio nevertheless attempts to rise above his situation within this society. Bassanio, in contrast to this, is fully adjusted to the mercantile world. His ideas regarding love and friendship are all bound up with money. He says to Antonio:

> to you, Antonio,
> I owe the greatest debt in money and in love,
> And from your love I have a warranty
> To unburthen all my plots and purposes
> How to get clear of all the debts I owe. (I. i. 130–4)

This hints that he wants to clear himself of the love-debt as much as of the financial one and shows at least that he regards them as strictly parallel. He is like Cordelia, loving Antonio *according to his bond*. When Antonio's life is put into the scale of obligations, Bassanio cannot make any repayment. It is beyond his imagination to see friendship as more than a matter of give-and-take.

Bassanio actively dissuades his cousin from accepting Shylock's 'merry bond', but Antonio's recklessness wins the day. Rather than showing careful mercantile husbandry, he romantically risks all. The standard tropes of romance suggest to most audiences that such a risk must gain reward, but the play is structured according to the more solemn belief, endorsed by Antonio himself, that there should be no such rewards.[25] One reward that he does receive is admiration, from an on-stage audience as well as that in the theatre. Salerio says 'A kinder gentleman treads not the earth' (II. viii. 35). There is something Christ-like about the man, but mercantile society, whilst admiring this, will also feel somewhat uncomfortable about it. Solanio's more telling comment is 'Let good Antonio look he keep his day, / Or he shall pay for this' (lines 25–6). This comment is full of one merchant's wise irony at another's folly. Solanio adds, regarding Antonio and Bassanio, 'I think he only loves the world for him' (line 50), a statement that may also imply bewildered scepticism. Antonio will find himself, like Timon of Athens, an object more of curiosity and wonder for his generosity than someone who is truly respected.

The only demand that Antonio makes is that Bassanio witness his martyrdom. It is couched in rather histrionic terms that recall the *Sonnets*. He is saying, as Shakespeare says in the poems, 'I don't mind if you don't repay my love, but at least acknowledge it.' His letter says, 'if your love do not persuade you to come, let not my letter' (III. ii. 321–2), and in person he prays that 'Bassanio come / To see me pay his debt, and then I care not' (III. iii. 35–6). He must not only do good but be seen to do good. His self-pity makes him seem not entirely selfless (and therefore more human and sympathetic). At the trial, he tells Bassanio 'You cannot better be employ'd, Bassanio, / Than to live still and write mine epitaph' (IV. i. 117–18); he is asking him to be his Horatio. The unbalanced friendship can only have its culmination in death, the writing of the epitaph sealing the friendship's ultimate perfection. In that way their putative one soul will be coherently in one body. This idea is hinted at by Portia, who thinks 'that this Antonio, / Being the bosom lover of my lord, / Must needs be like my lord' (III. iv. 16–18). The only true satisfaction that Antonio could get would be to coalesce with Bassanio as one person, but this impossibility is reduced to the demand that he be acknowledged and therefore be a part of Bassanio's married life, which Antonio's sacrifice has won:

> Commend me to your honourable wife,
> Tell her the process of Antonio's end,
> Say how I lov'd you, speak me fair in death;
> And when the tale is told, bid her be judge
> Whether Bassanio had not once a love. (IV. i. 273–7)

This implies a rivalry of affection between Antonio and Portia, and when Bassanio volunteers his life to save him, the disguised Portia acknowledges the rivalry with the acerbic comment 'Your wife would give you little thanks' (line 288). In the play's final scene, as Portia and Bassanio argue over the ring, Antonio says 'I am th' unhappy subject of these quarrels' (V. i. 238). He is an unnecessary gooseberry, the catalyst of their love that is no longer needed now that the two are bonded. He renounces Bassanio, in swearing to Portia that his friend will never break faith again. Such unequal friendship can only seek acknowledgement, even though it may want greater love. It can have no great scene of emotional recognition; even if it is acknowledged as the central relationship in the play, it is finally silenced.

Shakespeare's presentation of friendship in a larger social milieu reaches its peak in the *Henry IV* plays. When we first meet Hal he is alone with Falstaff in his apartment,[26] arguing about the latter's future role under Hal's kingship. Poins soon enters to make up a group with differing personalities, positions and priorities. Empson sees Poins as 'the Prince's own gentleman-in-waiting', but his status is not that clear.[27] We are given a gradual introduction to the 'unrestrained loose companions' that Hal's father spoke of in *Richard II* (V. iii. 7), and they appear in order of importance. First Falstaff, whose intimacy with the heir to the throne is surprising, addressing him as *thou*, and calling him 'sweet wag' (I. ii. 16), 'lad' (line 39) and 'mad wag' (line 44), terms which also serve to brush off Hal's insults. These are more biting than the witty banter with which Falstaff replies. The friendship here between age and youth, irresponsibility and ultimate political ambitions has vast inequalities which are only at all containable when placed in the larger social grouping. Hal chooses not to single out Falstaff as a particular friend when he gives his soliloquy at the end of the scene, saying merely 'I know you all' (line 195), a phrase that will be negatively echoed in his individual rejection of Falstaff. But Falstaff always tries to make them a pair. Hal has to attack Falstaff almost continually in order to drive away his friendly claims; this resembles the way in which masters treat their overfamiliar servants in earlier plays (see chapter 5, above). Poins's plan to rob Falstaff is therefore seized upon as a way of belittling the fat knight. In a childish manner Hal is ganging up with Poins to get one over on Falstaff, to diminish him and reduce his threat. Falstaff not only wants to be a particular friend, but in the group continually tries to be the leader, and Hal can only master him with Poins's help. (This resembles the behaviour of primate communities, in which two junior apes often join forces to remove an older dominant male.)[28] Poins is a much easier man for Hal to affect riotous friendship with, because he recognizes that some respect ought to be shown to 'my lord' (line 194), whom he tends to address as *you*, even though he does call him 'sweet Hal' (line 111). The problem with Hal's position in the group is that he pretends they are equal friends, a pretence that only Falstaff takes at face value. Empson is probably right to see Hal as a parasite, able to enter any world, who always destroys his 'host' (Falstaff, Hotspur, even the King),[29] but Falstaff tries to make a symbiotic connection with him.

Hal is able to have an easier intimacy with the more respectful Poins (who disappears without explanation once Hal has become king). The attack on Falstaff at Gad's Hill makes clear the limitations of Hal's affection for him but also binds Hal and Poins as comrades, youth playing a spiteful trick on age:

> Away, good Ned. Falstaff sweats to death,
> And lards the lean earth as he walks along.
> Were't not for laughing, I should pity him. (ii. ii. 108–10)

Only by laughing at Falstaff can Hal drive away the pity that would make for true friendship. He uses jokes primarily to maintain his distanced authority. Something similar happens in part 2, when Hal and Poins pretend to be drawers to eavesdrop on Falstaff's conversation (ii. iv). Hal repeatedly uses Poins as a buffer against Falstaff. With Poins himself, Hal also keeps his distance, and Poins is much readier than Falstaff is to accept this, giving no reply to Hal's extraordinarily ungracious exclamation – 'What a disgrace is it to me to remember thy name!' (ii. ii. 13). Instead Poins responds by trying to cheer the Prince up: 'Tell me, how many good young princes would do so, their fathers being so sick as yours at this time is' (lines 29–31). He makes the reasonable, if callous, assumption that Hal should be cheerful at his impending elevation to the throne. Hal insists he is not so eager for this, but does at least open his heart a little to his companion:

PRINCE. Shall I tell thee one thing, Poins?
POINS. Yes, faith, and let it be an excellent good thing.
PRINCE. It shall serve, among wits of no higher breeding than thine.
POINS. Go to, I stand the push of your one thing that you will tell.
PRINCE. Marry, I tell thee it is not meet that I should be sad, now my father is sick, albeit I could tell to thee – as to one it pleases me, for fault of a better, to call my friend, I could be sad, and sad indeed too. (lines 32–43)

Hal has a human need to unload his heart, but does not want friends – in avoiding 'better' men he avoids the risk of friendship. This is hardly the great intimacy that idealizations of friendship promise. In choosing lower-status men as his fellows, Hal has actually isolated himself from genuine social interaction. This is a matter of his temperament, which is solitary and seeks out only superficial intimacy. It also forces him to be graceless, treating his companions in a purely instrumental way, as he later will his subjects. Here, he is so burdened that he has to confide in Poins. In doing so, however, he feels compelled to insult him. Only being a prince allows him to behave so badly. That Falstaff, who receives much worse insults than Poins, is able to retain affection for him shows both Falstaff's magnanimity and Hal's inhumanity. Poins is clear that he is not one to claim excessive intimacy with the Prince. He shows his contempt for those who

never prick their finger but they say, 'There's some of the King's blood split.' 'How comes that?' says he that takes upon him not to conceive. The answer is ready as a borrower's cap – 'I am the King's poor cousin, sir'. (lines 112–16)

Falstaff, from his perspective, sees the Prince as 'too familiar' (line 127) with Poins, and warns Hal that Poins plans to marry the Prince to his sister Nell (lines 128–9). Falstaff's jealousy is laughable, but strongly felt, an indication of true friendly devotion. 'For fault of a better', though, Poins is Hal's closest friend. However, like Benvolio at the end of *Romeo and Juliet*, Poins disappears at the end of 2 *Henry IV*; such friendship is often a loose end in Shakespeare, treated as unimportant compared to the grand emotions of his plays' climaxes.

The rest of the Eastcheap crowd – Bardolph, Peto and Pistol – are much less important to Hal. Bardolph and Peto appear to be Falstaff's servants or hangers-on, related to Falstaff rather as Poins is to Hal. Pistol, the swaggerer, is treated as a joke in the tavern. Yet both he and Bardolph will survive into *Henry V*, having very different fates under Hal's kingship. Falstaff lords it over the tavern group, but he does so much more gracefully than Hal, accepting insults and not parrying them with more hurtful ones – only wittier ones. Hal breaks the rules of tavern intercourse by continually reminding the others, whether actively or passively, of his superior station. Hal's conviction is that he is genuinely loved by the lower orders, and this will come very much into question in *Henry V*, when he is asking them to die for him. In the first Boar's Head scene in part 1 he explains to his usual confidant Poins that this is his main purpose in living the riotous life. 'Sirrah, I am sworn brother to a leash of drawers, and can call them all by their names, as Tom, Dick, and Francis' (II. iv. 6 – 8). This patronizing idea comes back poignantly in part 2 when he feels disgraced by remembering Poins's name.

They take it already upon their salvation, that though I be but Prince of Wales, yet I am the king of courtesy, and tell me flatly I am no proud Jack like Falstaff, but a Corinthian, a lad of mettle, a good boy (by the Lord, so they call me!), and when I am King of England I shall command all the good lads in Eastcheap. (lines 8–15).

Hal supposes that he has touched the 'base string of humility', but it is very clear that his mock-humanity is full of baffled arrogance ('*but* Prince of Wales', 'so they call me!'). He shows here his pique at being called a boy or lad, terms which are frequently used by Falstaff and Poins. The regal self-confidence that he hopes to project is undercut by his desire to compete against Falstaff in a popularity contest with a 'leash of drawers', his sworn brotherhood to whom is as much a political fiction as his later brotherhood with his soldiers at Agincourt.

We saw in the previous chapter how Falstaff attempts to make his friendship for Hal the basis of the latter's royal status. When Hal gains a moral victory in the debate when each in turn pretends to be the King admonishing Hal, Falstaff's rhetoric saves him again, trapping Hal into a damaging admission of his true nature. Falstaff is clearly being extravagant when he says 'Banish plump Jack, and banish all the world', but when Hal replies 'I do, I will' (lines 479–81) he not only refuses Falstaff's continued company and affection, but in an ironically self-cursing way he drives away all human affection, for we can easily take Hal's emphatic two-part reply as *I do banish Jack, I will banish the world*. Falstaff may here be selfish in his desire to see Poins, Peto and Bardolph banished rather than him, but it is only because he genuinely wants to keep his friendship with Hal, and believes that it will be valuable to the future king. In any case, their friendship cannot perhaps flourish as it might in their present social group. Hal knows them all, making no discrimination, and will banish them all indiscriminately. Falstaff, as we saw in the previous chapter, plays a role whose significance extends beyond the fellowship group, but the rest can be easily dismissed, and Poins like Benvolio can disappear from the stage without comment.

Fellowship provides a means of representing a larger social world and showing how major characters interact with it, but it also allows comparatively minor characters to disappear because they try to do away with frictions between men. As we shall see in the next chapter, the frictions of false and betrayed friendship show a more recalcitrant sense of the individual's prominence. Perhaps because the good fellowship of normal social relations is indifferent to individuality, the individual needs to assert himself in ways that are antisocial.

CHAPTER 8

False friendship and betrayal

Despite the symbiotic if unequal and impermanent connections between men that can emerge in unpromising contexts such as service, politics or fellowship, friendship is most dramatically intense when it is betrayed, or when it is false in the first place. We have seen that betrayals of friendship for erotic purposes tend to be accepted in Shakespeare's plays, as erotic priorities must ultimately be accepted as taking precedence (as Benedick says, 'the world must be peopled' – *Much Ado About Nothing*, II. iii. 242). Betrayals of political friendship are also acceptable, if lamentable, because there is no place for true friendship in the world of politics. This chapter will deal with other varieties of false and betrayed friendship which more firmly unsettle the individual's sense of his own identity, but which paradoxically create the most powerful connections between men. In betraying or feigning friendship, selfish individuals come to see the emptiness of their individualism even as they act upon it. Parolles in *All's Well that Ends Well* is a false friend because he is a false man, something he comes to realize in a delicious balance of tragicomic irony. Iago makes a false friendship with Othello which comes, in its twisted way, to be the truest relationship either man has. The friendships of *Twelfth Night* are all false or treacherous in some way, but nonetheless motivate that play's gracious action. In *Antony and Cleopatra* it is only through betrayal that Enobarbus becomes a significant friend to Antony. Abandoning the Humanist ideal of friendship, these characters come to recognize themselves in differentiated interaction with others. The selfhood that emerges from false and treacherous relationships is reluctantly accepted, but is all the more resonant for that reason.

Being an untrustworthy friend is one of the standard qualities of villains in Renaissance drama, both in tragedies and comedies. John Marston's tragicomic *The Malcontent* is perhaps the best example of this. The villain Mendoza, whose name obviously suggests his lying, untrustworthy nature, is a perfect example of an anti-friend. He is a classic instance of the dangerous royal favourite in a play whose atmosphere of courtly corruption is primarily signified by the inversion and abuse of friendship. He either echoes or anticipates Shakespeare's Iago (it is not clear which play was written first), but is much more of a caricature than Shakespeare's great villain. Such a caricature can be helpful to our interpretation of a more mysterious character because he more readily explains himself; from Mendoza we can infer an outline to the false friend that Shakespeare left deliberately vague.

Mendoza is very clear about needing the ability to feign friendship in order to be an effective villain, saying 'Who cannot feign friendship can ne'er produce the effects of hatred' (I. ii. 167–8). Hammering home his self-definition as a self-made villain with no sense of human attachment, he goes on to say:

> Nothing so holy, no band of nature so strong,
> No law of friendship so sacred,
> But I'll profane, burst, violate
> 'Fore I'll endure disgrace, contempt and poverty. (II. i. 15–18)

He betrays no familial (or *natural*) bonds in the play (he has none); it is only friendship which he abuses. These lines seem more to emphasize his villainous character than to convince us that he is really concerned about the sacrilege of breaking the laws of friendship, which seem, as we have so often seen, to be rather a dead letter. More powerfully, he delights in his position as an anti-friend, in lines which influenced Shakespeare's Edmund ('I grow, I prosper' (*King Lear*, I. ii. 21)), but which are a more obvious acceptance of his own villainy than we see in Iago:

> O, I grow in prosperous treachery!
> As wrestlers clip, so I'll embrace you all,
> Not to support, but to procure your fall. (II. iv. 99–101)

This mode of inverting friendship reaches its peak when he befriends the disguised Pietro and Malevole/Altofronto, setting them to kill one another as part of the bond of friendship with him. In this scene, he tells Malevole 'Come, let's love; we must love, we two, soul and body' (IV. i. 202), even as he is plotting his murder. Like a paler Iago, he urgently grasps at new friends to betray. The play as a whole presents a world in which friendships are made too easily. The courtier Bilioso assents to

Malevole's ironic request for a 'strict friendship' (I. i. 255–6), saying 'let's hold betwixt us a firm correspondence, a mutual-friendly-reciprocal kind of steady-unanimous-heartily leagued – ', before this glib summary of the whole tradition of friendship theory is cut off by Malevole's cynicism. The play's hero cannot believe in friendship, something that comes out most clearly in his exchange with Pietro:

> Now God deliver me from my friends!
> PIETRO. Thy friends?
> MALEVOLE. Yes, from my friends, for from mine enemies I'll deliver myself. O,
>   cut-throat friendship is the rankest villainy. (IV. ii. 19–23)

This is ironic on a number of levels: Malevole himself has used friendship to get revenge on Pietro, telling him of his wife's infidelity; he is still using it to procure Mendoza's fall; and finally, he is at this stage developing something like a friendship with Pietro, the man who usurped him. This new friendship of forgiveness can defeat the false friendship of Mendoza, partly by using Mendoza's own methods. Malevole buys into this false friendship with absurd extravagance, telling Mendoza 'I am thy slave beyond death and hell' (III. i. 158) and saying 'In thee be all my spirit' (line 207). This fierce bonding resembles that between Othello and Iago (see below); Malevole is as ironic here as Iago, but the differences – that Mendoza is a villain being hoist with his own petard, and that Malevole has only contempt for Mendoza – are crucial. The play's conclusion insists on Mendoza's littleness, and in this it is he who resembles Iago. Malevole, restored to his ducal title, has returned to greatness, and scorns to avenge himself on Mendoza, saying that 'an eagle takes not flies' (V. ii. 195). The solitary grandeur of the ruler contrasts with the smallness of the traitor, who is, like Jonson's Mosca, a parasite, using friendship because he is dependent on another man. Mendoza has insisted that he trusts no one, but is not prepared to act alone; he needs to realize himself through others. False friendship emphasizes even more than friendship proper the dependence of small men on others. In Shakespeare, such a symbiotic dependence can be found in all classes, from the lowly hanger-on to the great hero.

The hanger-on Parolles has often been compared to Falstaff,[1] but he also bears some resemblance to Benedick, at least in Beatrice's account. Her view that if Claudio has 'caught the Benedick, it will cost him a thousand pounds ere it be cur'd' (I. i. 89–90), and that he is a false friend, who 'hath every month a new sworn brother' (lines 72–3), prejudices us against him as we are prejudiced against Parolles, at least until he decides to love Beatrice. Benedick's transition comes when he overhears his gulling friends talk about Beatrice's supposed love for him, and enumerating his character flaws. His comment on this is 'happy are they that can hear their own detractions and put them to mending' (II. iii. 229–30). Parolles hears his detractions all the time, but only tries to conceal his faults from his friend Bertram, who has to overhear detractions of himself before he can recognize Parolles' faults. Like Benedick, Parolles is introduced by a woman's negative assessment, but Helena is much more ambivalent, as his companionship with Bertram makes him worthy in her eyes. She sees him as

> One that goes with him [Bertram]. I love him for his sake,
> And yet I know him a notorious liar,
> Think him a great way fool, solely a coward;
> Yet these fix'd evils sit so fit in him,
> That they take place when virtue's steely bones
> Looks bleak i' th' cold wind. Withal, full oft we see
> Cold wisdom waiting on superfluous folly. (I. i. 99–105)

The lurching quality of the *yet* which is supposed to balance her love with all these ill qualities shows that Helena's beliefs about Parolles are deeply paradoxical and make us question her judgement; in fact Helena is deceiving herself in a different way from Beatrice's self-deception, as it is Bertram she is wrong about. Helena's generalization – 'Cold wisdom waiting on superfluous folly' – raises the possibility that her diagnosis is topsy-turvy, and that the supposed hanger-on is truly the wise one, the substantial young man the fool, as turns out in *Much Ado*. In fact, Bertram is even worse than Claudio, but Parolles' case is more complex. The fitness (or decorum) of his 'fix'd evils', like Falstaff's, gives him a certain licence. Parolles' riddling banter with Helena in the play's first scene almost makes him seem an official fool, which status would entitle him to some wisdom. David Ellis's excellent essay on Parolles perhaps goes too far in arguing that Parolles is taken into Lafew's service at the play's end as a fool,[2] but it certainly is a role to which he would be suited, and he does say that he intends to thrive 'by fool'ry' (IV. iii. 338). Whether or not he means this literally, he has thus far insisted on a social status above that of a fool, and has therefore had to rise above the mere talk of a fool to the gentleman's sphere of action.

As Helena suggests, Parolles is a 'superfluous' character in both social and plot terms. Lacking the blood or wealth that would make him *substantial*, he has to rely on two rather precarious resources – his own linguistic capacity (as indicated in his name) and his friendship with Bertram. In this, he not only resembles Falstaff, but the Shakespeare of the *Sonnets*. Parolles' attempt to be a man of words, relying on his wits rather than his actions or family, is doomed in the present world. The play as a whole has a superfluity of young men in its host of inter-changeable lords. These lords seem to have been tricked or let down by Parolles in the past. One of them says:

> You do not know him, my lord, as we do. Certain it is that he will steal himself into a man's favour, and for a week escape a great deal of discoveries, but when you find him out, you have him ever after. (III. vi. 90–3)

Parolles can only get temporary friendship as his social credit is no good. He may lack substance in their terms, but in the play's terms he is more vivid than they. As Rothman notes, he is on stage more than either Helena or Bertram;[3] he threatens to take over the play.

After centuries of critical orthodoxy attacking Parolles, the pendulum may have swung too far back in his favour, but it is easier for an audience to engage with what J. Dennis Huston calls his 'commitment to life'[4] than with Helena's pushiness or Bertram's gracelessness. In playing such a variety of roles, whilst having no real substance to back them up,[5] Parolles paradoxically manages to be the play's most impressive character. It may be going too far to suggest, as Jeremy Richard does, that Parolles develops 'a tragic acceptance of the world', but his role does provide a critique of the more supposedly substantial characters. David Scott Kastan, who does not discuss Parolles, argues tellingly that

> The contrivance of the romantic comedies ... establishes them literally as play worlds, worlds of make-believe, witnessing to Shakespeare's manipulation and control, and freeing us to delight in them. In the problem comedies the con-trivance is the characters' own and is throughout too self-regarding, too unre-sponsive to the needs and desires of others, to permit our delight.[6]

But Parolles does delight us, and he offers an escape from the selfishness of others even as he appears to betray friendship. When his cowardice and treachery are exposed by the lords he delights them rather than horrifies them, and his own self-awareness, which had earlier caused the lords to wonder 'Is it possible he should know what he is, and be that he is?' (IV. i. 44–5), disarms any criticism. It is Bertram who seems a fool for trusting him. Parolles essentially tells us not to take him as a tragic figure, or even a bitterly humiliated one like Malvolio:

> Yet I am thankful. If my heart were great,
> 'Twould burst at this. Captain I'll be no more,
> But I will eat and drink, and sleep as soft
> As captain shall. Simply the thing I am
> Shall make me live. (IV. iii. 319–23)

This is hardly Othello lamenting the going of his occupation. His humiliation is of course necessary, but it doesn't reflect any great glory on those who bring it about. Unlike Helena, Parolles cannot rise by his association with Bertram; friendship does not raise a man as marriage does a woman. But there is nothing wrong with accepting that one cannot be great. His claim on the audience's attention is now his own rather than based on the countenance given him by the supposed romantic hero Bertram. This self-recognition comes through friendship – of a sort – but it is ultimately a rejection of friendship.

In fact, the play makes little use of the discourse of ideal friendship, which is why we do not feel that Parolles has sinned too badly in betraying Bertram. The play associates the decline of chivalry and the decline of friendship; the idea may be commonplace but it has some force within the world of the play. The King speaks nostalgically of his youthful friendship with Bertram's late father: the two men fought side by sides many years ago, and their friendship is seen as a pattern of old-style martial companionship, just as Bertram's 'good father' (I. ii. 31) is a model for the son. Times have changed, though, and such friendships are a thing of the past; wars like friendships are more cynically motivated these days; Bertram will not be going off to war with a virtuous young friend in the manner of Pyrocles and Musidorus in the *Arcadia*. Pleasure not virtue motivates the young men of today, and Parolles is equipped with wit rather than moral discourses. Bertram too is not a heroic figure: he goes off to war against the King's express command because he wants to avoid sleeping with his unwanted new wife. The interchangeable lords have known him well at one time or other (IV. iii), but none have been his constant friend. This promiscuity of friendship signals Bertram's basic unreliability. The world of masculine friendship in *All's Well* is in decline, and this leads to its love affairs being settled by unsatisfactory compromises. Parolles is merely the most obvious instance of an unsatisfactory world, and his self-awareness gives him dignity above that of many others.

Given that Parolles has no discernible influence on Bertram, and given the insubstantiality of the friends' love triangle with Diana, what is the point of Parolles' role in the play? Disconcertingly, he is Helena's only intellectual equal in the play, as their witty, almost intimate banter in the first scene suggests. Like this woman, he is possessed of intellectual capabilities which are not joined with any substantial power in the court. He gives Helena some rather gnomic advice which sets the play's discourse of friendship going: 'When thou hast leisure, say thy prayers; when thou hast none, remember thy friends' (I. i. 212–14). Presumably this means that one should only remember one's friends when one has no leisure to do anything for them. This cynicism arises from Parolles' view of the court as a place in which no one does anything for anyone else's sake, a view that is borne out in the action that follows, in which even Helena's love is given to Bertram against the young earl's will. Parolles' cynicism about friendship is echoed by the Countess's clown, who asks leave to marry because

I am out a' friends, madam, and I hope to have friends for my wife's sake.
COUNTESS. Such friends are thine enemies, knave.
CLOWN. Y'are shallow, madam – in great friends, for the knaves come to do that for me that I am a-weary of. He that ears my crop spares my team, and gives me leave to in the crop. If I be his cuckold, he's my drudge. He that comforts my wife is the cherisher of my flesh and blood; he that cherishes my flesh and blood loves my flesh and blood; he that loves my flesh and blood is my friend; *ergo*, he that kisses my wife is my friend. (I. iii. 39–50)

The moral inversion that makes the cuckold-maker the truest friend is indicative of the play's atmosphere of friendship. Immediately after his advice to Helena on friendship, Parolles adds this on marriage – 'Get thee a good husband, and use him as he uses thee' (I. i. 214–15): in other words, be unfaithful in this instrumental world. There seems to be a suggestion in this that Parolles might desire Helena in his own peculiar way, but the play suppresses this potential love triangle. This will be brought up later in Parolles' conduct with Diana: Bertram finds letters from Parolles which advise the girl to get money from Bertram without losing her virtue. This is in curious parallel to his earlier advice to Helena (particularly that regarding her virginity as a 'commodity' to be sold at the right time (I. i. 153)). Bertram may call him a 'both-sides rogue' (IV. iii. 222), but it is clear that Parolles is, like Lucio and Pandarus in the other 'problem plays', a malcontent figure, unsuccessful but in tune with the real processes of the times, and therefore more clearly understanding the sexual economics to which women must submit. If he is not a chivalrous defender of women, as Benedick turns out to be, he is a man who understands the predicament of women and as such must be condemned by the martial world of masculine friendship. He pretends to defend Bertram when brought in as a witness for Diana's sake in the final scene, but he ultimately expresses the truth. It is not Parolles but the world that is inadequate. Forced by economic and political circumstance to try to befriend men, he is much more suited to female company, particularly because his lack of power means that he must rely on others to give him valid substance, as a woman must. Helena can take the world into her own hands, because she has semi-magical powers; Parolles' verbal skills do not similarly enable him.

Friendship is shown to be similarly powerless in *Twelfth Night*, which has three distinct plots of friendship, involving Sir Toby and Sir Andrew, Sebastian and Antonio, and Orsino and Cesario. The three contrasting friendships provide some of the play's structure, and their tensions are more than just a backdrop to the love plots. All these friendships are shown to be illusory in one way or another. Viola is a woman, Sir Toby is using Sir Andrew, and Antonio is apparently betrayed.

Sebastian and Antonio's friendship is the most extravagant in Shakespeare's plays, and Antonio's adoration of Sebastian has clear homoerotic overtones.[7] It also resembles the *Sonnets* in its pressing of the aspect of idolatry: Antonio says that he *adores* Sebastian (II. i. 47) and later, when disappointed in him, refers to him as an 'idol' (III. iv. 365). Antonio has done 'devotion' to Sebastian's 'image', rather than to his substance (line 363), as the Shakespeare of the *Sonnets* tended to adore the young man's 'outward fair' (sonnet 16, line 11). A further resemblance to the *Sonnets* is the social inequality of the two men, but the differential is less clear-cut than that between Shakespeare and the young man. The combination of homoeroticism (with its unspeakable underside of sodomy), false worship and uncertainty of status contributes to a sense of unreality in the men's friendship. When we first meet Sebastian at the start of act II, he has been a guest at Antonio's house for some months, but only now reveals his name, having previously said that he was called Roderigo (II. i. 17).[8] Their relationship therefore has a basis in false identity, but the scene demonstrates greater intimacy between the men than there was between Viola and her rescuing sea-captain: Sebastian and Antonio are alone together; Viola was with the captain and a silent group of sailors. This is only proper: a young gentlewoman could hardly be alone with a sea-captain. But this sense of propriety highlights the possibilities of intimacy between men that society denies between the sexes; male independence can apparently foster true friendship, female dependence makes all relationships more doubtful. Yet as the play develops it is heterosexual relationships that succeed, and male friendship that is shown to be uncertain. Like the *Sonnets'* young man, Sebastian needs no active emotions. The language of the two introductory scenes is contrasted as the characters are. Viola talks down to the captain (in verse), using 'thou', and is replied to (also in verse) with the respectful 'you'. Viola's confidence provokes no unseemly intimacy. Despite the length of their acquaintance, Sebastian and Antonio call each other 'you', bespeaking their mutual respect. The prose they speak suggests a lack of formal distance without hinting at any greater intimacy.[9] Indeed some of Antonio's language is almost servile: 'Pardon me sir, your bad entertainment' (II. i. 33) and he asks to be Sebastian's 'servant' (line 36).[10] There is considerable doubt about Antonio's social status: we know he has been a sailor as he claims to have done service against Orsino (III. iii. 26–7), but he is surely of higher status than Viola's captain (the simple fact of him having a name suggests that much), and he could be of as high a status as Drake or Ralegh. Even if not, Sebastian's 'you' would be more incongruous than polite if he were addressing someone genuinely humble as opposed to a deferential member of the lower gentry. Antonio's soliloquy shifts this ground – for he refers to the now absent Sebastian as 'thou', either equalizing him in his absence or figuring him as a deity.

Sebastian's true attitude to Antonio is hard to gauge, so cool is he (as stony as the young man in sonnet 94). His response to Antonio following him is maddeningly courteous again; adeptly refusing any sense of obligation:

> I would not by my will have troubled you,
> But since you make your pleasure of your pains,
> I will no further chide you. (III. iii. 1–3)

This insistence that he doesn't *will* Antonio to be with him, that Antonio is indulging himself by his service is exactly the sort of problem that the *Sonnets* identify in emotionally unequal friendship. Unable to rely on any will from Sebastian himself, Antonio has to attribute his friendly actions to an outside force, his 'desire / (More sharp than filed steel) [which] did spur me forth' (lines 4–5). He also claims that Illyria is 'Rough and inhospitable to strangers' (line 11), thus providing a reason for his assistance that might provoke a sense of obligation in Sebastian, but in fact the only danger is to himself. He wants credit for braving dangers for his friend's sake, but is in fact only braving unnecessary danger for the sake of seeing his friend. This excessive friendship is ultimately self-serving in a subtle way, but it would be wrong to think that Sebastian despises it – he in fact takes Antonio's friendship quite happily and simply, though he is not able to see its depths. When baffled by Olivia's advances, he wishes Antonio were with him, saying 'His counsel now might do me golden service' (IV. iii. 8), and this brings out a structural irony, for these, Sebastian's first truly friendly words about Antonio, come very soon after Antonio thinks that Sebastian has denied him. He can only recognize his friend in his absence.

The crucial feature of the betrayal of Antonio is that it is not really a betrayal, although it has the emotional effect of one on him. Because we know that Antonio is denied by Viola–Cesario rather than by Sebastian himself, our confident enjoyment of the structural ironies in the denial scene itself can mask the peculiarities of Antonio's behaviour here. In the first place, he denies himself, telling the officers that they've got the wrong man. This dishonest claim of a 'mistake' (III. iv. 327) suggests that Antonio's first impulse is self-preservation and chimes oddly with his anger at Viola's denial of him. Then, his appeal to Sebastian–Viola is presented in a self-assertive way: he seems both to be testing his friend, and to be prepared to make trouble for him rather than submit to his fate. His first words to Viola are clearly a reproach: 'This comes with seeking you' (line 332). He then asserts his self-sacrifice whilst associating his friend with him (a notorious outlaw): 'I shall answer it' (line 333), as if someone else might. Also, he seems to delight in the opportunity of testing Sebastian's friendship for him: 'What will you do, now my necessity / Makes me to ask you for my purse?' (lines 334–5). All this is histrionic, demanding recognition and attention from the friend in the same way as his namesake in *The Merchant of Venice* or, for that matter, Kent at the end of *King Lear*. Rather than submitting passively to Viola's denial, Antonio flings bitter reproaches at her, and tells the officers of his friend's ingratitude. This is an ungracious performance, reminiscent of the *Sonnets*' approach to reproaching an idealized friend, showing the subtle, almost unwilling self-assertion that emerges when friendship is tested to the uttermost. Antonio's idolatry here weakens and is perhaps permanently destroyed, regardless of the false basis of the discord with his friend:

> But O, how vile an idol proves this god!
> Thou hast, Sebastian, done good feature shame.

> In nature there's no blemish but the mind;
> None can be call'd deform'd but the unkind.
> Virtue is beauty, but the beauteous evil
> Are empty trunks, o'erflourish'd by the devil. (lines 365–70)

These are sentiments that, once felt, cannot be called back. It is a feeling that underlies the *Sonnets*, that 'good feature' is merely a vehicle for the projection of emotions that are irrelevant to the beloved's self. What Antonio cannot see, and the Shakespeare of the *Sonnets* can, is that neither good nor bad emotions about the friend have anything to do with the friend, for both exist only in the one who loves. Antonio's inability truly to know his friend is reflected in *Twelfth Night*'s final scene, where he again reproaches Viola, this time to Orsino. His resentment here seems designed to get his friend into trouble again, and he is again accused of madness, linking him to Malvolio. When he finds out the truth, all he can say is 'Sebastian are you?' (v. i. 221). Having doubted his 'god', he is baffled at his re-emergence. It is clear that he has forgotten his friend's back-story of having a twin (admittedly a sister), told him in act II scene i, or fails to see its relevance. What does this say about his interest in Sebastian's self? Olivia thinks the doubling of her beloved Cesario 'Most wonderful' (v. i. 225), but Antonio is almost reproachful when he asks 'How have you made division of yourself?' (line 222), because for him doubling is dishonesty and threatens their friendship through the recognition of a twin, more perfect in resemblance than a friend can be. Laurie E. Osborne explores the ways in which early eighteenth-century versions of the play at least ensured that Antonio was pardoned and thanked by Orsino, concluding that 'Shakespeare's *Twelfth Night* may accord Antonio a silence like that of silenced Shakespearean women, whose dramatic or ideological usefulness expires with their voices, but in the late eighteenth century Antonio becomes a problem to be solved.'[11] In the conclusion of the play Antonio can have no part. Having won a wife and found a sister, Sebastian speaks only one line to Antonio, ambiguously asserting his identity.[12] Antonio is not even offered consolations like Malvolio. Perhaps he goes quietly off to write some sonnets.

Barbara Everett identifies Antonio along with Malvolio as 'the play's solitaries'.[13] Given that he is an exemplar of friendship, this seems paradoxical, but it reflects his isolation from the main social integration of the play. He does not participate in the play's atmosphere of what Everett calls 'sheer adult social consideration, of people's steady and reflective judgment of one another'.[14] He is not easy in company as Viola–Cesario is, nor is he graceful like Sebastian or affable like Sir Toby. For him, Illyria is a dangerous place, not a festive one. It is a place in which friendships are false, and are recognized as such, almost happily.

The play's other friendships are less intense and easier-going, but fraught in their own way. Orsino's pseudo-homoerotic attraction to Cesario has a release in the fact that the younger 'man' is really a woman, but realization of this does not come until after the Duke has threatened to kill his beloved manservant after they have become apparent rivals in love. When Viola–Cesario tries to educate Orsino about women's love by telling him the story of 'his' sister, the Duke can only respond with a question that tries to prove his own point about the superiority of men's love – 'But died thy sister of her love, my boy?' (ii. iv. 119). Viola evades this, and turns the conversation back to Olivia, to which Orsino responds by saying 'Ay, that's the theme. /To her in haste' (lines 122–3). His own love takes precedence over all; there is no real inquisitiveness about his servant's life, no compassion. Orsino is fundamentally indifferent to others, which explains the ease with which he transfers his love from Olivia to Viola. In marrying Viola he says that 'I shall have share in this most happy wreck' (v. i. 266); like a spoiled child, he wants to make sure he gets his share of the happy spoils, and is not overly curious about its contents. He still calls Viola 'boy' (line 267), and will address him as Cesario until s/he is dressed as 'Orsino's mistress, and his fancy's queen' (lines 385–8); this suggests that the outer world is manipulable to Orsino's imagination, and is hardly a firm basis for a relationship with a real person. Everett argues that the play pursues 'a kind of wholeness beyond expression and perhaps even beyond possibility',[15] and in the case of Orsino this means a transcendence of real people. From illusory friendship to illusory marriage, Orsino seems to be living in a haze as far as other people are concerned.

A more calculatedly deceptive friendship is the one between Sir Toby and Sir Andrew. As Beatrice fears that friendship with Benedick will cost Claudio dear, so Maria feels that Andrew will 'have but a year in all these ducats' (i. iii. 23–4); but she says this principally because she thinks him a fool rather than because Toby is a parasite on him. Whilst it is clear that Toby is mocking his new friend, and we can infer that he is living off him, the latter fact is not made explicit at first. There is therefore some confusion about how much Toby is using Andrew, and therefore how untrustworthy he is as a friend. He does seem to enjoy his company, and whilst Toby may be gulling Andrew in insisting that the latter has a chance with Olivia, his motives may be as much a matter of fun as of avarice. It is as much a friendship of pleasure as of utility, even if the pleasure is often at Andrew's expense. The point at which we are first sure of Toby's financial use of Andrew is around halfway through the play, when Toby tells his other friend Fabian, 'I have been dear to him, lad, some two thousand strong, or so' (III. ii. 54–5). It is at this point that we see how much Toby despises his friend: in arranging the fight between Andrew and Cesario, Toby says, 'For Andrew, if he were open'd and you find so much blood in his liver as will clog the foot of a flea, I'll eat the rest of th' anatomy' (lines 59–63). This witty reflection on his friend's cowardice may contain an undertone of savagery, and he does put Andrew at some risk, though he is reasonably confident that the fight will come to nothing. Whilst Toby does try to make sure that there will be no fight, he does so in order to get Andrew's horse and perhaps to discourage Andrew from thoughts of leaving the house with his money.

Friendship in *Twelfth Night* is constructed as a danger and a humiliation: Andrew Aguecheek is put in danger by Sir Toby's plot against Cesario, and we often (e.g. at the end of II. v) see him in a humiliating posture of absurd agreement with everything that Sir Toby says. That the noble emotions of Antonio have a parallel in the cretinous Andrew Aguecheek demonstrates that excessive friendship can rob a man of his dignity entirely. It is noticeable that Antonio should fight Sir Toby (III. iv. 318), who is a treacherous friend, suggesting that at this moment he is defending the idea of friendship as much as he is defending his friend Sebastian (actually Viola); the fact that Antonio's arrival to defend Sebastian–Cesario–Viola (depending on one's perspective) prompts Sir Toby to defend Sir Andrew is a delicious irony, showing that a true friend can provoke friendship in even the most unpromising false friend (and, in the next scene, Sir Toby also defends Sir Andrew against Sebastian). Having got his comeuppance for starting all this in his 'bloody coxcomb' (V. i. 190) from Sebastian, Sir Toby leaves for the last time, the veil of his pretended friendship with Andrew lifted:

SIR ANDREW. I'll help you, Sir Toby, because we'll be dress'd together.
SIR TOBY. Will you help? – an ass-head and a coxcomb and a knave, a thin-faced knave, a gull? (lines 204–7)

The angry tone of this provokes audience laughter, of course, and a sense of justice that this silly and manipulative friendship has been broken up, but it is hard to say that we feel joy at this exposure of the rancour underlying the amusing pseudo-friendship we have been watching. The happy romantic ending of *Twelfth Night* is enabled by the realistic recognition of the limitation of various types of friendship, but each of those friendships has shaped the characters involved.

A tragedy motivated by the complex dynamic of human interactions rather than by metaphysical forces, friendship is absolutely central to *Othello*, principally in its abuse by Iago, and the feelings here are obviously deep, and have terrible consequences. Rather than being an end, as it is in *Twelfth Night*, rancour is Iago's starting point. His gulling of Roderigo is very similar to Toby's of Andrew: in both cases the gull thinks he can get a woman through his friend and spends money to do so – Iago repeatedly tells Roderigo to 'put money in thy purse' (I. iii. 341 etc.), just as Sir Toby tells Sir Andrew that 'Thou hadst need send for more money' (II. iii. 182–3); both gulls are tricked into fights. E. A. J. Honigmann, whilst drawing parallels between the plays, sees little similarity between Toby Belch and Iago,[16] and it is clear that the latter is more deeply malicious, but they occupy somewhat similar structural positions. (We might note one parallel, that both have servant wives. That Toby marries his at the play's end, and Iago kills his is part of the essential difference between tragedy and comedy.) Iago's plot has – at least at first – an apparently comic structure. If the actor who played Sir Toby Belch also played Iago and the plays were performed in repertory, the initial impression might be of a comic plotter against a socially unacceptable figure. Malvolio and Othello might also be played by one actor, the Moor and the puritan being seen as social outcasts to be mocked. Both Malvolio and Othello are authority figures, breaking up drunken revels, and thus showing themselves to be against the spirit of fun. They are also duped in love. These parallels suggest that we might read Iago, at least initially, as comic; and, given that we tend to side with plotters in comedy, we are therefore forced to recognize our sophisticated complicity in the destruction of the hero. Robert C. Evans argues that 'One of the most disquieting aspects of this play (at least in retrospect) is how much Iago can count on *our* friendly feelings, especially when he toys with Roderigo.'[17] Iago starts with hatred of the Moor, and it is clear that shared enmity to him is the basis of his friendship with Roderigo: they are to be 'conjunctive in our revenge against him' (I. iii. 367–8), suggesting the accidental, contingent basis of their friendship. In the abortive fight in the play's second scene Iago gratuitously says 'You, Roderigo! come, sir, I am for you' (I. ii. 58), and presumably attacks him. This anticipation of his later murder of Roderigo shows off his enmity and violence but conceals them as well as Poe's Purloined Letter.[18]

Iago's whole plot depends on his ability to inveigle his way into friendship with a number of men – Roderigo, Cassio and Othello. In a sense he resembles the promiscuous friend-makers Benedick and Parolles, but unlike Parolles in particular his credit is good: he is universally known to be 'honest'.[19] Desdemona says that his speech is suited to the 'alehouse' (II. i. 139): his slandering of women does not reduce his value, but rather stamps him as a trustworthy man's man. Whilst he is really leading his scenes, Iago always pretends to be a subordinate. A very common role for a friend in drama is to appear beside the main character as a kind of 'sidekick', and everyone treats Iago as if they were the focus, he the secondary friend. The importance of Iago's soliloquies, in addition to drawing us into awkward sympathy with him, is that we see the play from his inside-out perspective. Just as he inverts friendship, he inverts its structural role in drama.

The relationship between Iago and Cassio appears to be friendly. They banter matily about Bianca (IV. i. 107ff.), and Emilia reports that her husband is upset by Cassio's demotion 'as if the case were his' (III. iii. 4),[20] which of course is partly true, in that he wishes he were lieutenant. Iago really does seem to admire Cassio even as he hates and envies him, saying to Montano 'He is a soldier fit to stand by Caesar / And give direction' (II. iii. 122–3). His envy is powerful because it contains admiration, and here the compliment extends to Othello as well, presenting him as a Caesar. The horror of Iago's pretended friendship is that it is based on admiration without humility, but it can be understood in the hierarchical context of an army. Admiration and love flow upward, but do not reach back down. Iago is unappreciated by his superiors, and this rankles. This ambivalent attitude to Cassio has its fullest expression when Iago says 'He hath a daily beauty in his life / That makes me ugly' (v. i. 19–20). This admiring envy is rather similar to Antony's star being occluded by Octavius's, or Macbeth's by Banquo (see chapter 6, above). Iago's subordinate position, though, enables him to have an ironic position with regard to his superiors. He addresses Cassio after his disgrace in very double-edged terms:

> . . . good lieutenant, I think you think I love you.
> Cassio. I have well approved it, sir. (II. iii. 311–12)

The concept of *approval* or *proof* is central to *Othello*; it is an idea that underpins the play's apparent friendships (relying on the idea of 'longe deliberation and profe' that was supposed by Humanists to be necessary to friendship),[21] whilst being as untrustworthy as the proofs of Desdemona's infidelity. Not only does Iago taunt Cassio here with his lost rank, but he plays on the assumption of love flowing up the ranks. There is a sheer pleasure in fooling Cassio here, beyond the needs of his plot. We must presume a certain intimacy between Iago and Cassio: part of Iago's plot relies on the two sharing a bed, and there's something decidedly homo-erotic about Iago's description of the sleeping Cassio embracing him as if he were Desdemona (III. iii. 416–26). Iago seems here to be fantasizing closeness to other men that his treacherous nature really prevents, but the impression we get is that Iago is making a real claim that he is intimate friends with Cassio. There is a definite three-way friendship going on between Othello, Cassio and Iago and it creates its own jealousies. Iago juggles Othello and Cassio, keeping them apart, partly because of this jealousy, and partly so that his version of the world and the nature of the friendships can be presented to the others. Apparently the lowest member of the trio, he takes control of its workings.

At first we only see Cassio as Othello's lieutenant, but it later becomes clear that he is a real friend who has been in on his general's wooing of Desdemona. (Putting it rather strongly, Norman Sanders calls Cassio Othello's 'best friend', but surely Othello is too self-suffi-cient to have such a thing.)[22] We learn this quite late in the play (III. iii); and it is in part an afterthought device that lends credibility to Iago's suggestions of a love affair between Cassio and Desdemona. What is important is that Iago only learns from overhearing Desde-mona that he has been kept out of Othello's confidence and feels betrayed, innocently asking about it as soon as he is alone with Othello. As Empson puts it, 'Iago feels that he has been snubbed, as too coarse to be trusted in such a matter, and he takes immediate advantage of his discomposure.'[23] Whilst betrayed friendship between Othello and Cassio is not an emotionally important aspect of the play, as it would be in a standard jealousy/friendship plot, such a plot is invoked immediately by Iago, who is jealous of Othello's friendship with Cassio. The assumption of friendship between Othello and Cassio is important to the play's plot, even if the betrayal of the friendship is not a major issue for Othello. Othello tells us that Desdemona's first hints of her love came couched in coy terms that later on might seem a seed of jealousy. He says she

> ... bade me, if I had a friend that loved her,
> I should but teach him how to tell my story
> And that would woo her. (I. iii. 164–6)

The play makes no direct connection between this and the later revelation that Cassio was his companion, but the standard trope of a jealousy/friendship plot – one man bringing his friend when he comes wooing, and the friend and woman falling in love – is invoked in both cases. As Laurens J. Mills observes, 'Iago makes use of the whole suggested background of the false-friend tradition.'[24] The upshot is that Othello is prepared to believe in Desdemona's infidelity with Cassio, precisely because Cassio was his friend. Cassio considers himself a true friend, and even at the end calls Othello 'dear General' (v. ii. 299), but this friendship binds him too closely to Othello's marriage. When he presses his suit to Desdemona he wants again to be 'a member of his love' (iii. iv. 112): this suggests that he was not only Othello's intermediary, but almost his penis, or his sexual proxy. The very idea of Cassio's lieutenancy suggests taking his place in bed, as he later takes his place as governor. Iago's plot works so well precisely because of assumptions about the nature of friendship.

As a woman in a man's military world Desdemona is forced into the play's discourse of male friendship. Desdemona overheard Othello say 'Cassio I love thee / But never more be officer of mine' (ii. iii. 248–9), and she is prepared to speak on Cassio's behalf because she is convinced that Cassio really loves Othello (iii. iii. 10), and she vows a 'friendship' (line 21) to Cassio for Othello's sake. She tells Othello, when suing for Cassio's place, that he 'so many a time, / When I have spoke of you dispraisingly, / Hath ta'en your part' (iii. iii. 71–3). Of course Desdemona only wanted to hear Othello praised, but in the circumstances this is bound to enrage Othello, who knows little of such guiltless feminine subtlety. In the end the woman is the victim of jealousies developed in the male friendships. The development of her own friendship with Emilia is one of the play's more emotionally constructive aspects. In the source (Cinthio's *Hecatommithi*, iii. 7) Emilia is her close friend rather than her servant, but here we are presented with a developing friendship which culminates in Emilia's passionate and self-destructive defence of her mistress's reputation. The irony is that Desdemona trusts Iago partly because of her friendship with his wife. When she asks him to intervene on her behalf, she calls him 'Good friend' (iv. ii. 150). It is hard to agree with Evans that Iago really loves Desdemona,[25] as the double jealousy plots that Iago imagines between himself and Othello are overdone, but affectless: his supposed desire for Desdemona, and his suspicion of Othello leaping into his 'seat' (ii. i. 296), are simply ways of binding himself imaginatively to his general in a parody of the sharing and intermingling of friendship.

Iago's claimed hatred for Othello (1. i. 154; 1. iii. 366) is really an inverted form of a desire for friendship. His plot to displace Cassio as lieutenant may simply be vengeance for his disappointment, but he still wants to be thought worthy of the lieutenancy himself. Not entirely driven by bitterness, he still wants to be Othello's right-hand man (rather than the sinister left-hand man?). The problem is that in order to gain Othello's good graces, Iago has not only to displace Cassio, but also Desdemona. This is partly practical – he is not immediately made lieutenant on the dismissal of Cassio, so he has to perform some service in order to get appointed. As Cassio may have got the lieutenancy partly by his aid in the wooing of Desdemona, so Iago wants to perform a similar though inverse personal service in 'exposing' her. He takes some pleasure in the idea that the one he hates will have to be grateful to him, thus implying that Othello's gratitude is of value to him: he says that he wants to 'Make the Moor thank me, love me, and reward me, / For making him egregiously an ass' (11. i. 308–9). His love of irony is primary here, but it is also affective, in that having come to desire the post so rancorously, he wants no one to come between himself and the general. There is no malice towards Desdemona in this – and little enough towards Cassio – but the destruction of these impediments (and, in the end, Emilia) binds Iago closer to Othello. Iago's desire to *possess* Othello, at once demonic and servile, based on radical difference and the desire to identify with his military leader, is the fullest and most savagely excessive form of what Eve Kosofsky Sedgwick calls 'homosocial desire' (see chapter 1, above).[26]

Othello's greatness separates him from the rest of mankind, accentuated in his case by his racial difference from the play's other characters. He claims to have a 'perfect soul' (1. ii. 31), suggesting absolute and unselfconscious integration which does not need the soul-completion of a friend. The play enacts the processes of disintegration of this perfect soul, and Othello's consequent need for a symbiotic connection to another man. First, he makes himself vulnerable by his marriage to Desdemona: she, although a soul complement, cannot be integrated into Othello's soul. In a sense she is the reward he has taken for martial endeavour, but she is not just an object; she brings in the element of emotional consciousness to Othello's life, as indicated in his description of their courtship:

> She loved me for the dangers I had pass'd,
> And I lov'd her that she did pity them. (1. iii 167–8)

All would be well if this was the only move toward self-awareness that Othello made, but the process of seeing himself emotionally goes further.

He is inducted into the imperfect world of the 'super-subtle Venetian' (I. iii. 356) by Iago. The *pity* which had been exclusively Desdemona's is transferred to Othello by Iago's agency. Once he has been convinced of his wife's infidelity, Othello exclaims, 'But yet the pity of it, Iago. O, Iago, the pity of it Iago!' (IV. i. 195–6). This is a non-specific emotion, combining shame, self-pity and proleptic pity of Desdemona (whom he must now murder). The conglomeration of feeling here expresses the general's bafflement – unable to deal with the new concept of pity, the weakened hero turns insistently to Iago to help him deal with the situation, calling his name repeatedly as an emotional prop. The unusually intimate bond between these men becomes an inversion of friendship which infects Othello with the disease of self-consciousness. Iago becomes the most distorting of mirrors, leading Othello to doubt himself, his wife, his occupation.

The binding together of Othello and Iago comes as part of Iago's technique of insinuation. In echoing his general, Iago says nothing directly and seems to become a part of Othello:

> OTHELLO. Is he not honest?
> IAGO.   Honest, my lord?
> OTHELLO. Honest? ay, honest.
> IAGO.   My lord, for aught I know.
> OTHELLO. What dost thou think?
> IAGO.   Think, my lord?
> OTHELLO. Think, my lord? By heaven, thou echo'st me
> As if there were some monster in thy thought
> Too hideous to be shown. (III. iii. 103–7)

This verbal parasitism seems to give Othello the initiative but turns all Othello's thoughts back on themselves, distorted. Whereas a hero's friend in narrative and drama is often a sounding-board (Horatio, Dr Watson), here the echo causes subtle alterations, using the tropes of humility from unequal friendship to bind the men together, and the humility of a servant to create mastery. Servants, in the words of Dromio of Syracuse, 'must their masters' minds fulfil' (*Comedy of Errors*, IV. i. 113; see chapter 5, above), but here Iago fills his master's mind full of his own ideas. His idea of service is skewed: as he says to Roderigo, 'We cannot all be masters, nor all masters / Cannot be truly follow'd' (I. i. 43–4). Iago insists on his 'duty', but also reminds Othello that he is not a slave and does not therefore have to utter his thoughts (III. iii. 134–5). What he is doing now is a favour, above and beyond the call of duty, the act of a friend, not of a servant.

Immediately thereupon Othello calls himself Iago's 'friend' (line 142) for the first time (ironically saying that Iago must be conspiring against him if he won't tell all). Iago manages to make it seem that his actions are, if anything, based on an excess of friendship. There is more than a simple ironic charge in utterances like 'I humbly do beseech you of your pardon / For too much loving you' (III. iii. 212–13). This implies 'I love you really – but I'm destroying you, so I'm pretending to love you. My love is really *too much*, for it's made me jealous of Desdemona and Cassio and forced me to destroy you as well as them – which is too much.' He seems almost to be begging Othello to notice his irony. When Othello acts suspicious of him, Iago takes on the stance of injured friend,[27] saying, 'I'll thank you for this profit, and from hence / I'll love no friend, sith love breeds such offence' (lines 379–80). The double truths here are terrifying – Iago cannot love a friend in a constructive way, and his perverted version of love breeds offence to all. Earlier he had said that he could 'counsel Cassio to this parallel course / Directly to his good' (II. iii. 349–50), thinking this makes him unvillainous. He is *parallel* to friendship, his course apparently good but going to the wrong destination (the term is clearly maritime). So he guides Othello away from love into their demonic friendship, resembling a blood-brotherhood as Othello calls 'O blood, blood, blood!' (III. iii. 451). Iago is as inevitably bound into the new special relationship as Othello. It results in a ceremony of friendship that is more like a marriage than the off-stage ceremony with Desdemona. Iago calls the stars as his witness, and turns himself into Othello's private instrument (in military terms, he should already have been his devoted instrument). He binds the friendship further by sacrificing Cassio to it, saying in anticipation of the murder, 'My friend is dead' (line 474), and ends the ceremony by saying 'I am your own for ever' (line 480), once he has been given the lieutenancy. This echoes Othello's words more than 200 lines previously, immediately after Iago's talk of 'too much loving': 'I am bound to thee for ever' (line 213). A drawn-out process is needed for this, which is surely the grandest ceremony of friendship in all literature. Desdemona is sacrificed to this ultimate male bond, which is wholly destructive.

As far back as Plato's *Lysis*, the doctor was a crucial metaphor and analogy for the friend, and the idea still had currency in Burton's *Anatomy of Melancholy* (see chapter 1, above). When Othello collapses in his fit, Iago crows 'Work on, / My medicine, work!' (IV. i. 44–5). Of course Iago's medicine is really poison, causing rather than curing Othello's sickness, but perhaps there is a sense in which he really thinks he is purging Othello of a disease. The disease is being a 'credulous fool' (line 45), not only in trusting Iago, but in trusting *anyone*. Iago thinks that he is curing Othello of his disease of unconsciousness, but we might consider in this case that consciousness itself is the disease. Iago is less a demon than a creature from a parallel moral universe,[28] an 'Anti-Friend', as Evans calls him.[29] We might now call him a sociopath, capable of manipulating others, but incapable of seeing others' feelings as real; but the diagnosis is inadequate, for this is a sociopath who is fascinated by others' capacity to feel. When Lodovico enquires about Othello's sanity, Iago gnomically replies,

> He's that he is; I may not breathe my censure
> What he might be. If what he might he is not,
> I would to heaven he were! (lines 270–2)

To get the full force of these lines we need to go back to Iago's similarly cryptic statements early in the play. He told Roderigo 'Were I the Moor, I would not be Iago' (I. i. 57) – is there a suggestion therefore that Iago now has swapped identities with the Moor in their demonic friendship? Soon after he also told Roderigo that 'I am not what I am' (line 65): now we may wonder if this condition of divided selfhood has been given to Othello. Iago has been identified as an example of the Elizabethan New Men,[30] who believed they might become anything; he has transferred this onto Othello here. He *might* possibly be mad, but now, Iago says, I have freed him from himself, from his integrated perfect soul, and he *might* have the power to be anything. As a true friend increases his friend's virtues, Iago has broadened the world of possibilities for Othello in turning him into a murderer.

Iago has prompted a certain hysteria of insistence that he is evil, indeed sub- or superhumanly so, an agent of the devil or the devil himself. Modern attempts to understand him have either pathologized him or insisted on his status as an unworrying literary construct. All these efforts seem to me aimed at denying that anything of Iago can be found in normal human beings. Even Coleridge abstracts him in calling him 'a motiveless malignity', but it is Coleridge who gives us the most purchase on why we must acknowledge this thing of darkness as human in identifying his crucial motivation as envy.[31] Coleridge thought deeply about envy, writing in his notebook:

one important part of the Process in the growth of envy is the Self-degradation (a painful, self-referent Feeling) consequent on the first consciousness of the pang – the Obscurity & Darkness of mind from ignorance of the Cause – dim notion that our nature is suddenly altered for the worse.&c.&c.[32]

The process of envy in Iago is a process of the recognition of his own smallness, a recognition that he uncomfortably shares with us. Envy makes us *small*, and we therefore refuse to associate ourselves with it, not least because its inverse and corollary, scornful superiority, makes us disdain it in others. Iago is hated because he is like ourselves at our pettiest, and this pettiness brings down something we admire – and envy – in Othello. John Bayley comes close to this recognition of Iago's human side in saying that 'He is the person known at some time in every community – school, regiment, office, household – who hates quietly and deeply, hates others for being what they are.'[33] At least Iago hates the real Othello rather than an image of him – in this, he is a truer friend than *Twelfth Night*'s Antonio. Most literature asks us to identify with a hero, however flawed. *Othello* is the greatest work to ask us to identify with a villainous coward. Iago is a stark reminder of our own capacity for petty malice and of our fear that we are not the hero of our own life's story. Iago's silence absorbs him wholly into Othello's tragedy – it is the ultimate act of friendly identification.

It is highly significant that this ultimate male bond should emerge in the high-stakes context of a military expedition; such contexts put men's affiliations to other men more vigorously to the test than any other. A soldier trusts in his general and puts a considerable amount of his self-worth into his leader. The relationship is therefore a powerful one and betrayal of it on either side has as much force as the betrayal of a private friendship. Alexander's love for Hephaestion (one of his subordinate generals) is often represented as one of the iconic friendships of the classical world, and the general's relationship with his second-in-command or *aide de camp* is a peculiarly close one. In particular, a lieutenant has to take over his leader's place should he die or be called away: as such, he is something of a second self, in a more practical sense than a private friend can be. To betray one's general, then, is one of the greatest betrayals possible, almost amounting to a self-betrayal. It is much more than a matter of betraying a cause, and becomes a betrayal of all that makes one a man.

Like Iago, Enobarbus in *Antony and Cleopatra* is a lieutenant to an heroic leader. As a subordinate general, his status is higher than Iago's, but his manner sometimes suggests a similar social bearing: like Iago, he has a reputation as a plain-speaking truth-teller. This may seem incompatible with his role as poetic commentator on Cleopatra and Egypt, but his bluff demeanour serves to underpin and validate his grand speech capturing the imaginative appeal of Cleopatra on the barge. His role in the play suggests that the titular heroes' relationship is not a *folie à deux*. The lovers may be absorbed with one another, but Enobarbus is crucial to the way the audience assesses them; in a play that is deeply concerned with reputation, this makes him an important part of an alternative triumvirate. Michael Redgrave commented that 'Enobarbus creates Antony's nobility and Cleopatra's fascination as much as the protagonists can hope to do.'[34] Like Antony, but at a simpler and less political level, Enobarbus is amphibious between the masculine world of Rome and war, and the feminine world of Egypt and luxury. His doubleness is reflected in the fact that Dryden gave Antony two friends in *All for Love*: one the soldier Ventidius, the other the epicene Dolabella. Shakespeare presents us with a deeply ambiguous figure. At times he is a mere follower of Antony (even at times a fool), but at others he takes the role of a senior and trusted *aide de camp*. Like most of Antony's supporters, he is ambivalent about the general's love for Cleopatra. He sarcastically comments on Cleopatra's first entrance, 'Hush, here comes Antony' (i. ii. 79), a theatrically effective joke that raises the question of who the play's true hero is. Both Dryden's Ventidius and his Dolabella have desires for Cleopatra, the former's sternly repressed, the latter's working out into a love triangle that is crucial to the play's plot. Enobarbus is not involved in such a plot, and his attachments are more disinterested. He prides himself on being a truth-teller, almost upsetting the reconciliation of the triumvirs (ii. ii) by his plain speech. He is distanced from political machinations and causes, loyal only to truth and to the man Antony. He can get on with the bluff and honourable Pompey (ii. vi) and with Antony in Egyptian mode, but not with the political triumvirs. At various stages of the play he takes on the roles of chorus, fool, servant and gossip, without ever being defined by them. Only in death, a suicide in a ditch, does he become defined as an honourable Roman: even here, there is the paradox of him finding this role through being a traitor and deserter.

There cannot be true equality and mutuality between Antony and Enobarbus. Antony is of unparalleled significance in Enobarbus's life, but Enobarbus barely registers in Antony's. Cleopatra consumes not only his political alliances but also his military friendships. He absorbs loyalty without giving much return, though no one resents him for that exactly. Enobarbus's betrayal oddly makes Antony recognize him much more than he did when he was loyal. Although Enobarbus did not take offence at it, Antony's comment 'Thou art a soldier only' (II. ii. 107) has clear significance for their relationship. It implies, 'and I am so much more than you', and, even more cuttingly, 'to be a soldier is not very much'. To Antony, his men are somewhat expendable: he even lacks Hal's nominal concern for the rightness of leading them into battle (because it never occurs to him to question it), and is prepared to sacrifice them for the sake of his love. Enobarbus has been taken for granted, but this does not mean that Antony is indifferent to him. Whenever something or someone is brought to his attention he engages his full passionate nature on the matter. He is no butterfly – rather he is a man whose passion can never be divided to attend to more than one thing at once. When the news comes of Enobarbus's desertion, this passionate intensity is engaged. He sends Enobarbus's treasure after him in a doomed but characteristically magnanimous gesture, and adds a message –

> Say that I wish he never find more cause
> To change a master. O, my fortunes have
> Corrupted honest men! Dispatch. Enobarbus! (IV. v. 15–17)

The message itself is more a reproach than a well-wishing. Fear for Enobarbus's fate may also be a component: Enobarbus in the next scene mentions how those who have gone over to Caesar have been killed by him. Antony's private ejaculation is almost a touch of self-awareness – except that Antony blames his 'fortunes' rather than himself. The final cry of Enobarbus's name, though, is heavily loaded: he finally appreciates the value of the honest man, realizes what he has lost, and sees this loss as a true self-reproach. Antony's passionate greatness has made him incapable of friendship and gratitude until too late. Calling the man's name is the only way he can express this mingling of reproach and self-blame that will lead to his own suicide. It is perhaps Antony's truest moment of recognition.

The arrival of the treasure has the effect of pushing Enobarbus to the shame that will soon lead him to death. He takes it as a reproach. The soldier who brings the gold – who is Caesar's follower and therefore may be thought disinterested – says, 'Your emperor / Continues still a Jove' (IV. vi. 28–9), acknowledging Antony's superiority to Caesar in good treatment of his followers and friends – that is, magnanimity. Enobarbus reflects:

> I am alone the villain of the earth,
> And feel I am so most. O Antony,

Thou mine of bounty, how wouldst thou have paid
My better service, when my turpitude
Thou dost so crown with gold! This blows my heart.
If swift thought break it not, a swifter mean
Shall outstrike thought, but thought will do't, I feel.
I fight against thee? No, I will go seek
Some ditch wherein to die; the foul'st best fits
My latter part of life. (IV. vi. 29–38)

Outward signs – the payment of friendship – are the key to Enobarbus's emotional loyalty, but it is still heartfelt; unlike Parolles', his heart is great, and it bursts. Antony is the source of goodness, a *mine*, perhaps with a pun on Enobarbus's inability to possess such a man. Like Antony, he only recognizes the value of their friendship after it has been lost. We have not actually seen Enobarbus's decision to leave Antony: before the arrival of the treasure we only see him contemplating going over to Caesar. Antony's own tragic histrionics after his defeat (IV. ii) were the last cause that might have driven Enobarbus away. It is as if Antony *wants* his men to leave him, thus heightening his own tragedy, refusing to *share* his fame as Enobarbus hoped. A similar suspicion might be entertained regarding Christ's attitude to Judas and Simon Peter. Antony and Christ have an individual greatness that cannot be shared. They therefore cannot be true friends to anyone.

Enobarbus's betrayal of Antony is nobler than Iago's of Othello, and less directly undermines the hero, but it is just as crucial to his own identity. The name Enobarbus, meaning *red-bearded*, suggests Judas Iscariot, the greatest traitor of them all.[35] After his desertion of Mark Antony, he dies in a ditch, the lowest of the low, apparently a suicide; this again recalls Judas and indicates the self-betrayal that is involved in his treachery to Antony. His treachery is incomplete: he merely abandons Antony, and does not ultimately go over to the other side, reproached by Antony's generosity. The minor but parallel figure of Dolabella does go over to Caesar, and is present on stage at the end as Caesar arranges the whole play as a contribution to his own glory. In a play full of betrayals and desertions, Enobarbus's stands out because of his integrity and because he is the audience's point of access to the drama, sharing our ambivalence about Antony and Cleopatra, who are characters of such historical resonance that we cannot quite sympathize with them. Like the audience, he has no time for Octavius and wavers in his loyalty to Antony. Very rarely, though, does he make direct comment on Antony's personality: in the first acts of the play his loyalty is implicit. He tries to do the best for Antony, urging Cleopatra not to join the battle of Actium in person (III. vii), and his military advice is articulate and impeccably sensible. Even after the defeat he will still follow Antony against his better judgement (III. x). It is Antony himself who urges his followers to abandon him, saying, 'let that be left / Which leaves itself' (III. xi. 19–20). Enobarbus in this scene is more Antony than Antony himself; his shift away from Antony is a gradual one. In consoling Cleopatra he tells her that Antony not she is to blame for the defeat at Actium (III. xii), and after this he confronts himself as the most resolutely soliloquizing and therefore thoughtful and accessible character in the play, whose confrontation with honesty is as profound in its way as Iago's:

> Mine honesty and I begin to square.
> The loyalty well held to fools doth make
> Our faith mere folly; yet he that can endure
> To follow with allegiance a fall'n lord
> Does conquer him that did his master conquer,
> And earns a place i' th' story. (III. xiii. 41–6)

Like Cleopatra, he is aware that history and drama are being made, and is motivated by a desire that he should be represented well to future ages. There may be an element of envy of Antony here – he wants to share some of his fame – but it is a productive envy so long as he gains his fame through loyalty. He gains a more defined fame, however, by betraying Antony and becoming, in the play's terms, infamous, though in history's terms he is insignificant, hidden in a ditch. As he is ultimately disloyal, Antony and Enobarbus will not go into the pantheon of great historical friends; but Shakespeare finds a place for the friend, gaining his importance through his ambiguous treachery. Enobarbus is not allowed an operatic suicide like Cleopatra's, or a Roman (if botched) suicide like Antony's. Instead, he almost wills himself to death, leaving himself. He may be hidden from history, but as an honest friend to Antony, rehabilitating the idea of honesty from Iago's abuse of it, he has a place in Shakespeare's story.

The characters in *Antony and Cleopatra* are not only engaged in a competition of power, but also in a competition for theatrical centrality. The critical question of who is the tragic hero is of particular force in this play because of this rivalry for our attention. Fredson Bowers may be right to see Cleopatra as the play's moving spirit and ultimate protagonist, pushing Antony aside,[36] but both heroes' tragic stories are ultimately absorbed into the triumph of Octavius Caesar. Caesar does not have as great a significance in terms of the play's emotional *story*, but in terms of its political *history* he is obviously the most significant figure. This difference between historical importance and theatrical emotional significance is also played out in the character of Enobarbus. Friendship's importance for him, as it is for so many Shakespearean characters, is to give him theatrical significance by association with the truly heroic and significant. It is through friendship with the great, Shakespeare suggests, even though that friendship may be severely compromised, that the ordinary man's life becomes meaningful, both in theatrical terms, and in terms of his own significance to himself. It is also through such characters that we, the audience, gain access to the great and heroic figures who are beyond us. Yet Enobarbus fails Antony (and vice versa), and Iago destroys Othello: friendship between the great man and the ordinary does not necessarily do either any good, but it is through the connections forged here that each finds his full identity.

This dramatic use of friendship is particularly acute in tragedies: in different ways Kent, Horatio, Enobarbus and Iago stand as our proxies on stage, allowing us to feel a connection with the tragic hero, but also suggesting that we keep a proper distance from them, preventing us from easy empathy or identification with these recalcitrant individuals. The contrast between the hero and his friend allows us to see the hero more clearly, and makes us recognize the limitations of dramatic identification with others, as well as allowing non-heroic modes of selfhood to find expression. Far from promoting equalization, dramatic friendship is ultimately a mode of recognizing and respecting human difference.

CHAPTER 9

Conclusion: 'Time must friend or end'

In *Troilus and Cressida*, Pandarus tells his niece that 'time must friend or end' (I. ii. 77–8). This proverbial cliché means little in context, but has some resonance. Idealized and, as we have seen, imaginary perfect friendship is seen as permanent. In dramatic plots, however, friendship is presented as fleetingly impermanent, fragile, illusorily existing in the moment; its value is only fully recognized when it has passed. To be fully realized in a plot it must *end*. Iago's final silence is the ultimate closure of friendship. He has won his place in the story, but in doing so he has cancelled himself out.

Shakespeare's plays show the dependence of even the most apparently self-sufficient individual on other people. Just as the great tragic actor needs bit-part players to focus attention on him and to enable the emergence of his full dramatic range, so the most central character needs his friends and others to situate him in the drama of his life, and to bring out all the harmonics of his selfhood. Louis MacNeice, in his *Autumn Journal*, put this better than anyone:

> Aristotle was right about the Alter Ego
> But wrong to make it only a halfway house:
> Who could expect – or want – to be spiritually self-supporting,
> Eternal self-abuse?
> Why not admit that other people are always
> Organic to the self, that a monologue
> Is the death of language and that a single lion
> Is less himself, or alive, than a dog and another dog?[1]

Yet all dogs are not equal; friendship which relies too much on the concept of equality ultimately makes people less themselves. The plays and characters which centralize friendship are the ones which lead to the most attenuated selves. It is in difference between men – between dogs and lions, as it were – that people come to themselves. Yet the dream of equality is needed to make momentary connections and shape the self. The Humanist ideal of friendship tries to promote a notion of individual integrity, but it is in the recognition of the varieties of human connectedness – and their arbitrariness – that Shakespearean men come to recognize themselves; they recognize their own variety, and the arbitrariness of being themselves. Even as they have most fully asserted themselves, their selfhood becomes a matter of indifference, separated from others, but determined by the fictions of connection.

Notes

I TRUE FRIENDS?

1 For female friendship, see Lilian Faderman, *Surpassing the Love of Men: Romantic Friendship and Love between Women from the Renaissance to the Present* (New York: Morrow, 1981).

2 Stephen Orgel, *Impersonations: The Performance of Gender in Shakespeare's England* (Cambridge: Cambridge University Press, 1997), points out that masculinity and femininity were seen as a continuum, with masculinity something to be attained and preserved. Being a man was something you had to be educated, and dressed, into. See also Bruce R. Smith, *Shakespeare and Masculinity* (Oxford: Oxford University Press, 2001), Coppélia Kahn, *Man's Estate: Masculine Identity in Shakespeare* (Berkeley: University of California Press, 1981), Stephen Greenblatt, 'Fiction and Friction', in *Shakespearean Negotiations* (Oxford: Oxford University Press, 1988).

3 *Between Men: English Literature and Male Homosocial Desire* (New York: Columbia University Press, 1985), p. 45.

4 *Ibid.*, p. 25.

5 *Friends and Lovers: The Phenomenology of Desire in Shakespearean Comedy* (New York: Columbia University Press, 1985), p. 12.

6 *Man's Estate*, p. 1.

7 *Ibid.*, p. 193.

8 Robert Burton, *The Anatomy of Melancholy*, 3 vols. (London: J. M. Dent, [1932]), 3: 23.

9 *Ibid.*, 3: 29.

10 *Between Men*, p. 117.

11 See Diarmaid MacCulloch, *Reformation: Europe's House Divided 1490–1700* (London: Allen Lane, 2003), pp. 647–62.

12 Alan Bray, *The Friend* (Chicago: University of Chicago Press, 2003), p. 41.

13 References are to Thomas Heywood, *A Woman Killed with Kindness*, ed. Brian Scobie (London: A&C Black, 1985).

14 *The Friend*, p. 112.

15 References are to Thomas Middleton, *A Mad World, My Masters and Other Plays*, ed. Michael Taylor (Oxford: Oxford University Press, 1995).

16 Reference is to Philip Massinger, *A New Way to Pay Old Debts*, ed. T. W. Craik (London: A&C Black, 1964).

17 A. W. Price, *Love and Friendship in Plato and Aristotle* (Oxford: Clarendon Press, 1989), p. 131.

18 Laurens J. Mills, *One Soul in Bodies Twain: Friendship in Tudor Literature and Stuart Drama* (Bloomington, IN: Principia Press, 1937), p. 378 and *passim*.

19 Laurie Shannon, *Sovereign Amity: Figures of Friendship in Shakespearean Contexts* (Chicago: University of Chicago Press, 2002), p. 6.

20 *The Works of Plato*, trans. Benjamin Jowett (New York: The Modern Library, 1928), p. 32.

21 *The Works of Francis Bacon*, ed. J. Spedding, R. L. Ellis, and D. D. Heath, 7 vols. (London: Longman's, 1857–74), 6: 390.

22 See Price, *Love and Friendship*, pp. 124–30.

23 Though as Alan Stewart, *Close Readers: Humanism and Sodomy in Early Modern England* (Princeton: Princeton University Press, 1997), and Lisa Jardine, *Erasmus: Man of Letters* (Princeton: Princeton University Press, 1993), have shown, it was sixteenth-century Humanists who constructed the idea of feudalism for their own purposes.

24 Sir Thomas Elyot, *The Boke Named the Governour*, ed. Henry Herbert Stephen Croft, 2 vols. (London, 1880), 2: 122–3. The idea of friendship as sun of man's life is echoed in Walter Dorke, *A Tipe or Figure of Friendship* (1589), B1V.

25 Thomas Churchyard, *A Sparke of Friendship* (1588), sig. C[1]v–C2r.

26 *Songes and Sonnets, written by the Right Honorable Lord Henrie Haward late Earl of Surrey, and others* [aka *Tottel's Miscellany*] (1587 edition), fols. 107v–108r.

27 *The Friend*, p. 136.

28 Arthur F. Marotti, 'Patronage, Poetry and Print', in Cedric C. Brown (ed.), *Patronage, Politics and Literary Traditions in England 1558–1658* (Detroit: Wayne State University Press, 1993), p. 22, notes that writers saw themselves 'as parties to an (albeit unequal) gift-exchange', whose ability to print enabled them to reciprocate their patron's friendly gestures.

29 See Stewart, *Close Readers*, and Jardine, *Erasmus*.

30 See Lorna Hutson, *The Usurer's Daughter: Male Friendship and Fictions of Women in Sixteenth Century England* (London: Routledge, 1994).

31 Francis Bacon, 'Of Followers and Friends', *Works*, 6: 438.

32 Thomas Nashe, *Pierce Pennilesse*, in *Works*, ed. Ronald B. McKerrow, corr. F. P. Wilson, 5 vols. (Oxford, 1958), 2: 176.

33 *Sovereign Amity*.

34 Francis Bacon, 'Of Friendship', *Works*, 6: 443.

35 Allan Bloom, *Shakespeare on Love and Friendship* (Chicago: University of Chicago Press, 2000), p. 110.

36 *The Book of the Courtier*, trans. Thomas Hoby (London: Dent, 1928), p. 119.

37 *Discourse of Ciuill Life*, in Lodowick Bryskett, *Literary Works*, ed. J. H. P. Pafford (Farnborough: Gregg, 1972), p. 136.

38 See Bray, *The Friend*, p. 54.

39 For a full treatment of this effect, rooted in actors' experience of playing Shakespeare's parts, see Jonathan Holmes, *Merely Players: Actors' Accounts of Performing Shakespeare* (London: Routledge, 2004).

40 'Of Friendship', *Works*, 6: 442.

41 See Keith Wrightson, *English Society 1580–1680* (London: Routledge, 1982), pp. 48–55.

42 *The Usurer's Daughter*, pp. 2–3.

43 *Ibid.*, p. 6.

44 Robert C. Evans, *Ben Jonson and the Poetics of Patronage* (London: Associated University Presses, 1989), p. 194.

45 *Anatomy*, 3: 22.

46 *A Tipe or Figure of Friendship*, A3r.

47 *The Four Loves* (London: Fount, 1977), pp. 62–3.

48 References are to John Marston, *The Malcontent and other Plays*, ed. Keith Sturgess (Oxford: Oxford University Press, 1997).

49 *The Four Loves*, p. 63.

50 Alan Bray, 'Homosexuality and the Signs of Male Friendship in Elizabethan England', *History Workshop Journal* 19 (1990), and *Homosexuality in Renaissance England* (London: Gay Men's Press, 1982).

51 Jonathan Goldberg, *Sodometries: Renaissance Texts, Modern Sexualities* (Stanford, CA: Stanford University Press, 1992).

52 *The Homoerotics of Early Modern Drama* (Cambridge: Cambridge University Press, 1997), pp. 1–2.

53 *Ibid.*, p. 12.

54 E.g. Orgel, *Impersonations*, p. 51.

55 See Paul Hammond, *Figuring Sex Between Men from Shakespeare to Rochester* (Oxford: Oxford University Press, 2002), pp. 72–84.

56 *Anxious Masculinity in Early Modern England* (Cambridge: Cambridge University Press, 1996), p. 157.

57 See Bray, 'Signs'.

58 *Between Men*, p. 2.

59 See Wrightson, *English Society*, p. 44 and *passim* for the turnover of population in early modern England.

60 John Donne, *The Complete English Poems* (Harmondsworth: Penguin, 1971), p. 207.

61 Shannon, *Sovereign Amity*, p. 2, pp. 32–4.

62 Joel Fineman, *Shakespeare's Perjured Eye: The Invention of Poetic Subjectivity in the Sonnets* (Berkeley: University of California Press, 1986), p. 25.

63 Shannon, *Sovereign Amity*, p. 98.

64 Friedrich Nietzsche, *Human, All Too Human*, trans. R. J. Hollingdale (Cambridge: Cambridge University Press, 1996), p. 149.

65 Maurice Blanchot, *Friendship*, trans. Elizabeth Rottenberg (Stanford: Stanford University Press, 1971); Jacques Derrida, *Politics of Friendship* (London: Verso, 1997), p. 5.

66 *Human, All Too Human*, p. 370.
67 *Ben Jonson and the Poetics of Patronage*, p. 212.
68 *Shakespeare's Perjured Eye*, p. 5.
69 *Anatomy*, 3: 108.
70 Translated as 'Sympathy', in *The Colloquies of Erasmus*, trans. Craig R. Thompson (Chicago: University of Chicago Press, 1965).
71 Aristotle, *Poetics*, trans. M. E. Hubbard, in *Classical Literary Criticism*, ed. D. A. Russell and M. Winterbottom (Oxford: Oxford University Press, 1989), p. 64.
72 *The Praise of Folly*, in *The Essential Erasmus*, trans. John P. Dolan (New York: New American Library, 1964), p. 112.
73 *Ibid.*, pp. 113–14.
74 *The Colloquies of Erasmus*, p. 527.
75 *Ibid.*, p. 518.

2 MOMENTARY MUTUALITY IN *SHAKESPEARE'S SONNETS*

1 I shall refer to him as the young man rather than as the friend, given that I am trying to establish the nature of the relationship, and calling him the friend would prejudge the issue. The poetic persona of the sequence is clearly not to be absolutely identified with Shakespeare himself, but given the full title *Shakespeare's Sonnets*, printed on the top of each verso sheet in the 1609 edition, it is hard to get away from the insistent suggestion that we are to take 'Shakespeare' as the literary character here, the equivalent of Sidney's 'Astrophel'.
2 *Between Men*, pp. 31, 43.
3 See Heather Dubrow, '"Incertainties now crown themselves assur'd": The Politics of Plotting Shakespeare's Sonnets', in James Schiffer (ed.), *Shakespeare's Sonnets: Critical Essays* (New York: Routledge, 1999). See also Colin Burrow in his edition of *Complete Sonnets and Poems* (Oxford: Oxford University Press, 2002), p. 118, who also makes the valuable point that 'The addressee is a different thing depending on how he or she is addressed, and on how the epithet by which he or she is addressed is inflected in its context. To impose a single scenario on these poems is to deny this vital poetic fact' (p. 123).
4 *Shakespeare's Perjured Eye*, p. 25 and *passim*.
5 Plato's works were available in Ficino's Latin translation, e.g. *Diuini Platonis opera omnia, Marsilio Ficino interprete* (1588).
6 Ronald A. Sharp, *Friendship and Literature* (Durham, NC: Duke University Press, 1986), p. 7.
7 See, for example, Helen Vendler, *The Art of Shakespeare's Sonnets* (Cambridge, MA: Harvard University Press, 1997), p. 103, and her identification of some poems as 'reply poems'. Ilona Bell, ' "That which thou hast done": Shakespeare's Sonnets and *A Lover's Complaint*', in Schiffer (ed.), *Sonnets: Critical Essays*, p. 466, argues that 'In the Sonnets Shakespeare "dialogued for" the young man, anticipating his response, blurring the identities of poet and

lover, expressing his feelings ("my love") so as to imply that the young man ("my love") acts as Shakespeare wills, even though Shakespeare always seems to succumb to the young man's will.'

8 George T. Wright, 'The Silent Speech of Shakespeare's Sonnets', in Schiffer (ed.), *Sonnets: Critical Essays*, p. 136, argues that 'these sonnets, unlike many others by other writers, are more about absence than presence, more about the absence – experienced, feared, or forecast – of their radiant center than about the enjoyment of its presence, though there is enough testimony about its presence to make its absence seem all the more poignant.'

9 *Plato and Aristotle on Love and Friendship*, p. 91.

10 *Lysis*, in *The Works of Plato*, the Jowett translation, ed. Irwin Edman (New York: Simon & Schuster, 1928), p. 6.

11 Aristotle, *The Nicomachean Ethics*, 9. 8, trans. Terence Irwin (Indianapolis: Hackett Publishing, 1985).

12 Price's Afterword is worth quoting at some length: 'Aristotle's ideal is mutual and reciprocal: each owes his actions to the other. Effectiveness may come just of joint action: two shoulders may move a wheel too heavy for one. Here their contributions may be identical, though both are necessary. Success may also come of the variations in ingenuity or experience that differentiate even the closest and most equal of friends: good men "are thought to become better too by their activities and by improving each other; for from each other they take the stamp of the characteristics that please them – whence the saying 'Fine deeds from fine men'" (9. 12. 1172a 10–14). And here the causal play is two-way: fine men also come from fine deeds as co-operation becomes education, so that each partly owes to the other not only his actions but his qualities. In such ways, all the features that constitute acting well – doing the good thing, with knowledge out of choice, and out of a firm and stable character (2. 4. 1105a 28–33) – may be owed by each to the other, so that their *eudaimonia* may be said to overlap. Each, in pursuing his own *eudaimonia*, will in part be pursuing that of the other', *Plato and Aristotle on Love and Friendship*, p. 267. He sees Shakespeare as expressing this ideal in *A Midsummer Night's Dream*, III. ii. 201–14.

13 References are to *Shakespeare's Sonnets*, ed. Katherine Duncan-Jones (London: Arden Shakespeare, 1997).

14 *The Art of Shakespeare's Sonnets*, p. 162.

15 Fineman, *Shakespeare's Perjured Eye*, p. 151.

16 *Complete Sonnets and Poems*, p. 442.

17 Lars Engle, ' "I am that I am": Shakespeare's Sonnets and the Economy of Shame', in Schiffer (ed.), *Sonnets: Critical Essays*, p. 193.

18 'To Mr T. W.' ('All hail, sweet poet'), lines 9–11, *Complete English Poems*, p. 208.

19 'The Storm', 1–2, *Complete English Poems*, p. 197.

20 J. B. Leishman, *Themes and Variations in Shakespeare's Sonnets* (London: Hutchinson, 1961), pp. 95–101.

21 *The Art of Shakespeare's Sonnets*, p. 135.

22 *Ibid.*, p. 60 and *passim.*

23 See Price, *Plato and Aristotle on Love and Friendship*, p. 17.

24 *The Art of Shakespeare's Sonnets*, p. 103.

25 See Wilfrid Hooper, 'The Tudor Sumptuary Laws', *English Historical Review* 30 (1915), 433–49.

26 Margreta de Grazia, 'The Scandal of Shakespeare's Sonnets', in Schiffer (ed.), *Sonnets: Critical Essays*, p. 101, argues that in the *Sonnets* 'Fair is the distinguishing attribute of the dominant class.'

27 G. W. F. Hegel, *Phenomenology of Spirit*, trans. A. V. Miller (Oxford: Clarendon Press, 1977), pp. 115ff.

28 *The Sonnets and A Lover's Complaint*, ed. John Kerrigan (London: Penguin, 1986), p. 287.

29 *The Art of Shakespeare's Sonnets*, p. 395.

30 'The Name of the Rose: Christian Figurality and Shakespeare's Sonnets', in Schiffer (ed.), *Sonnets: Critical Essays*, p. 253.

31 See Goldberg, *Sodometries*.

32 'Hal's Desire, Shakespeare's Idaho', in Nigel Wood (ed.), *Henry IV, Parts One and Two* (Buckingham: Open University Press, 1995), p. 41.

33 In *The Boke Named the Governour*; see chapter 4, below.

34 *The Force of Poetry* (Oxford: Oxford University Press, 1984), p. 231.

35 'To Mr T. W.' ('Haste thee harsh verse'), line 6, *Complete English Poems*, p. 209.

36 It is significant that George Herbert continually regards Christ as a *friend* in *The Temple* (pub. 1633 – e.g. 'The Holdfast', 'Love Unknown').

37 Vendler, *The Art of Shakespeare's Sonnets*, p. 278, notes that this poem's 'vocabulary approaches the theological'.

38 *Shakespeare's Sonnets*, ed. Stephen Booth (New Haven: Yale University Press, 1977), p. 236.

39 I capitalize to indicate that this is an omniscient, perfect, monotheistic god rather than a flawed polytheistic one.

40 John Donne, *The Complete English Poems*, p. 233.

41 John Kerrigan (ed.), *Sonnets*, p. 26, notes that Shakespeare 'takes the path towards tautology, through "you alone are you" to "you are you". Shakespeare has few mannerisms, but his habit of celebrating particularity and being through this kind of reflexive structure is one of them.' This mannerism is based, I think, on his idolatry.

42 *Lysis*, p. 20.

43 This gives a clear basis for Fineman's view that 'what allows the poet to commit himself to what is, at least in some respects, a cosmeticizing, *because* idealizing, rhetoric is that his poetry is itself intended, as itself says, to make up for, rather than to point up, the distance between what is ideal and what is the mundane actualization of the ideal', *Shakespeare's Perjured Eye*, p. 60.

44 *Shakespeare's Sonnets*, ed. Duncan-Jones, p. 363.

45 *Between Men*, p. 43.

46 Gerard Manley Hopkins, *Poetry and Prose*, ed. Walford Davies (London: J. M. Dent, 1998), p. 98.

47 *The Poems of Andrew Marvell*, ed. Nigel Smith (London: Longman, 2003), pp. 109–11.

3 FRIENDS AND BROTHERS

1 *The Friend, passim.*

2 Michel de Montaigne, *The Essayes*, translated by John Florio, 3 vols. (London: Everyman, 1928), 1: 197.

3 *The Boke Named the Governour*, 2: 164. Based on *de Amicitia*, cap. 4.

4 'Of Followers and Friends', *Works*, 6: 495.

5 *Ibid.*, 6.

6 Edmund Spenser, *The Faerie Queene*, ed. A. C. Hamilton *et al.*, 2nd edition (London: Longman, 2001).

7 Michel de Montaigne, *Essayes*, 1: 197.

8 *Ibid.*, 1: 204.

9 *Toxaris*, ¶ 37 *Lucian*, with translations by A. M. Harmon, K. Kilburn and M. D. McLeod, 5 vols. (London: W. Heinemann, 1913–67), 5: 162.

10 *Toxaris*, ¶ 62, 5: 204.

11 *Works*, 6: 390.

12 References to Cyril Tourneur, *The Atheist's Tragedy*, ed. Brian Morris and Roma Gill (London: A&C Black, 1976).

13 *The Colloquies of Erasmus*, p. 520.

14 William Kerrigan, 'Female Friends and Fraternal Enemies in *As You Like It*', in Valeria Finucci and Regina Schwarz (eds.), *Desire in the Renaissance: Psychoanalysis and Culture* (Princeton: Princeton University Press, 1994), p. 184.

15 Thomas Kelly, 'Shakespeare's Romantic Heroes: Orlando Reconsidered', *SQ* 24 (1973), 12–24, p. 16.

16 *Shakespeare: The Invention of the Human* (New York: Riverhead Books, 1998), p. 491.

17 Michael Billington, Review of *Lear* directed by Bill Alexander, *The Guardian*, 2 July 2004, calls the role 'almost unplayable'.

18 See Bray, *The Friend*, p. 112.

19 Patricia Parker, 'Elder and Younger: The Opening Scene of *The Comedy of Errors*', *SQ* 34 (1983), 325–7.

20 Judiana Lawrence, 'Natural Bonds and Artistic Coherence in the Ending of *Cymbeline*', *SQ* 35 (1984), 440–60, p. 444.

4 LOVE AND FRIENDSHIP

1 It is these plots that are the chief interest of Mills, *One Soul in Bodies Twain*.

2 *Anatomy of Melancholy*, 3: 263.

3 Pamela Mason (ed.), *Shakespeare: Early Comedies – A Casebook* (Basingstoke: Macmillan, 1995), p. 23.

4 *The Usurer's Daughter*, p. 57.

5 *The Boke Named the Governour*, 2: 161–2.

6 *Sovereign Amity*, p. 43.

7 *Euphues: The Anatomy of Wyt*, in *The Complete Works of John Lyly*, ed. R. Warwick Bond, 3 vols. (Oxford: Clarendon Press, 1902), 1: 185.

8 *One Soul in Bodies Twain*, p. 187.

9 Richard A. McCabe, 'Wit, Eloquence and Wisdom in *Euphues: The Anatomy of Wit*', *SP* 81 (1984), 299–324.

10 Theodore L. Steinberg, 'The Anatomy of *Euphues*', *SEL* 17 (1977), 27–38, p. 38.

11 *The Usurer's Daughter, passim*.

12 And her allegorical name (meaning wisdom) implies that she isn't really to be taken as a person.

13 William Rosky, '*The Two Gentlemen of Verona* as Burlesque', *ELR* 12 (1982), 210–19, p. 215.

14 *The Usurer's Daughter, passim*.

15 Shannon, *Sovereign Amity*, p. 6.

16 Shannon, *Sovereign Amity*, p. 187, argues that these lines reflect Polixenes' 'nostalgia for private status'.

17 Nora Johnson, 'Ganymedes and Kings: Staging Male Homosexual Desire in *The Winter's Tale*', *Sh. St.* 26 (1998), 187–217.

18 *Shakespeare: The Poet and his Plays* (London: Methuen, 1997), p. 341.

19 *Sovereign Amity*, chapter 6.

20 Introduction to *The Two Gentlemen of Verona*, ed. William Carroll (London: Arden Shakespeare, 2004), p. 33.

21 E. M. Waith, 'Shakespeare and Fletcher on Love and Marriage', *Sh. St.* 18 (1986), 235–50.

22 Alan Stewart, '"Near Akin": The Trials of Friendship in *The Two Noble Kinsmen*', in Jennifer Richards and James Knowles (eds.), *Shakespeare's Late Plays* (Edinburgh: Edinburgh University Press, 1999), pp. 58, 71.

23 Laurie J. Shannon, 'Emilia's Argument: Friendship and "Human Title in *The Two Noble Kinsmen*', *ELH* 64 (1997), 657–82, p. 672, rightly sees these lines as 'delicately erotic', but that does not necessarily imply lesbianism as Richard Malette, 'Same-Sex Erotic Friendship in *The Two Noble Kinsmen*', *Renaissance Drama* 26 (1995), 29–52, argues. Even the erotic banter between Emilia and her woman in II. ii only suggests a prurient interest (on the part of the male spectator and the spectating Palamon and Arcite) in Emilia's burgeoning sexuality. Hugh Richmond, 'Performance as Criticism: *The Two Noble Kinsmen*' in Charles H. Frey (ed.), *Shakespeare, Fletcher and 'The Two Noble Kinsmen'* (Columbia: University of Missouri Press, 1989), argues that any homoeroticism does not come across on the stage.

24 Barry Weller, '*The Two Noble Kinsmen*, the Friendship Tradition, and the Flight from Eros', in Frey (ed.), *Shakespeare, Fletcher*, p. 100.

25 Donald K. Kendrick, '"Be Rough With Me": The Collaborative Arenas of *The Two Noble Kinsmen*', in Frey (ed.), *Shakespeare, Fletcher*, p. 63.

26 Derrida, *Politics of Friendship*, p. 261.

27 Weller, '*The Two Noble Kinsmen*', p. 108.

28 This has been seen as a parallel to the problem of distinguishing between the play's two authors. See Kendrick, '"Be Rough With Me"', p. 48.

29 See Richmond, 'Performance as Criticism: *The Two Noble Kinsmen*', in Frey (ed.), *Shakespeare, Fletcher*, p. 167.

30 In Anthony Trollope's *Phineas Finn, The Irish Member* (1869), we see a similarly perverse chivalry, when the hero is prepared to fight a duel for pride's sake, though his friend clearly loves Violet Effingham and he does not.

31 '*The Two Noble Kinsmen*', p. 93.

32 *Poetics*, p. 64.

33 References to *The Dramatic Works in the Beaumont and Fletcher Canon*, ed. Fredson Bowers, 10 vols. (Cambridge: Cambridge University Press, 1966–96).

5 SERVANTS

1 See Bray, *The Friend*, pp. 146–52.

2 See Ann Kussmaul, *Servants in Husbandry in Early Modern England* (Cambridge: Cambridge University Press, 1981).

3 Thomas Moisan, ' "Knock Me Here Soundly": Comic Misprision and Class Consciousness in Shakespeare', *SQ* 42 (1991), 276–90, pp. 279–80.

4 Francis E. Dolan, 'The Subordinate(s) Plot: Petty Treason and the Forms of Domestic Rebellion', *SQ* 43 (1992), 317–40, p. 324.

5 A. D. Nuttall, *Timon of Athens* (London: Harvester Wheatsheaf, 1989), p. 88.

6 References are to *The Collected Works of Richard Edwards*, ed. Ros King (Manchester: Manchester University Press, 2001).

7 Elliot Krieger, *A Marxist Study of Shakespeare's Comedies* (London: Macmillan, 1979), p. 3.

8 George Meredith, *The Ordeal of Richard Feverel* (London: Chapman and Hall, 1889), p. 325.

9 Mark Thornton Burnett, *Masters and Servants in English Renaissance Drama and Culture: Authority and Obedience* (Basingstoke: Macmillan, 1997), p. 79.

10 *Ibid.*, p. 81.

11 E. M. W. Tillyard, *Shakespeare's Early Comedies* (London: Chatto & Windus, 1965), p. 92.

12 See Carroll, Introduction to *The Two Gentlemen of Verona*, p. 125.

13 Maurice Hunt, 'Slavery, English Servitude, and *The Comedy of Errors*', *ELR* 27 (1997), 31–56, p. 39.

14 References are to Ben Jonson, *Every Man in His Humour*, ed. Robert N. Watson, 2nd edition (London: A&C Black, 1998).

15 William Rowley, Thomas Dekker and John Ford, *The Witch of Edmonton*, ed. Peter Corbin and Douglas Sedge (Manchester: Manchester University Press, 1999).

16 William Gifford in his General Introduction to Jonson's *Works* (1816) argues that 'Mosca is not the servant, but the humble friend of Volpone.' Reprinted in Jonas Barish (ed.), *Jonson: Volpone: A Casebook* (Basingstoke: Macmillan, 1992), p. 48.

17 Brian F. Tyson, 'Ben Jonson's Black Comedy: A Connection between *Othello* and *Volpone*', *SQ* 29 (1978), 60–6.

18 References are to Ben Jonson, *Volpone*, ed. Brian Parker, revised edition (Manchester: Manchester University Press, 1999).

19 See Goldberg, *Sodometries*.

20 Laurie E. Maguire, *Studying Shakespeare: A Guide to the Plays* (Oxford: Blackwell, 2004), p. 8.

21 References are to Christopher Marlowe, *The Jew of Malta*, ed. N. W. Bawcutt (Manchester: Manchester University Press, 1978).

22 References are to Christopher Marlowe, *Doctor Faustus: A- and B-Texts*, ed. David Bevington and Eric Rasmussen (Manchester: Manchester University Press, 1993), A-Text.

23 Judith Weil, '"Full Possession": Service and Slavery in *Doctor Faustus*', in Paul Whitfield White (ed.), *Marlowe, History and Sexuality* (New York, 1998), p. 148.

24 Helen Gardner, 'The Theme of Damnation in *Doctor Faustus*', in John Jump (ed.), *Marlowe: Doctor Faustus – A Casebook* (Basingstoke: Macmillan, 1969), pp. 97–8.

25 David Lucking, 'Our Devils Now are Ended: A Comparative Analysis of *The Tempest* and *Doctor Faustus*', *Dalhousie Review* 80 (2000), 151–67.

26 Krieger, *A Marxist Study*, p. 55.

27 Derek Cohen, 'The Culture of Slavery: Caliban and Ariel', *Dalhousie Review* 76 (1996), 153–75, argues that their lack of rights and wages makes Caliban and Ariel slaves, rather than servants (p. 154). Andrew Gurr, 'Industrious Ariel and Idle Caliban', in Jean-Pierre Maquerlot and Michèle Willems (eds.), *Travel and Drama in Shakespeare's Time* (Cambridge: Cambridge University Press, 1996), p. 198, points out that 'The peculiar difference in the relationships is that in Ariel's case but not Caliban's it is not perpetual slavery but has a defined limit.' He goes on to argue that in both cases, they are something like apprentices.

28 Empson, *Some Versions of Pastoral* (London: Chatto & Windus, 1935), p. 17.

29 Gurr, 'Industrious Ariel and Idle Caliban', p. 204, on the other hand, argues that Caliban 'is a servant and needs to continue in service', hence his desire to 'seek for grace' from Prospero. It is, however, unclear whether Caliban will return to Milan as a servant, or stay alone on the island. Perhaps he will serve the newly freed Ariel. Jonathan Bate, 'Caliban and Ariel Write Back', in Catherine M. S. Alexander and Stanley Wells, (eds.), *Shakespeare and Race* (Cambridge: Cambridge University Press, 2000), p. 175, observes that 'We don't know where Caliban goes at the end of the play, but we do know that Ariel is free and that the island will be his again.' Another possibility is that he will be shown off as a freak: Antonio says that he is 'no doubt marketable'

(v. i. 266), and Antonio will presumably be looking for a way to make a living now that he is no longer a duke.

30 Shannon, *Sovereign Amity*, pp. 48–9, argues that the true friend in the Renaissance is registered by his speech, particularly 'by its acidity in a conflict situation'. But in a play we can hardly react emotionally to this as a mark of friendship; rather, we see it as a sign that he is not a flatterer, whilst also holding his intemperance and attention-seeking in mind.

31 Shannon, *Sovereign Amity*, p. 192, observes that in Plutarch 'the predominant metaphor for the friend is that of a medical doctor'.

32 *The Yale Edition of the Works of Samuel Johnson*, 16 vols. (1958–), vol. 8, *Johnson on Shakespeare*, ed. Arthur Sherbo, p. 675, note to these lines.

33 *King Lear*, ed. R. A. Foakes (London: Arden Shakespeare, 1997), p. 231, note to these lines.

34 A. C. Bradley, *Shakespearean Tragedy: Lectures on 'Hamlet', 'Othello', 'King Lear', 'Macbeth'*, 3rd edition (Basingstoke: Macmillan, 1992), p. 269.

35 A. C. Bradley, *Shakespearean Tragedy*, p. 220, wonders 'Why does Kent so carefully preserve his incognito till the last scene? He says he does it for an important purpose, but what the purpose is we have to guess.' His purpose is, at least in part, self-dramatizing. Hugh Maclean, 'Disguise in *King Lear*: Kent and Edgar', *SQ* 11 (1960), 49–54, argues, p. 54, that Kent has become a 'prisoner' of his own disguise.

6 POLITICAL FRIENDSHIP

1 Elements of this chapter appear in my essay 'Favourites in Shakespeare', in a forthcoming volume edited by Richard A. McCabe and David Womersley (University of Delaware Press).

2 See Peter Saccio, *Shakespeare's English Kings: History, Chronicle and Drama*, 2nd edition (Oxford: Oxford University Press, 2000), p. 235.

3 *Sovereign Amity*, p. 184.

4 'Of Friendship', *Works*, 6: 442.

5 In line 20, I make use of the F rather than the Q reading, 'Cosin (Cosin)' rather than 'Coosens Coosin;' I think this makes more sense; Bolingbroke is Richard's cousin, and Aumerle's. All three are bound in bonds of kinship, which the repetition stresses almost to absurdity.

6 E.g. *A Declaration of the True Causes of the Great Troubles, Presupposed to be Intended Against the Realm of England* (1592).

7 References are to Christopher Marlowe, *Edward the Second*, ed. Charles R. Forker (Manchester: Manchester University Press, 1999).

8 References are to *Woodstock: A Moral History*, ed. A. P. Rossiter (London: Chatto & Windus, 1946).

9 A. L. French, '*Richard II* and the Woodstock Murder', *SQ* 22 (1971), 337–44.

10 Introduction to *Richard II*, ed. Charles R. Forker (London: Arden Shakespeare, 2002), p. 161.

11 *Ibid.*, p. 47.

12 Richard Helgerson, '*1 Henry IV* and *Woodstock*', *NQ* 23 (1976), 153–4, p. 154, suggests that Falstaff's desire for this post may be derived from the use of Tresilian as lawless Lord Chief Justice in *Woodstock*.

13 Introduction to *Henry IV Part 1* (London: Arden Shakespeare, 2002), p. 46.

14 In the *Nicomachean Ethics*. For a full exploration of this idea, see Price, *Love and Friendship*, and chapter 1, above.

15 *Shakespeare on Love and Friendship*, p. 132.

16 David Womersley, 'Why Is Falstaff Fat?' *RES* 47 (1996), 1–22, p. 21.

17 *Works*, 7: 521.

18 See Phyllis Rackin, *Stages of History: Shakespeare's English Chronicles* (London: Routledge, 1991), p. 227.

19 See Kiernan Ryan, *Shakespeare*, 2nd edition (London: Harvester Wheatsheaf, 1995), p. 90.

20 Geoffrey Bullough (ed.), *Narrative and Dramatic Sources of Shakespeare*, 8 vols. (London: Routledge & Kegan Paul, 1957–75), 7: 496.

21 *Works*, 6: 443; see chapter 1, above.

22 *The Boke Named the Governour*, 2: 163.

23 *The First Quarto of Hamlet*, ed. Kathleen O. Irace (Cambridge: Cambridge University Press, 1998), scene 14.

24 *Works*, 6: 442.

25 Dennis Kay, ' "To hear the rest untold": Shakespeare's Postponed Endings', *RQ* 37 (1984), 207–27.

26 James Shapiro, *1599: A Year in the Life of William Shakespeare* (London: Faber & Faber, 2005), p. 335.

7 FELLOWSHIP

1 Montaigne, 'On Friendship', *The Complete Essays*, trans. M. A. Screech (Harmondsworth: Penguin, 1993), p. 207. Montaigne's actual word is 'société', and Florio translates it as 'societie'. I have used the word chosen for the translation by M. A. Screech as it avoids the ambiguity of the word *society*. It is also used by Bacon, 'Of Friendship', *Works*, 6: 437.

2 *The Four Loves*, p. 61.

3 *Ibid.*, p. 55.

4 Nuttall, *Timon of Athens*, p. xvii, observes that 'in *Timon of Athens* the drama is purged of all natural relations of affection, leaving instead the cold structures of an extreme yet somehow vacuous liberality, succeeded by an inhuman and therefore unsympathetic misanthropy'.

5 G. Wilson Knight, *The Wheel of Fire: Interpretations of Shakespearian Tragedy with three New Essays*, 4th edition (London: Methuen, 1949), p. 235.

6 *Timon of Athens*, ed. Karl Klein (Cambridge: Cambridge University Press, 2001), p. 35.

7 *Sovereign Amity*, p. 1.

8 'Timon of Athens: The Iconography of False Friendship', *HLQ* 43 (1980), 181–200, p. 186.

9 'Timon of Athens: An Unfinished Play', *RES* 18 (1942), 270–83, p. 282.

10 'Timon of Athens', *SQ* 12 (1961), 3–20, p. 15.

11 *Timon of Athens*, Introduction, p. 11.

12 *Timon*, p. 41.

13 *Ibid.*, p. 127.

14 For Shakespeare's collaboration with Middleton on *Timon*, see *Timon of Athens*, ed. John Jowett (Oxford: Oxford University Press, 2004), Introduction.

15 *Timon*, p. 40, see also 108, where he is called 'that most sociable of misanthropes'.

16 References to Ben Jonson, *Epicene*, ed. Richard Dutton (Manchester: Manchester University Press, 2003).

17 See Andrew Gurr, *Playgoing in Shakespeare's London*, 2nd edition (Cambridge: Cambridge University Press, 1996).

18 Adrian Streete, 'Charity and Law in *Love's Labour's Lost*: A Calvinist Analogue', *NQ* 247 (2002), 224–5, notes that there is a 'diffuse' influence of Calvin's thought at work in the play.

19 See Cyrus Hoy, '*Love's Labour's Lost* and the Nature of Comedy', *SQ* 13 (1962), 31–40.

20 David Bevington, '"Jack Hath Not Jill": Failed Courtship in Lyly and Shakespeare', *Sh. Surv.* 42 (1990), 1–13, p. 9.

21 Herbert McArthur, 'Romeo's Loquacious Friend', *SQ* 10 (1959), 35–44, p. 44.

22 Joseph A. Porter, *Shakespeare's Mercutio: His History and Drama* (Chapel Hill: University of North Carolina Press, 1988), pp. 150–1.

23 *Jew of Malta*, 1. ii. 219–22.

24 See Hutson, *The Usurer's Daughter, passim.*

25 Lorna Hutson argues that 'it is the Jew, with his murderous insistence that he may "be assured" of Antonio's bond (1. iii. 26), who personifies the anxiety that is always latent in the idea of *amicitia* – the anxiety that the "love" between like-minded men will not be able to sustain the pressure of the uncertainty, the strategic lack of assurance, that contributes vitally to the rhetorical, and therefore the economic success of their collective endeavour', *The Usurer's Daughter*, p. 228.

26 The location is not absolutely clear (Hal's apartment being suggested by Theobald), but it is not Eastcheap – see line 187.

27 William Empson, *Essays on Shakespeare*, ed. David B. Pirie (Cambridge: Cambridge University Press, 1986), p. 41.

28 See Matt Ridley, *The Origins of Virtue* (London: Viking, 1996), pp. 161–2.

29 *Some Versions of Pastoral*, p. 43.

8 FALSE FRIENDSHIP AND BETRAYAL

1 Jules Rothman, 'A Vindication of Parolles', *SQ* 23 (1972), 183–96: p. 183.

2 David Ellis, 'Finding a Role for Parolles', *EC* 39 (1989), 289–304.

3 'A Vindication of Parolles', p. 189.

4 J. Dennis Huston, '"Some Stain of Soldier": The Functions of Parolles in *All's Well that Ends Well*', *SQ* 21 (1970), 431–8, p. 436.

5 See R. J. Schork, 'The Many Masks of Parolles', *PQ* 76 (1997), 263–69, for the clever balance of New Comedy roles that Parolles plays.

6 David Scott Kastan, '*All's Well that Ends Well* and the Limits of Comedy', *ELH* 52 (1985) 575–89, p. 579.

7 Joseph Pequigney, 'The Two Antonios and Same-Sex Love in *Twelfth Night* and *The Merchant of Venice*', *ELR* 22 (1992), 201–21, is right to see homoerotic desire on Antonio's part, but is unjustified in his assertion that the men are lovers.

8 Pequigney, 'The Two Antonios', p. 205, argues that he uses a false name to cover up an illicit love affair, but the stranded man's use of a false name to his host is a romance trope that goes back to the *Odyssey*.

9 Some productions go so far as to have the men in bed together: see Stanley Wells, *Looking for Sex in Shakespeare* (Cambridge: Cambridge University Press, 2004), pp. 77–8.

10 Krieger, *A Marxist Study of Shakespeare's Comedies*, pp. 112–13, regards Antonio as literally a servant, and thus rather downplays the significance of their friendship.

11 Laurie E. Osborne, 'Antonio's Pardon', *SQ* 45 (1994), 108–14.

12 Pequigney, 'The Two Antonios', p. 206, fondly imagines that Sebastian, Olivia and Antonio can all go off arm in arm towards their new '*ménage à trois*'.

13 'Or What You Will', *EC* 35 (1985), 294–314, p. 297.

14 *Ibid.*, p. 306.

15 *Ibid.*, p. 312.

16 Appendix to *Othello*, ed. E. A. J. Honigmann (London: Arden Shakespeare, 1997), pp. 346–9. It is just possible, as Honigmann suggests, that the two plays were produced in the same season: they have remarkably similar casting demands.

17 Robert C. Evans, 'Friendship in Shakespeare's *Othello*', *Ben Jonson Journal* 6 (1999), 109–46, p. 131.

18 This is an example of what John Bayley calls Iago's 'kidding on the level', *Shakespeare and Tragedy* (London: Routledge & Kegan Paul, 1981), p. 217.

19 For the role of this word, see William Empson, *The Structure of Complex Words* (London: Chatto & Windus, 1951), pp. 218–49.

20 I prefer here the reading of the Quarto; the Folio reads 'cause'.

21 See Elyot, *The Boke Named the Governour*, p. 163, and chapter 4, above.

22 Introduction to *Othello*, ed. Norman Sanders (Cambridge: Cambridge University Press, 1984), p. 8.

23 *Structure*, p. 222.

24 Mills, *One Soul*, p. 283

25 Evans, 'Friendship', p. 122.

26 *Between Men*, p. 2.

27 See Evans, 'Friendship', p. 139, for an excellent analysis of the use of friendship tropes in this scene.

28 For a discussion of Iago as devil, see Leah Scragg, 'Iago – Vice or Devil?' *Sh. Surv.* 21 (1968), 53–68.

29 Evans, 'Friendship', p. 123. See also his excellent analysis of friendship and its relevance to IV. i in 'Flattery in Shakespeare's *Othello*: The Relevance of Plutarch and Sir Thomas Elyot', *Comparative Drama* 35 (2001), 1–41.

30 Paulette Michel-Michot, 'Sir Walter Raleigh as a Source for the Character of Iago', *English Studies* 50 (1969), 85–9.

31 Jonathan Bate (ed.), *The Romantics on Shakespeare* (Harmondsworth: Penguin, 1992), p. 146.

32 *Coleridge's Notebooks: A Selection*, ed. Seamus Perry (Oxford: Oxford University Press, 2002), p. 41.

33 *Shakespeare and Tragedy*, p. 217.

34 Cit. Allyson P. Newton, '"At the Very Heart of Loss": Shakespeare's Enobarbus and the Rhetoric of Remembering', *Renaissance Papers* (1995), 81–91, p. 81.

35 See R. MacG. Dawson, 'But Why Enobarbus?' *NQ* 34 (1987), 216–17, for a discussion of Enobarbus's roots in the miracle plays' depiction of Judas.

36 'The Concept of Single or Dual Protagonists in Shakespeare's Tragedies', *Renaissance Papers* (1982), 27–33.

9 CONCLUSION: 'TIME MUST FRIEND OR END'

1 Louis MacNeice, *Collected Poems* (London: Faber & Faber, 1979), p. 135.

Bibliography

TEXTS OF SHAKESPEARE'S TIME AND EARLIER

Anon., *A Declaration of the True Causes of the Great Troubles, Presupposed to be Intended Against the Realm of England* (1592) [aka *Leicester's Commonwealth*].

Anon., *Woodstock: A Moral History*, ed. A. P. Rossiter (London: Chatto & Windus, 1946).

Aristotle, *The Nicomachean Ethics*, trans. Terence Irwin (Indianapolis: Hackett Publishing, 1985).

Bacon, Francis, *Works*, ed. J. Spedding, R. L. Ellis and D. D. Heath, 7 vols. (London: Longman's, 1857–74).

Beaumont, Francis and Fletcher, John, *The Dramatic Works in the Beaumont and Fletcher Canon*, ed. Fredson Bowers, 10 vols. (Cambridge: Cambridge University Press, 1966–96).

Bryskett, Lodowick, *Literary Works*, ed. J. H. P. Pafford (Farnborough: Gregg, 1972).

Burton, Robert, *The Anatomy of Melancholy*, 3 vols. (London: J. M. Dent, [1932]).

Castiglione, Baldessare, *The Book of the Courtier*, trans. Thomas Hoby (London: Dent, 1928).

Churchyard, Thomas, *A Sparke of Friendship* (London: [J. Windet], 1588).

Donne, John, *The Complete English Poems* (Harmondsworth: Penguin, 1971).

Dorke, Walter, *A Tipe or Figure of Friendship* (London: T. Orwin and H. Kirkham, 1589).

Edwards, Richard, *The Collected Works of Richard Edwards*, ed. Ros King (Manchester: Manchester University Press, 2001).

Elyot, Sir Thomas, *The Boke Named the Governour*, ed. Henry Herbert Stephen Croft, 2 vols. (London, 1880).

Erasmus, Desiderius, *The Colloquies of Erasmus*, trans. Craig R. Thompson (Chicago: University of Chicago Press, 1965).

The Essential Erasmus, trans. John P. Dolan (New York: New American Library, 1964).

Heywood, Thomas, *A Woman Killed with Kindness*, ed. Brian Scobie (London: A&C Black, 1985).

Jonson, Ben, *Epicene*, ed. Richard Dutton (Manchester: Manchester University Press, 2003).

Every Man in His Humour, ed. Robert N. Watson, 2nd edition (London: A&C Black, 1998).

Volpone, ed. Brian Parker, revised edition (Manchester: Manchester University Press, 1999).

Works, 11 vols., ed. C. H. Herford and Percy and Evelyn Simpson (Oxford: Clarendon Press, 1925–52).

Kyd, Thomas, *The Spanish Tragedy*, ed. Philip Edwards (London: Methuen, 1959).

Lucian, *Lucian*, with translations by A. M. Harmon, K. Kilburn and M. D. McLeod, 5 vols. (London: W. Heinemann, 1913–67).

Lyly, John, *The Complete Works of John Lyly*, ed. R. Warwick Bond, 3 vols. (Oxford: Clarendon Press, 1902).

Marlowe, Christopher, *Doctor Faustus: A- and B- Texts*, ed. David Bevington and Eric Rasmussen (Manchester: Manchester University Press, 1993).

Edward the Second, ed. Charles R. Forker (Manchester: Manchester University Press, 1999).

The Jew of Malta, ed. N. W. Bawcutt (Manchester: Manchester University Press, 1978).

Marston, John, *The Malcontent and Other Plays*, ed. Keith Sturgess (Oxford: Oxford University Press, 1997).

Massinger, Philip, *A New Way to Pay Old Debts*, ed. T. W. Craik (London: A&C Black, 1964).

Middleton, Thomas, *A Mad World, My Masters and Other Plays*, ed. Michael Taylor (Oxford: Oxford University Press, 1995).

Montaigne, Michel de, *The Complete Essays*, trans. M. A. Screech (Harmondsworth: Penguin, 1993).

The Essayes, translated by John Florio, 3 vols. (London: Everyman, 1928).

Nashe, Thomas, *Pierce Pennilesse*, in *Works*, ed. Ronald B. McKerrow, corr. F. P. Wilson, 5 vols. (Oxford, 1958).

Plato, *Diuini Platonis opera omnia, Marsilio Ficino interprete* (London: 1590).

The Works of Plato, trans. Benjamin Jowett (New York: The Modern Library, 1928).

Rowley, William, Dekker, Thomas and Ford, John, *The Witch of Edmonton*, ed. Peter Corbin and Douglas Sedge (Manchester: Manchester University Press, 1999).

Shakespeare, William, *The First Quarto of Hamlet*, ed. Kathleen O. Irace (Cambridge: Cambridge University Press, 1998).

Henry IV Part 1, ed. David Scott Kastan (London: Arden Shakespeare, 2002).

Othello, ed. Norman Sanders (Cambridge: Cambridge University Press, 1984).

Othello, ed. E. A. J. Honigmann (London: Arden Shakespeare, 1997).

Richard II, ed. Charles R. Forker (London: Arden Shakespeare, 2002).

Complete Sonnets and Poems, ed. Colin Burrow (Oxford: Oxford University Press, 2002).

Shakespeare's Sonnets, ed. Stephen Booth (New Haven: Yale University Press, 1977).

Shakespeare's Sonnets, ed. Katherine Duncan-Jones (London: Arden Shakespeare, 1997).

The Sonnets and A Lover's Complaint, ed. John Kerrigan (London: Penguin, 1986).

Timon of Athens, ed. Karl Klein (Cambridge: Cambridge University Press, 2001)

Timon of Athens, ed. John Jowett (Oxford: Oxford University Press, 2004)

The Two Gentlemen of Verona, ed. William C. Carroll (London: Arden Shakespeare, 2004).

Songes and Sonnets, written by the Right Honorable Lord Henrie Haward late Earl of Surrey, and others [aka *Tottel's Miscellany*] (1587 edition).

Spenser, Edmund, *The Faerie Queene*, ed. A. C. Hamilton *et al.*, 2nd edition (London: Longman, 2001).

Tourneur, Cyril, *The Atheist's Tragedy*, ed. Brian Morris and Roma Gill (London: A&C Black, 1976).

Webster, John, *The Duchess of Malfi and Other Plays*, ed. René Weis (Oxford: Oxford University Press, 1996).

LATER TEXTS AND CRITICISM

Barish, Jonas (ed.), *Jonson: Volpone: A Casebook* (Basingstoke: Macmillan, 1992).

Barthes, Roland, 'Introduction to the Structural Analysis of Narratives', in *Image – Music – Text*, trans. Stephen Heath (London: Fontana, 1977), pp. 79–124.

Bate, Jonathan, 'Caliban and Ariel Write Back,' in Catherine M. S. Alexander, and Stanley Wells (eds.), *Shakespeare and Race* (Cambridge: Cambridge University Press, 2000), pp. 165–76.

The Genius of Shakespeare (London: Picador, 1997).

(ed.), *The Romantics on Shakespeare* (Harmondsworth: Penguin, 1992).

Bayley, John, *Shakespeare and Tragedy* (London: Routledge & Kegan Paul, 1981).

Bevington, David, ' "Jack Hath Not Jill": Failed Courtship in Lyly and Shakespeare', *Sh. Surv.* 42 (1990), 1–13.

Blanchot, Maurice, *Friendship*, trans. Elizabeth Rottenberg (Stanford: Stanford University Press, 1971).

Shakespeare on Love and Friendship (Chicago: University of Chicago Press, 2000).

Bloom, Harold, *Hamlet: Poem Unlimited* (Edinburgh: Canongate, 2003).

Shakespeare: The Invention of the Human (New York: Riverhead Books, 1998).

Bowers, Fredson, 'The Concept of Single or Dual Protagonists in Shakespeare's Tragedies', *Renaissance Papers* (1982), 27–33.

Bradley, A. C., *Shakespearean Tragedy: Lectures on 'Hamlet', 'Othello', 'King Lear', 'Macbeth'*, 3rd edition (Basingstoke: Macmillan, 1992).

Bray, Alan, *The Friend* (Chicago: University of Chicago Press, 2003).
'Homosexuality and the Signs of Male Friendship in Elizabethan England', *History Workshop Journal* 19 (1990), 1–19.
Homosexuality in Renaissance England (London: Gay Men's Press, 1982).
Breitenberg, Mark, *Anxious Masculinity in Early Modern England* (Cambridge: Cambridge University Press, 1996).
Bullough, Geoffrey (ed.), *Narrative and Dramatic Sources of Shakespeare*, 8 vols. (London: Routledge & Kegan Paul, 1957–75).
Burnett, Mark Thornton, *Masters and Servants in English Renaissance Drama and Culture: Authority and Obedience* (Basingstoke: Macmillan, 1997).
Carroll, Joseph, *Evolution and Literary Theory* (Columbia: University of Missouri Press, 1995).
Cohen, Derek, 'The Culture of Slavery: Caliban and Ariel', *Dalhousie Review* 76 (1996), 153–75.
Coleridge, Samuel Taylor, *Coleridge's Notebooks: A Selection*, ed. Seamus Perry (Oxford: Oxford University Press, 2002).
Davenant, Sir William, *The Rivals* (London, 1668).
Dawson, R. MacG., 'But Why Enobarbus?' *NQ* 34 (1987), 216–17.
Derrida, Jacques, *Politics of Friendship* (London: Verso, 1997).
DiGangi, Mario, *The Homoerotics of Early Modern Drama* (Cambridge: Cambridge University Press, 1997).
Dolan, Francis E., 'The Subordinate(s) Plot: Petty Treason and the Forms of Domestic Rebellion', *SQ* 43 (1992), 317–40.
Dryden, John, *All for Love*, ed. N. J. Andrew (London: A&C Black, 1975).
Duck, Steve, *Friends, for Life: The Psychology of Personal Relationships*, 2nd edition, (London: Harvester Wheatsheaf, 1991).
Ellis, David, 'Finding a Role for Parolles', *EC* 39 (1989), 289–304.
Ellis-Fermor, Una, '*Timon of Athens*: The Iconography of False Friendship', *HLQ* 43 (1980), 181–200.
'*Timon of Athens*: An Unfinisher Play', *RES* 18 (1942), 270–83.
Empson William, *Essays on Shakespeare*, ed. David B. Pirie (Cambridge: Cambridge University Press, 1986).
Some Versions of Pastoral (London: Chatto & Windus, 1935).
The Structure of Complex Words (London: Chatto & Windus, 1951).
Erskine-Hill, Howard, *Poetry and the Realm of Politics: Shakespeare to Dryden* (Oxford: Clarendon Press, 1996).
Evans, Robert C., *Ben Jonson and the Poetics of Patronage* (London: Associated University Presses, 1989).
'Flattery in Shakespeare's *Othello*: The Relevance of Plutarch and Sir Thomas Elyot', *Comparative Drama* 35 (2001), 1–41.
'Friendship in Shakespeare's *Othello*', *Ben Jonson Journal* 6 (1999), 109–46.
Everett, Barbara, 'Or What You Will', *EC* 35 (1985), 294–314.
Faderman, Lilian, *Surpassing the Love of Men: Romantic Friendship and Love between Women from the Renaissance to the Present* (New York: Morrow, 1981).

Fineman, Joel, *Shakespeare's Perjured Eye: The Invention of Poetic Subjectivity in the Sonnets* (Berkeley: University of California Press, 1986).

French, A. L., '*Richard II* and the Woodstock Murder', *SQ* 22 (1971), 337–44.

Frey, Charles H. (ed.), *Shakespeare, Fletcher and 'The Two Noble Kinsmen'* (Columbia: University of Missouri Press, 1989).

Gardner, Helen, 'The Theme of Damnation in *Doctor Faustus*', in John Jump (ed.), *Marlowe: Doctor Faustus – A Casebook* (Basingstoke: Macmillan, 1969), pp. 95–100.

Goldberg, Jonathan, 'Hal's Desire, Shakespeare's Idaho', in Nigel Wood (ed.), *Henry IV, Parts One and Two* (Buckingham: Open University Press, 1995), pp. 35–64.

Sodometries: Renaissance Texts, Modern Sexualities (Stanford, CA: Stanford University Press, 1992).

Greenblatt, Stephen, *Renaissance Self-Fashioning: From More to Shakespeare* (Chicago: The University of Chicago Press, 1980).

Shakespearean Negotiations (Oxford: Oxford University Press, 1988).

Gurr, Andrew, 'Industrious Ariel and Idle Caliban', in Jean-Pierre Maquerlot and Michèle Willems (eds.), *Travel and Drama in Shakespeare's Time* (Cambridge: Cambridge University Press, 1996), pp. 193–208.

Playgoing in Shakespeare's London, 2nd edition (Cambridge: Cambridge University Press, 1996).

The Shakespearean Stage 1574–1642, 3rd edition (Cambridge: Cambridge University Press, 1992).

Hammond, Paul, *Figuring Sex Between Men from Shakespeare to Rochester* (Oxford: Oxford University Press, 2002).

Hegel, G. W. F., *Phenomenology of Spirit*, trans. A. V. Miller (Oxford: Clarendon Press, 1977).

Helgerson, Richard, '*1 Henry IV* and *Woodstock*', *NQ* 23 (1976), 153–4.

Holmes, Jonathan, *Merely Players: Actors' Accounts of Performing Shakespeare* (London: Routledge, 2004).

Honigmann, E. A. J., '*Timon of Athens*', *SQ* 12 (1961), 3–20.

Hooper, Wilfrid, 'The Tudor Sumptuary Laws', *English Historical Review* 30 (1915), 433–49.

Hopkins, Gerard Manley, *Poetry and Prose*, ed. Walford Davies (London: J. M. Dent, 1998).

Hoy, Cyrus, '*Love's Labour's Lost* and the Nature of Comedy', *SQ* 13 (1962), 31–40.

Hunt, Maurice, 'Slavery, English Servitude, and *The Comedy of Errors*', *ELR* 27 (1997), 31–56.

Huston, J. Dennis, ' "Some Stain of Soldier": The Functions of Parolles in *All's Well that Ends Well*', *SQ* 21 (1970), 431–8.

Hutson, Lorna, *The Usurer's Daughter: Male Friendship and Fictions of Women in Sixteenth Century England* (London: Routledge, 1994).

Jardine, Lisa, *Erasmus: Man of Letters* (Princeton: Princeton University Press, 1993).

Johnson, Nora, 'Ganymedes and Kings: Staging Male Homosexual Desire in *The Winter's Tale*', *Sh. St.* 26 (1998), 187–217.

Johnson, Samuel, *The Yale Edition of the Works of Samuel Johnson*, 16 vols. (1958–), vol. 8, *Johnson on Shakespeare*, ed. Arthur Sherbo.

Kahn, Coppélia, *Man's Estate: Masculine Identity in Shakespeare* (Berkeley: University of California Press, 1981).

Kastan, David Scott, '*All's Well that Ends Well* and the Limits of Comedy', *ELH* 52 (1985), 575–89.

Kay, Dennis, ' "To hear the rest untold": Shakespeare's Postponed Endings', *RQ* 37 (1984), 207–27.

Kelly, Thomas, 'Shakespeare's Romantic Heroes: Orlando Reconsidered', *SQ* 24 (1973), 12–24.

Kermode, Frank, *Shakespeare's Language* (London: Allen Lane, 2000).

Kerrigan, William, 'Female Friends and Fraternal Enemies in *As You Like It*', in Valeria Finucci and Regina Schwartz (eds.), *Desire in the Renaissance: Psychoanalysis and Culture* (Princeton: Princeton University Press, 1994), pp. 184–206.

Knight, G. Wilson, *The Wheel of Fire: Interpretations of Shakespearian Tragedy with three New Essays*, 4th edition (London: Methuen, 1949).

Krieger, Elliot, *A Marxist Study of Shakespeare's Comedies* (London: Macmillan, 1979).

Kussmaul, Ann, *Servants in Husbandry in Early Modern England* (Cambridge: Cambridge University Press, 1981).

Lawrence, Judiana, 'Natural Bonds and Artistic Coherence in the Ending of *Cymbeline*', *SQ* 35 (1984), 440–60.

Leishman, J. B., *Themes and Variations in Shakespeare's Sonnets* (London: Hutchinson, 1961).

Lewis, C. S., *The Four Loves* (London: Fount, 1977).

Lucking, David, 'Our Devils Now Are Ended: A Comparative Analysis of *The Tempest* and *Doctor Faustus*', *Dalhousie Review* 80 (2000), 151–67.

MacCulloch, Diarmaid, *Reformation: Europe's House Divided 1490–1700* (London: Allen Lane, 2003).

Maclean, Hugh, 'Disguise in *King Lear*: Kent and Edgar', *SQ* 11 (1960), 49–54.

MacNeice, Louis, *Collected Poems* (London: Faber & Faber, 1979).

Maguire, Laurie E., *Studying Shakespeare: A Guide to the Plays* (Oxford: Blackwell, 2004).

Malette, Richard, 'Same-Sex Erotic Friendship in *The Two Noble Kinsmen*', *Renaissance Drama* 26 (1995), 29–52.

Marotti, Arthur F., 'Patronage, Poetry and Print', in Cedric C. Brown (ed.), *Patronage, Politics and Literary Traditions in England 1558–1658* (Detroit: Wayne State University Press, 1993), pp. 21–46.

Marvell, Andrew, *The Poems of Andrew Marvell*, ed. Nigel Smith (London: Longman, 2003).

Mason, Pamela (ed.), *Shakespeare: Early Comedies – A Casebook* (Basingstoke: Macmillan, 1995).

McArthur, Herbert, 'Romeo's Loquacious Friend', *SQ* 10 (1959), 35–44.

McCabe, Richard A., 'Wit, Eloquence and Wisdom in *Euphues: The Anatomy of Wit*', *SP* 81 (1984), 299–324.

McCary, Thomas, *Friends and Lovers: The Phenomenology of Desire in Shakespearean Comedy* (New York: Columbia University Press, 1985).

Michel-Michot, Paulette, 'Sir Walter Raleigh as a Source for the Character of Iago', *English Studies* 50 (1969), 85–9.

Mills, Laurens J., *One Soul in Bodies Twain: Friendship in Tudor Literature and Stuart Drama* (Bloomington, IN: Principia Press, 1937).

Moisan, Thomas, ' "Knock Me Here Soundly": Comic Misprision and Class Consciousness in Shakespeare', *SQ* 42 (1991), 276–90.

Newton, Allyson P., ' "At the Very Heart of Loss": Shakespeare's Enobarbus and the Rhetoric of Remembering', *Renaissance Papers* (1995), 81–91.

Nuttall, A. D., *A New Mimesis: Shakespeare and the Representation of Reality* (London: Methuen, 1983).

Timon of Athens (London: Harvester Wheatsheaf, 1989).

Orgel, Stephen, *Impersonations: The Performance of Gender in Shakespeare's England* (Cambridge: Cambridge University Press, 1997).

Osborne, Laurie E., 'Antonio's Pardon', *SQ* 45 (1994), 108–14.

Pahl, Ray, *On Friendship* (Cambridge: Polity, 2000).

Palliser, D. M., *The Age of Elizabeth: England under the Later Tudors 1547–1603* (London: Longman, 1992).

Parker, Patricia, 'Elder and Younger: The Opening Scene of *The Comedy of Errors*', *SQ* 34 (1983), 325–7.

Pequigney, Joseph, 'The Two Antonios and Same-Sex Love in *Twelfth Night* and *The Merchant of Venice*', *ELR* 22 (1992), 201–21.

Porter, Joseph A., *Shakespeare's Mercutio: His History and Drama* (Chapel Hill: University of North Carolina Press, 1988).

Price, A. W., *Love and Friendship in Plato and Aristotle* (Oxford: Clarendon Press, 1989).

Rackin, Phyllis, *Stages of History: Shakespeare's English Chronicles* (London: Routledge, 1991).

Richards, Jennifer, *Rhetoric and Courtliness in Early Modern Literature* (Cambridge: Cambridge University Press, 2003).

Ricks, Christopher, *The Force of Poetry* (Oxford: Oxford University Press, 1984).

Ridley, Matt, *The Origins of Virtue* (London: Viking, 1996).

Russell, D. A. and Winterbottom, M. (eds.), *Classical Literary Criticism* (Oxford: Oxford University Press, 1989).

Rosky, William, '*The Two Gentlemen of Verona* as Burlesque', *ELR* 12 (1982), 210–19.

Rothman, Jules, 'A Vindication of Parolles', *SQ* 23 (1972), 183–96.

Ryan, Kiernan, *Shakespeare*, 2nd edition (London: Harvester Wheatsheaf, 1995).

Saccio, Peter, *Shakespeare's English Kings: History, Chronicle and Drama*, 2nd edition (Oxford: Oxford University Press, 2000).

Schiffer, James (ed.), *Shakespeare's Sonnets: Critical Essays* (New York: Routledge, 1999).

Schork, R. J., 'The Many Masks of Parolles', *PQ* 76 (1997), 263–69.

Scragg, Leah, 'Iago – Vice or Devil?' *Sh. Surv.* 21 (1968), 53–68.

Sedgwick, Eve Kosofsky, *Between Men: English Literature and Male Homosocial Desire* (New York: Columbia University Press, 1985).

Shannon, Laurie, 'Emilia's Argument: Friendship and "Human Title" in *The Two Noble Kinsmen*', *ELH* 64 (1997), 657–82.

   Sovereign Amity: Figures of Friendship in Shakespearean Contexts (Chicago: University of Chicago Press, 2002).

Shapiro, James, *1599: A Year in the Life of William Shakespeare* (London: Faber & Faber, 2005).

Sharp, Ronald A., *Friendship and Literature* (Durham, NC: Duke University Press, 1986).

Smith, Bruce R., *Homosexual Desire in Shakespeare's England* (Chicago: University of Chicago Press, 1991).

   Shakespeare and Masculinity (Oxford: Oxford University Press, 2001).

Steinberg, Theodore L., 'The Anatomy of *Euphues*', *SEL* 17 (1977), 27–38.

Stewart, Alan, *Close Readers: Humanism and Sodomy in Early Modern England* (Princeton: Princeton University Press, 1997).

   '"Near Akin": The Trials of Friendship in *The Two Noble Kinsmen*', in Jennifer Richards and James Knowles (eds.), *Shakespeare's Late Plays* (Edinburgh: Edinburgh University Press, 1999), pp. 57–71.

Stone, Lawrence, *The Family, Sex and Marriage in England 1500–1800* (London: Weidenfeld & Nicholson, 1977).

Streete, Adrian, 'Charity and Law in *Love's Labour's Lost*: A Calvinist Analogue', *NQ* 247 (2002), 224–5.

Tate, Nahum, *The History of King Lear. Acted at the Duke's Theatre. Reviv'd with Alterations* (London, 1689).

Tillyard, E. M. W., *Shakespeare's Early Comedies* (London: Chatto & Windus, 1965).

Tyson, Brian F., 'Ben Jonson's Black Comedy: A Connection between *Othello* and *Volpone*', *SQ* 29 (1978), 60–6.

Vendler, Helen, *The Art of Shakespeare's Sonnets* (Cambridge, MA: Harvard University Press, 1997).

Vernon, Mark, *The Philosophy of Friendship* (Basingstoke: Palgrave Macmillan, 2005).

Waith, E. M., 'Shakespeare and Fletcher on Love and Marriage', *Sh. St.* 18 (1986), 235–50.

Weil, Judith, '"Full Possession": Service and Slavery in *Doctor Faustus*', in Paul Whitfield White (ed.), *Marlowe, History and Sexuality*, (New York, 1998), pp. 143–54.

Wells, Stanley, *Looking for Sex in Shakespeare* (Cambridge: Cambridge University Press, 2004).

   Shakespeare: The Poet and his Plays (London: Methuen, 1997).

Womersley, David, 'Why Is Falstaff Fat?' *RES* 47 (1996), 1–22.

Wrightson, Keith, *English Society 1580–1680* (London: Routledge, 1982).

Index

Aeschylus, *Oresteia*, 139
All's Well that Ends Well, 2, 21, 27, 169
Antony and Cleopatra, 11, 21, 169, 183, 190–5
Aristotle, 6, 9, 27, 31, 32, 76, 85, 129
As You Like It, 1, 24, 57–8, 96

Bacon, Francis, 8, 11, 12, 14, 48, 52, 119, 135, 137
Beaumont, Francis and Fletcher John
  The Maid's Tragedy, 88–9
  Philaster, 110
betrayal, 169–95
Blanchot, Maurice, 25
Bray, Alan, 5–6, 11, 48
Breitenberg, Mark, 18
Breme, Thomas, 10
Bryskett, Lodowick, 13
Burrow, Colin, 34
Burton, Robert, 4, 15, 26, 65, 188

Castiglione, Baldesar, 12
Cecil, William, 1st Lord Burghley, 121
Churchyard, Thomas, 9
Cicero, Marcus Tullius, 6–7, 74, 121
Coleridge, Samuel Taylor, 189
The Comedy of Errors, 61–2, 95, 96, 187
Coriolanus, 21, 147
countenance, 13, 91
Cymbeline, 62–4

Derrida, Jacques, 25, 81
DiGangi, Mario, 17
Donne, John, 19, 35, 41, 44
Dorke, Walter, 16
Dryden, John, *All for Love*, 191

Edwards, Richard, *Damon and Pythias*, 93–5
envy, 33, 189
Erasmus, Desiderius, 9, 26, 28, 57
Elyot, Sir Thomas 9, 41, 48, 66–8, 135, 143

family, opposed to friendship, 4–5, 12, 37, 48–64, 78–9, 107, 121
favouritism, royal, 121–31
fellowship, 141–68
female friendship, 3, 79–80, 185
fineman, Joel, 20, 25, 31, 34
friendship, false, 169–95
friendship in military contexts, 190

Grimald, Nicholas, 10

Hamlet, 4, 20, 21, 24, 27, 54, 74, 114, 132, 135–40, 155
Hegel, G. W. F., 38
Henry IV Part 1, 20, 22, 65, 125–7, 129, 131, 150, 164–8
Henry IV Part 2, 55–6, 101, 127–30, 131, 164–8
Henry V, 130–1, 167
Henry VI Part 1, 22, 117, 120
Henry VI Part 2, 120
Henry VI Part 3, 23, 55, 117–19
Henry VIII, 23
Herbert, William, Earl of Pembroke, 33
Heywood, Thomas, *A Woman Killed with Kindness*, 5
homoeroticism, 17–18, 40, 82, 101, 104, 162, 184
homosexuality, *see* homoeroticism
Hopkins, Gerard Manley, 46
Hutson, Lorna, 14, 67

James VI and I, King of Scotland and England, 18
Jardine, Lisa, 11
jealousy (sexual), 65–90, 183–5
Jonson, Ben, 96
  The Alchemist, 102
  Epicene, 149
  Every Man in His Humour, 102, 149
  Volpone, 96
Julius Caesar, 21

Kahn, Coppélia, 4
King Lear, 13, 21, 27, 58–9, 110–14, 170, 178

Lewis, C. S., 16, 141
love (romantic/sexual), opposed to friendship, 65–90, 152–60, 164, 169, 183–5
Love's Labour's Lost, 7, 149–54
Lucian, *Toxaris*, 52
Lyly, John, *Euphues*, 66, 68–72

Macbeth, 132–5, 183
MacCary, W. Thomas, 3
MacNeice, Louis 196
Marlowe, Christopher
  Doctor Faustus, 105–6
  Edward II, 122–3, 127
  The Jew of Malta, 105, 161
marriage, opposed to friendship, 40, 106, 164 *see also* family
Marston, John, *The Malcontent*, 16, 169–71
Marvell, Andrew, 46
Massinger, Philip, *A New Way to Pay Old Debts*, 6
The Merchant of Venice, 4, 13, 16, 18, 24, 142, 150, 160–4, 178
Meredith, George, 95
Middleton, Thomas
  as co-author of *Timon of Athens*, 146
  The Revenger's Tragedy, 54
  A Trick to Catch the Old One, 6
Middleton, Thomas, and Rowley, William, *The Changeling*, 108
A Midsummer Night's Dream, 45
Mills, Laurens J., 7, 69
Montaigne, Michel de, 25, 48, 51, 141
Much Ado about Nothing, 24, 27, 56, 157–60, 169, 171

Nashe, Thomas, 11
Nietzsche, Friedrich, 25

Othello, 20, 27, 103, 169, 182–90, 196

patronage, 9–11
Plato, 7–9, 31–2

Lysis, 7, 31, 43, 45, 111, 145, 188
  Symposium, 8–9, 130, 147
politics, 55, 116–40

Ralegh, Sir Walter, 121
Richard II, 22, 27, 120–2, 123, 124–5, 142, 164
Richard III, 54–5, 119–20
Romeo and Juliet, 150, 154–7
Rowley, William, Dekker, Thomas and Ford, John, *The Witch of Edmonton*, 103
royal friendship, 116–40

Sedgwick, Eve Kosofsky, 3, 4, 18, 30, 46, 186
service, 91–115, 143, 187
Shannon, Laurie, 7, 12, 20, 74, 117, 142
Shakespeare's Sonnets, 7, 18, 30–47, 96, 104, 141, 163, 176–9
Sidney, Sir Philip
  Astrophel and Stella, 40
  The Countess of Pembroke's Arcadia, 15, 174
Sonnets, see Shakespeare's Sonnets
Spenser, Edmund, *The Faerie Queene*, 49–52, 57
status, 19, 37, 38, 44, 91, 95, 141
Stewart, Alan, 11

The Taming of the Shrew, 38, 95, 97–8, 150
The Tempest, 26, 59–61, 107–10
Timon of Athens, 92–3, 141–9
Tourneur, Cyril, *The Atheist's Tragedy*, 52–3
Troilus and Cressida, 101–2, 196
Twelfth Night, 17, 108, 110, 169, 176–82
The Two Gentlemen of Verona, 7, 72–5, 77, 88, 95, 98–100, 103, 110
The Two Noble Kinsmen, 53, 77–86, 88

Vendler, Helen, 36

Webster, John, *The Duchess of Malfi*, 108
  The White Devil, 53
Webster, John and Rowley, William, *A Cure for a Cuckold*, 86–8
The Winter's Tale, 74–7
Wodehouse, P. G., 106
Woodstock (anon.), 123–4

4058742R00142

Printed in Germany
by Amazon Distribution
GmbH, Leipzig